"Tony Dungy's life is a living testimony of a man's faith in God. He has given us a new picture and definition of a 'Coach.' Good guys do come in first!"

LOVIE SMITH, *Head Coach, Chicago Bears*

"Winning the Super Bowl is an extraordinary achievement. Being the first African American coach to do so is monumental. But the Lombardi trophy does not reflect even a fraction of the greatness of this man and his message. Tony Dungy is an inspiration—a true champion both on and off the field. Now, in *Quiet Strength*, you can learn the principles that have propelled him to the top of his game."

PETER LOWE, *President and CEO, Get Motivated Seminars, Inc.*

"In this fast-paced American culture with so many people driven by the lure of material success, Tony Dungy reminds us what truly matters in the game of life. At the pinnacle of NFL success, he has taken time to show us the value of making memories and not just money, focusing on family instead of fame, and building up a storehouse of eternal wealth that can never be depleted. Don't just read this book; listen to it with the ears of your soul."

PRISCILLA SHIRER, *Author and Speaker*

"In today's world where sports figures and movie stars are idolized, Tony Dungy is a true hero because his life is a testimony to the fact that if you 'do your best and let God do the rest,' not only will success follow, but your life will have a positive impact on others. This is the reason I consider Tony a great friend and role model."

BENJAMIN S. CARSON, SR., MD, *Professor and Director of Pediatric Neurosurgery, Johns Hopkins Medical Institutes*

"My good friend Tony Dungy has demonstrated in his personal life and in this powerful book that it is possible to be a committed Christian on and off the field and still come out a winner. This insightful work will challenge, encourage, and inspire all who read it to uncompromisingly integrate our faith into every aspect of our lives, so that we too, will be victorious in spite of the challenges and obstacles that life brings our way."

TONY EVANS, *Senior Pastor, Oak Cliff Bible Fellowship; President, The Urban Alternative*

"'No excuses, no explanations.' I first heard Coach Dungy say these words in 1996, when he explained how we were going to turn the Bucs franchise around. But Coach challenged us to be more than just a winning football team. He wanted us to be winners in life—and he led by example. There are not enough pages in this book to share all the stories of the lives Coach Dungy has touched. You don't have to win a ring to be a champion . . . but I am so glad he has won a Super Bowl ring so he can continue to use the platform God has given him."

DERRICK BROOKS, *Outside Linebacker, Tampa Bay Buccaneers*

"Amid the deafening roar surrounding the machinery of earthly glory, the spiritual man leaves quiet footsteps of inspired faith. Tony Dungy's footprints can be traced back to God and family. This foundation has provided him with the love, strength, compassion, and tolerance to fill his earthly run with man's greatest gift and purpose . . . to be of service to God and his fellow man."

JIM IRSAY, *Owner, Indianapolis Colts*

"In the twenty-one years I've known Tony Dungy, I have consistently found him to be a man of integrity, sincerity, and openness. As a man of faith, no matter what trials or tribulations he's faced, he has embodied the Scripture found in Proverbs 16:32—'Better to be patient than powerful; better to have self-control than to conquer a city.' Dungy has followed the biblical prescription for success. In football and in the game of life, Tony Dungy is a winner."

JAMES BROWN, *Host,* The NFL Today, *CBS Sports*

"Tony Dungy is a world champion in every way. His quiet strength both on and off the field has been an inspiration to millions. His sense of priority is uncommon and uncompromised. His purposeful desire to turn the spotlight off of himself and onto Christ is admirable. Even more impressive, however, is the character and dignity he exemplifies when there are no cameras . . . when there is no spotlight. This is a man of tremendous faith, and he lives it every day of his life. He has inspired me, and I'm so thankful for his friendship."

MICHAEL W. SMITH, *Singer/Songwriter*

"To say that I am a football fan is an understatement. I love it. But I love even more my friend and coach of the Indianapolis Colts, Tony Dungy. He has had a profound impact on Indianapolis that goes far beyond football. Tony Dungy is a man who uses football and its lessons to share with all of us his journey with the Lord. He walks with quiet strength each and every day."

SANDI PATTY, *Singer/Songwriter*

"For over a decade, Tony Dungy has quietly taught me significant lessons in leadership and in life. Now he's sharing them with you in this thought-provoking book. In *Quiet Strength*, Tony leads us on a journey that reveals profound principles for living and our ultimate purpose in life."

MARK W. MERRILL, *President, Family First and All Pro Dad*

"Tony Dungy has become an icon of strength, character, perseverance, and faith. *Quiet Strength* is a road map that can help each of us draw on the God-given reserve of 'character, fortitude, and peace' that will allow us to stand tall during the low points of life and to be humble during the times of celebrated triumphs. I applaud Tony for his inspiring testimony that he has penned in this work."

S. TRUETT CATHY, *Founder and CEO, Chick-Fil-A*

QUIET STRENGTH

A MEMOIR

TONY DUNGY

WITH NATHAN WHITAKER

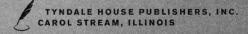
TYNDALE HOUSE PUBLISHERS, INC.
CAROL STREAM, ILLINOIS

Visit Tyndale's exciting Web site at www.tyndale.com

TYNDALE and Tyndale's quill logo are registered trademarks of Tyndale House Publishers, Inc.

Quiet Strength: The Principles, Practices, & Priorities of a Winning Life

Designed by Dean H. Renninger

Published in association with the literary agency of Legacy LLC, Winter Park, Florida 32789.

Library of Congress Cataloging-in-Publication Data

Dungy, Tony.
    Quiet strength : the principles, practices & priorities of a winning life / Tony Dungy with Nathan Whitaker.
        p. cm.
    ISBN-13: 978-1-4143-1801-1 (hc)
    ISBN-10: 1-4143-1801-4 (hc)
    ISBN-13: 978-1-4143-1802-8 (sc)
    ISBN-10: 1-4143-1802-2 (sc)
    1. Dungy, Tony. 2. Spiritual biography. 3. African American football coaches—Religion. 4. African American football coaches—Biography. 5. Christian life. I. Whitaker, Nathan. II. Title.
    BR1725.D738A3 2007
    277.3′083092—dc22
    [B]   2007015181

Printed in the United States of America

13 12 11 10 09 08 07
 9   8   7   6

CONTENTS

FOREWORD

We are hard pressed on every side, but not crushed;
Perplexed, but not in despair;
Persecuted, but not destroyed.
We always carry around in our body the death of Jesus,
so that the life of Jesus may also be revealed in our body.
For we who are alive are always being given over to
death for Jesus' sake, so that His life may be revealed in our
mortal body.
    2 CORINTHIANS 4:8-11

WE ARE BLESSED and privileged to write the foreword to a book that truly represents the power of God and the rewards of obedience to God's Word.

On February 4, 2007, millions of people witnessed Coach Tony Dungy confirm his faith after winning the greatest award in football, the Super Bowl Championship. Coach Dungy made history as the first African American coach to win the Super Bowl. Although that is significant, it is only a small part of his journey toward fulfilling his life's purpose.

It has been said that we get good at whatever we practice. Coach Dungy practices proactive faith. This faith is not a gimmick or magic or the will of a strong mind. It is not a short-order request to receive what we want when we want it. Proactive faith is receiving everything that has been promised to us by God's Word for His purpose and in His timing.

Because of his proactive faith, Tony Dungy has been able to climb many mountains. Great achievements require great effort, and Coach Dungy's greatest accomplishment is that through it all, he has stayed obedient to God's will.

Coach Dungy's life displays his steadfast belief in God and his submission to God's Word. His story is a guide for basic living and a confession of his belief in Jesus Christ, the Son of God. This account is proof that Coach Dungy's beliefs have sustained him consistently throughout his life.

To follow Coach Dungy's life from his beginnings to the present is most inspiring. For him to have been rejected, ignored, praised, and denied—yet still maintain dignity, strength, and hope—is a testament to his unwavering faith. At times his choices have not been popular, but he has stood his ground. He has remained commited to the will of God.

The payoff of such faith is far better than anything the material world can offer. In this world, one can never be satisfied. The reward of remaining patient and obedient to the will of God is that life becomes fulfilling and satisfying . . . complete.

Hebrews 11:6 says, "Without faith it is impossible to please God, because anyone who comes to Him must believe that He exists and that He rewards those who earnestly seek Him."

We see a beautiful testimony of such faith in this man of courage.

Pauletta and Denzel Washington

ACKNOWLEDGMENTS

BY NATHAN WHITAKER

TONY WAS RELUCTANT to single out people specifically, noting how many people made this book possible, both by direct participation as well as in the entwining of their very lives into Tony and Lauren's, and thereby into the fabric of these pages. Although he's right—we're bound to forget people—I had far too much help with this book to not attempt to recognize those who assisted.

We are grateful for the time and memories of Jerry Angelo, Jim Caldwell, Vernon Cheek, Clyde Christensen, Jackie Cook, Mark Dominik, Herm Edwards, Leslie Frazier, Loren Harris, John Idzik, Craig Kelley, Tom Lamphere, Rich McKay, Mark Merrill, Veronica Pinto, Tim Ruskell, Donnie Shell, Alan Williams, and Ruston Webster.

Recognition is also due the pastors who have ministered to Tony and Lauren so faithfully through their married life: Richard Farmer, Charles Briscoe, Steve Gould, Ken Whitten, Abe Brown, Jeff Singletary, John Ramsey, and Clarence Moore.

D.J. Snell of Legacy, LLC, in his dual roles as our literary agent as well as a brother in Christ, has been invaluable with his guidance and vision for this book, as has Jim Dodson, with his assistance and encouragement on manuscript concepts.

Our faith in Tyndale House Publishers has been borne out by the work of Jan Long Harris, Todd Starowitz, Sarah Atkinson, Doug Knox, Mark Taylor, Dan Elliott, Lisa Jackson, Jeremy Taylor, Bonne Steffen, Erin Smith, Sarah Rubio, Dean Renninger, and the rest of the outstanding staff.

In addition, I have been carried by the assistance—sometimes through encouraging word or prayer, other times through more direct roles with the book—of Don Buerkle, Dom and Karen Capers, Brian and Cindy Clark, Jeff and Shaunti Feldhahn, David French, Chan Gailey, Matthew Hartsfield, John Kingston, Buddy Moore, Betsy and Mike Mularkey, Phil Pharr, Rob Rose, Heath Schiesser, Charlie Skalaski, Todd and Christine Stockberger, George Woods, and John Wunderli.

I am incredibly thankful for the assistance of Lauren Dungy, who balanced a desire to shield their already public life with the knowledge that sharing their experiences might affect lives. I pray that the Lord will continue to bless her tremendous impact through her partnership with Tony.

I couldn't have done this without the support of my wife, Amy, who kept faith in me long after mine had started to falter; my precious daughters, Hannah, for sharing me and for finding the comma we needed on page 72, and Ellie Kate, for stopping the banging on my office door long enough for me to finish; and my parents, Scott and Lynda Whitaker, for their belief in my vision and substantial editing assistance.

Tony, you were "Jesus with skin on" throughout this process, in good times and tough. I will forever be grateful for your faith in me and this project and for allowing your story to be told so that others might be encouraged and edified by it. You are a remarkable man with a remarkable story.

Most of all, Tony and I are grateful to our Lord and Savior, Jesus Christ, for bringing us this far in the journey of our lives, a journey of hope, joy, and the promise of eternal life.

INTRODUCTION

If you want to lift yourself up, lift up someone else.
    BOOKER T. WASHINGTON

"ABSOLUTELY NOT." I have been approached many times over the last few years about writing a book, and my answer has always been the same.

In 2004 I had lunch with my good friend Nathan Whitaker in Indianapolis, and we talked about doing a book that would be more about life than about football. Could I see how such a book could help others? Yes. But still my answer was no.

And then my team, the Indianapolis Colts, won Super Bowl XLI in February 2007.

Still no.

But then cards and letters and e-mails started to roll in.

> *"Thank you for your witness before the game. . . ."*

> *"My son and I watched your comments after the game together. I could take him to church twenty times, and it wouldn't have opened up a chance for us to talk the way watching the Super Bowl did. . . ."*

*"My husband moved out three weeks ago but heard
one of your comments about putting your family first.
He has since called and wants to come talk. . . ."*

I like the saying, "Life is hard, but God is good." It's because of God's goodness that we can have hope, both for here and the hereafter. And it's the desire to share that hope that finally changed my no to yes.

But before we begin, I want to make sure we're starting at the same place. The point of this book is not the Super Bowl. In fact, it's not football.

Don't get me wrong—football is great. It's provided a living and a passion for me for decades. It was the first job I ever had that actually got me excited about heading to work.

But football is just a game. It's not family. It's not a way of life. It doesn't provide any sort of intrinsic meaning. It's just football. It lasts for three hours, and when the game is over, it's over.

And frankly, as you'll see throughout this book, that fact—that when it's over, it's over—is part of football's biggest appeal to me. When a game ends, win or lose, it's time to prepare for the next one. The coaches and players really don't have time to celebrate or to stay down, because Sunday's gone and Monday's here. And no matter what happened yesterday, you have to be ready to play next Sunday.

That's how it works—just like life.

It's the journey that matters. Learning is more important than the test. Practice well, and the games will take care of themselves. Whether you've been kicked in the teeth or life just couldn't get any sweeter, it keeps rolling on . . . and then there's another game.

If football were the only thing that mattered to me, I would have left coaching after the 2001 season, when I had finished with the Tampa Bay Buccaneers—or when they had finished with me. At that time, I thought God might be moving me into some other walk of life. There were a lot of things I had always wanted to do "someday," and my family certainly wanted to stay in Tampa. I figured God was simply telling me that "someday" had arrived.

If it were all about football, I would have left after the 2005 season, when I was reminded—in the most painful context I can imagine—that football really occupies a spot far down my list of priorities.

If it were all about football, I would have moved on after the 2006 season, when the Colts won Super Bowl XLI, accomplishing the ultimate team goal in the National Football League. After all, if football were all that mattered, what else would be left to do?

It would have been easy enough to do: "Ladies and gentlemen, I've achieved the ultimate victory. I'm stepping down." Everyone would have understood.

But winning the Super Bowl is not the ultimate victory. And once again, just to make certain we're on the same page, it's not all about football. It's about the journey—mine and yours—and the lives we can touch, the legacy we can leave, and the world we can change for the better.

I'm still not totally comfortable putting my story in a book, but here's how I see it: although football has been a part of my life that I've really enjoyed, I've always viewed it as a means to do something more. A means to share my faith, to encourage and lift up other people. And I see this book as a way of expanding the platform that football has provided.

Despite my day job, I am by nature a very private person in a very private family. So you won't see a whole lot about my children in this book. I love them dearly, and it's impossible to tell my story without mentioning them. At the same time, a tension exists because my wife, Lauren, has worked very hard to make our kids' upbringing as normal as possible with a father who is the head coach of an NFL team. So with one notable, obvious exception, you won't find much discussion of my children in this book. I hope you, as well as they, understand and appreciate why.

This book is not only about me, either. It's about the priorities, choices, approaches, and habits that lead to being a winner, to experiencing true success. It's about you and me and our journey in this world together. It's about the things I've learned, the mistakes I've made, and the heartaches that have made me lean into the Father's presence. I hope that when it's all said and done, you'll see that it's really all about Him.

TAMPA RAIN

CHAPTER ONE

*We are pressed on every side by troubles, but we are not crushed. We
are perplexed, but not driven to despair. We are hunted down, but never
abandoned by God. We get knocked down, but we are not destroyed.*
    2 CORINTHIANS 4:8–9

IT WAS TIME. I figured I had waited long enough. Darkness
had fallen on that winter evening, two days after our team's
business had concluded for the season. The building was otherwise deserted as I pulled up and parked at the small wooden
shack guarding the entrance to One Buccaneer Place.

One Buc, as we all called it, stood quiet. The one-story,
stucco and concrete block building was located on the edge
of the Tampa International Airport. The color of butter pecan
ice cream, this was the original building that housed the newly
formed Buccaneers in 1976. Rather than expand the building
as the organization exploded in size over the years—as personnel were added for coaching, scouting, marketing, public
relations, ticketing, and other functions—the Bucs had simply
added a series of trailers on the other side of a small parking
lot in the late 1990s. The trailers were collectively known as
Two Buc.

Oscar, the guard on duty, escorted me through the locked

gate on the side of the building; my security code no longer worked. Silently I gathered six years' worth of my professional life from my office—three-ring binders with notes, play diagrams, and play-calling sheets; various books and photographs; my sons' video games; and a couple of Buccaneers hats, although I'd never wear them again. I was lost in my memories as I placed these things rather haphazardly in cardboard boxes thoughtfully left out for me by my administrative assistant. *No, I realized, Lora is somebody else's administrative assistant now.*

I stopped to contemplate a wood-framed picture in the stack. It had been taken our first year in Tampa, and we were all beaming: my daughter, Tiara; my sons, Jamie and Eric; my wife, Lauren; and me. The stadium grass behind us was a vibrant green, the shade of an Irish meadow, sliced into five-yard increments by crisp, white stripes. A teeming throng of humanity, dressed in orange and red and squinting in the unforgiving Florida sun, filled the stands in the picture's background.

The summer of 1996 had been a long time ago.

Now, in the winter of 2002, that same Florida sky was dark. Dark, cold, and damp. The mist that had begun in the afternoon had turned to light drops. The weather mirrored my dark inner world on that night of January 14.

I finished packing the last of the items. Not that much, really. A few boxes stood by the door, ready to be carried home. Nothing else of note remained. That office of mine had been lived in pretty hard, I had to admit. Most of the homework completed by my sons Jamie and Eric over the previous six years had been done in there, and the office had seen countless games of catch, video-game competitions, and other pursuits geared around young boys.

I later learned that Rich McKay, general manager of the

Bucs during my tenure as head coach, had asked the facility manager to clean and paint the office that week, noting that my replacement was "about to move into an office that two boys have been living in every day for the last six years."

As I wrapped things up, I noticed that the light drops falling outside had turned into a heavy rain.

I should have just walked out, since by then it was getting late. Instead, I wandered out of my office and through the building, stopping in the coaches' locker room. Standing in the middle of the room, I let my gaze sweep over the cramped, worn twelve-by-fifteen room. I looked from locker to locker, reading some names, imagining others.

Monte Kiffin. Chris Foerster. Clyde Christensen. Rod Marinelli.

We had shared this locker room and many memories, these men and I. We had spent hours, weeks, and years together. These men had walked off the frozen, concrete-hard synthetic turf in Philadelphia with me just two days earlier, their careers critically stung by the Bucs' 31–9 loss. So much had been at stake for all of us—and the players too—yet the outcome had never really been in doubt.

It was a difficult season punctuated by a painful ending.

And now God had something different in mind for all of us.

I tried to take solace in the things we had accomplished together—three straight playoff appearances, more wins than any other staff in team history—but they seemed hollow, even within me. I stared at the lockers, the enormity of the moment suddenly overwhelming as I remembered names of guys long gone from my staff.

Lovie Smith. Herm Edwards. Mike Shula.

The prognosticators had been circling for weeks. And amid season-long rumors that a new head coach was being courted, their speculations had finally become reality. I had been fired.

Many of the assistant coaches—maybe all of them—would be let go as well. They would all come out fine. I knew that. But I also ached for the inevitable pain I knew they would face as they dealt with the uncertainty of their futures, that their children would face when they were uprooted from their schools, that their wives would face when ripped from their support systems.

Joe Barry. Mike Tomlin. Alan Williams. Jim Caldwell.

These men had just come that year. Why did they have to go? It was hard to figure. My family had come to Tampa for a reason. God had led us here, opened doors that we didn't expect would be open, and allowed us to connect deeply with this community. But for what purpose?

Not football, apparently. I felt certain that the Buccaneers were my best, and possibly last, chance to lead an NFL team. For whatever reason, God had closed the door. For what?

Possibly some sort of ministry. I was heavily involved in the All Pro Dad organization and Abe Brown's prison ministry, both based in Tampa, as well as our church, Idlewild Baptist Central. Maybe God was trying to turn my focus toward those.

But did He have to close this door already?

And close it so firmly?

It really was hard to fathom. I had been faithful, hadn't I? So faithful in the mission that surely—*surely*—it was going to be blessed by Him. I had come here in 1996 with dreams of creating an organization based on values and character, and my staff and I had succeeded in doing just that. But God obviously wanted something else from me now.

It wasn't really the firing itself that was a shock but rather the thought that God was allowing this great experiment to end. Hadn't we tried to do things right?

Oscar reappeared. It was late, approaching midnight.

I walked out, traversing a path between the squat racks,

benches, and other weight-lifting machines in the weight area attached to the building. A cool mist blew in under the awning, dampening my forty-six-year-old face. This half of the weight room was outside and open on its ends and side, but at least the Glazers, the Bucs' owners, had partially covered it with a vinyl awning. Although the weights were cooled and heated—mostly heated—according to the daily whims of the southwest Florida climate, they were usually out of direct reach of the elements.

I looked to my left, past the row of squat racks and away from the building. Through the dark and rain, I could barely make out the two shadowy practice fields. The runway lights of the airport were clearly visible just yards beyond.

Where was the burning bush? Where was that still, small voice? Or, even better, the loud, booming one.

The only voice I could hear clearly was my own, crying out in the wilderness. *When will I hear Your voice, Lord?*

I returned from my thoughts as Oscar quickly maneuvered between and around the weight machines to beat me to the next door. He pressed the electronic pad, releasing the magnetic lock on the chain-link gate that separated the weight area and practice fields from the waiting parking lot.

The Bay News 9 reporter had been waiting all night for this shot. For two days, news trucks had been parked along the street, on the front lawn, in the surrounding ditches—wherever they could fit close to One Buc.

I thought everyone had abandoned the vigil hours earlier, when the Buccaneers had issued a statement that there would be a press conference the following morning. But on a hunch, this reporter had doubled back in the dark and rain, and he was about to hit the jackpot.

He must have seen my head over the dark green screen of the fence; he began filming just as I carried the boxes through the gate and into the open area. He was across the street, sitting in the back of a news van on airport property, but given the narrow street and small parking area, he was no more than fifty feet away. The lens on his video camera more than compensated for that short distance as I walked directly toward him.

His nighttime footage of me would air repeatedly over the next several days. Everyone in the Tampa viewing area would have multiple opportunities to see Tony Dungy, former head coach of the Tampa Bay Buccaneers, placing boxes into his SUV in the pouring rain.

As I drove away from One Buc, I knew that my real and painful experience of being fired was an all-too-common part of the human condition in the young 21st century. I reminded myself that it was temporary. I took comfort in the knowledge that this, too, would pass. But my emotions were a mixture of peace and bewilderment with a swirl of unanswered questions.

What's next? What could we have done differently?

I kept driving, across Columbus Drive and up Dale Mabry Highway. I went past Raymond James Stadium, where I'd experienced so many highs. Fittingly, it was now empty. As I reached Bearss Avenue, I took a deep breath and let it out slowly. I kept reminding myself that I would move on, that things would turn out all right professionally, that Lauren and the children were resilient enough to handle all of this. And it was obvious to me that God had something else for us, or He wouldn't have closed off what we were doing with the Bucs.

When will I hear Your voice, Lord? Soon, I hope.

I knew everything would ultimately be fine, but at that moment—on that rain-swept night of January 14, 2002—my Explorer and my spirits traveled under the same dark clouds.

GROWING UP
A DUNGY

CHAPTER TWO

What are you going to do to make the situation better?
Dr. Wil Dungy

GROWING UP IN JACKSON, to my way of thinking, was the way growing up was meant to be. Jackson is a small town in Michigan, about an hour from Detroit and twenty-five minutes from East Lansing. In addition to being my birthplace, it lays claim to being the site of the first official meeting of the Republican Party (brought together by the group's common opposition to slavery), and for years it housed the largest walled prison in the world. If those three items are linked, I haven't yet figured out how.

Most of the jobs in Jackson revolved around the auto industry. Guys played high school sports, got out of school, and went to work at one of the big factories. They'd buy a car and get married. That's the way most of the guys I knew approached life.

But because of our parents, we Dungy kids never thought that way. Both my parents were college graduates, and it was always assumed that my siblings and I would go to college. Our parents talked regularly about what we wanted to do and their visions of what we could do. Early on, I thought everyone's parents were like that, but later I learned that I was unusually blessed to have this sort of background. Growing up with educators gave me a different slant on things. More than anything, my mom and dad focused on exercising our brains, building both knowledge and character.

My mom and dad wouldn't tell us, "Here are the steps: A, B, C, and D." Instead, they allowed us to figure things out for ourselves and to explore and grow. Who I am today and the way I think were shaped by that time with my parents. This is true of all the Dungy children. Our parents encouraged us to follow our dreams and told us that if we wanted to do something, we could do it. And, they said, if we did it the Lord's way, for the right reasons, we would be successful. Not that we would win every game or be wealthy, but that we would be successful in God's eyes if we did the things that glorify Him.

Herm Edwards, a longtime friend and now head coach of the Kansas City Chiefs, is always quick to remind me that, of all the Dungy children, I'm the one who is a football coach. I'm pretty sure he means that in a bad way. All three of my siblings are in professions dedicated to serving others. Sherrie is a nurse at the Southern Michigan Correctional Facility near Jackson, devoting her life to inmate care. Linden is a dentist and recently opened his own dental practice. His dream has always been to give care to people who otherwise might not be able to afford it. Lauren, Linden's twin, is a perinatologist. She deals with high-risk pregnancies in Indianapolis and throughout Indiana. All three are exceptional at what they do. My line of work gives me more notoriety in some circles, but they're all doing things that are much more important in the long run. The three of them are definitely a living tribute to our parents and their values.

✝   ✝   ✝

I can still see my mother sitting quietly, intently reading every word, looking for more from the students she believed had been entrusted to her care and nurturing. Many times I was more than just an observer of this scene, as my mom enlisted me to grade papers for her students at Jackson High, where she taught English and public speaking. While I pored over the multiple-choice questions that could easily be graded by an elementary school child, she marked up the essays. Once she had given a grade to each test, she let me record the grades in her book. Although I don't remember the exact names, here's how it went:

> *"John Smith, A. Steve Jones, B. Steve can do better than this. How am I going to get Steve to earn an A? He's not working to his potential."*

While my mom wanted to make sure she provided enough instruction for the voracious learners, she was more concerned with the students who didn't earn As. She never really commented on the ones who got the highest grades; she was more worried about the one getting a B who should have been getting an A. She always had an eye toward her students' God-given potential.

In my mom's mind, the burden was hers: "How can I make the subject more interesting and keep their attention?"

My mom wasn't afraid to go against the grain of how things were usually taught if she could come up with a better way to reach and motivate her students. And when she did go against the grain, she always practiced it on us Dungy kids the night before. In football terms, we were her "scout team."

My mom ultimately did find a way to reach many of her

students. I have received countless cards, letters, and calls from an entire generation who took classes from Mrs. Dungy during her twenty years of teaching, starting in 1966.

I received a letter one day from a man in Detroit:

> *I took public speaking from your mother at Jackson*
> *High in 1979. I have gone on to a career in business,*
> *and my ability to get up in front of groups can be*
> *traced back to that tenth-grade class.*

I think the only downside my mom found to teaching at Jackson High—and it was my fault, I guess—is that when I played football and basketball at rival Parkside High, she had to listen to her students talk about how they were going to shut her son down during any given game.

My mom always insisted on teaching at least one elective English or Public Speaking class. She believed that many of the kids in Jackson decided far too early in life to finish high school and then immediately get a job at the glassworks, the metal shop, or the prison. My mom was concerned—almost fanatical—about making sure her students saw the many different opportunities the world held before deciding to end their education. She used Shakespeare and anything else at her disposal to do it.

One student who took an elective from my mom has called me many times through the years. He had spent his entire childhood in the special-education track of the Jackson schools. Although in special ed, he was able to take public speaking as an elective. Somehow, early in the semester, my mom realized that this student had been mislabeled a "special-ed kid." My mom did not rest until she got his counselor to place him in regular classes. Once he was reassigned, this student began to blossom, and eventually he went on to attend and graduate from Western Michigan University. He gives my mom complete credit for the career he has today.

A life changed.

Our home was a small, green two-story house with wood siding and a dirt backyard. Any grass bold enough to try to come up would be instantly trampled by all the neighborhood kids—and my mom—playing whatever game was in season.

I was in seventh grade before I beat my mom in a foot-race. She and I often raced the sixty or seventy yards around the house. But until that memorable day in junior high, I had never once beaten her.

CleoMae Dungy was tall, athletic, energetic, and quick to laugh. But even as I remember that, my mind also sees her late in life, shrunken and withered, in a wheelchair from years of battling the diabetes that ultimately took her life in 2002.

My mom was born in Amherstburg, Ontario, and she played on Canadian junior basketball teams as a young girl. She carried the title of Most Athletic Dungy throughout her life. Between her love of basketball and serving as adviser to the cheerleading squad at Jackson High, she made sure we Dungy kids were exposed to all kinds of sports. All four of us—Sherrie, the oldest; the younger twins, Linden and Lauren; and I—always looked forward to Tuesdays and Fridays. On those afternoons, we rode on the activity bus to wherever Jackson High was playing, provided we'd been good that week and had completed our schoolwork.

In contrast, my father was more interested in individual sports. I think he was motivated by the desire to continually measure his progress—and by the idea that he could improve by an act of will. As a boy, my dad participated in boxing and track and field; throughout his adulthood, he still followed both regularly. Team sports, from his perspective, existed primarily for the life lessons they could teach his children.

✝   ✝   ✝

My dad was usually a quiet, thoughtful man. A scientist at heart and by training, Wilbur Dungy loved to be outside, enjoying the scenery. Fishing allowed him time to contemplate, to listen, and to marvel at God's creation. My dad used fishing to teach his children to appreciate the everyday wonders of the natural world God created—the sandy shoreline, the dark pine forests, the shimmering water, and the abundant wildlife. The lessons were always memorable, whether we caught a lot of fish or not.

Although we fished countless times together throughout our lives, one particular day stands out in my mind. It was a summer day in 1965. Summers in Michigan are beautiful, with comfortable temperatures and clear, blue skies. I was nine years old, and my brother was five. My dad had taken us fishing at one of the many small lakes around Jackson. On that day, my dad was teaching my brother and me how to cast. We were both working on it, mostly in silence, until my dad's voice finally broke a period of stillness.

"Hey, Linden, don't move for a minute, please." I looked back and watched my dad move his hand toward his face. Calm and deliberate, he continued to speak.

"Now, Linden, always make sure that you know not only where your pole is while you're starting to cast"—at this point, I realized my dad was working my brother's hook out of his own ear—"but also make certain that you know where every-one else is around you."

I learned something about proper casting that day, but I also learned something about patience. Years later, when I got hooked myself, in my hand, I realized *how much it hurts.* Remembering my dad's patience that day when Linden's hook was caught in his ear, I finally understood the importance of staying calm and communicating clearly.

My father taught physiology at Jackson Community College. Both he and my mom had advanced degrees from Michigan State: she an MA in English and he a PhD in physiology. But you'd have been hard-pressed to know that my dad was *Dr.* Wilbur Dungy. He always introduced himself as Wil, and that was how everyone knew him. In fact, after he had known my dad for eight years, my friend Lovie Smith, now the head coach of the Chicago Bears, ran across something that referred to my dad as "Dr. Dungy."

"Tony, is this right? I've talked with your father countless times over the years and spent many a practice with him. He's a *doctor*?"

My dad didn't have the financial means to attend the University of Michigan coming out of high school, so he started at Jackson Community College, which gave him the experience of learning in a college setting. He then went to the University of Michigan in Ann Arbor. After earning his undergraduate degree, he joined the Army Air Corps. Then, after returning and teaching for a year at a segregated high school in Alexandria, Virginia, my dad went back to Jackson Community College, where he became one of the first African American professors in the state community college system. While working on his PhD at Michigan State, my dad continued to teach one class a week at JCC.

Although my dad always considered the University of Michigan his alma mater, those three years at Michigan State—while my mom and dad earned their advanced degrees—had a dramatic impact on me. We were there from 1963 to 1966, and while I vividly remember looking at microscope slides with my dad, I remember being just as enthralled by Duffy Daugherty's Spartan football teams. Those Michigan State teams ultimately altered the trajectory of my life in an unexpected way.

As for the slides, my dad earned his doctorate by studying the effects of cigarette smoking on laboratory rats. He never did tell me how he got the rats to smoke all those cigarettes, but that wasn't the point. I saw many slides of normal rat hearts and lungs, and I also saw stunning slides of rat hearts and lungs that had been exposed to and damaged by cigarette smoke. From the third grade on, I've never had any desire to experiment with any of that stuff—a valuable side benefit of my dad's education. It also taught me something I have put to use as a coach: if I want my players to remember something, one picture isn't worth a thousand words—it's *better*.

We moved back to Jackson in 1966 after my dad's graduation, and he resumed teaching full-time. His goal was to provide students who needed to start at JCC the same eye-opening college experience he had enjoyed. Like my mom, he focused on squeezing every bit of potential from his students, especially those who were struggling. My mom and dad were a perfectly matched set.

My father often said, "If you're going to be a good teacher, you can't just teach the A students. A good teacher is one who helps everybody earn an A." Note that he didn't say he would *give* anybody an A but that he would help his students *earn* it. There's an important difference.

I remind my assistant coaches of that approach every so often. My dad believed you can't teach only one way with only one syllabus, because while some students might get it, others won't. Students have different ways of learning and connecting, and it's the teacher's job to make sure they are all doing so. In the same way, coaches must help players earn an A—that is, learn the material we're presenting—by communicating in a way that makes sense for each individual player. That's one reason I've always hired coaches who value teaching and communication.

My dad was always fascinated by how and why things worked, but at the end of the day, he was most concerned with character. He believed that most of life was an object lesson, and he always found ways to pass those lessons on to his kids.

One day I was complaining to him about the unfairness of life. I forget the situation, but I know he agreed that I had been wronged. His response has stayed with me for many years, even though it took me a while to completely figure it out.

"When I was in the service," he said, "they didn't want to teach us how to fly planes, so we taught ourselves to fly."

We. Blacks. African Americans.

Tuskegee is located about forty miles east of Montgomery, in the heart of Alabama. Founded by General Thomas Simpson Woodward in 1833, the town was allegedly named for a nearby Native American tribe, the Taskigis. Through the years, it has been best known for Tuskegee University, which dates back to 1881, and the school's first president, Booker T. Washington.

In 1940, the United States Army Air Corps selected Tuskegee as the training ground for its fledgling program to train black pilots, who up to that point had been barred from flying in the military. This was the Tuskegee Experiment. Until 1946, when blacks were fully integrated into military training, Tuskegee trained roughly a thousand pilots, none of whom were shot down during World War II bombing runs in Europe. Tuskegee also trained all the support personnel that kept those planes operational throughout the war.

My father was part of the Tuskegee Experiment.

I never knew this until my dad's funeral service in 2004, when someone shared the story during one of the eulogies. Why hadn't he told me about Tuskegee? Maybe it's because he believed the greater point was the lesson. What's important is not the accolades and memories of success but the way you respond when opportunities are denied.

Because I was just a kid, I didn't think to ask for more details when he said, "We taught ourselves to fly." It sounded easy. The lesson, which I did not understand clearly until much later, was that you shouldn't allow external issues to be a hindrance, whether those issues are based on race or any other factor. Things will go wrong at times. You can't always control circumstances. However, you can always control your attitude, approach, and response. Your options are to complain or to look ahead and figure out how to make the situation better.

I use what I learned from that lesson daily—and almost minute by minute on game day.

My siblings and I learned about the unfairness of life in the Dungy household on a regular basis—or so it seemed to us at the time. My parents believed in treating us all as the individuals we were, which didn't fully make sense to me until I became a parent myself.

I often got in trouble for getting home late. I might have a curfew of eight o'clock, and if I stayed out playing basketball until nine or nine-thirty, my father would reprimand me. But at least he always knew where I was. Not being where you said you would be at the time you said you would be there—*that* was a big deal in our house, as was not doing what you said you would do. I learned that pretty early. If you said you were going to do something, you'd better do it.

Of course, our parents gave us the latitude to learn those lessons. They trusted us in a lot of ways that parents aren't able to today. When my parents were getting their advanced degrees at Michigan State in East Lansing, our family lived in the married-student housing units on campus. My parents usually allowed me to play basketball with local high school kids or even Michigan State students, even though I was still in elementary school. They didn't need to be there—it was a different era.

Initially, I could play at the elementary school until the streetlights came on. Later, they'd let me play with some of the high school kids at MSU's intramural building even after dark. My sister Sherrie often got upset because I usually stayed later than I was supposed to and didn't seem to get in as much trouble as my siblings did for the same infraction.

The problem I faced—which my dad understood—was that because I was so little, I rarely got picked for a team. The winning team stayed on the court to face the challengers, comprised of the guy whose turn it was to be captain (he had "next") plus four guys he picked. If my team lost, I'd have to wait until *my* "next" came up and it was my turn to pick a team. Those were usually the times I came home an hour late, and my dad never seemed to get too mad.

After we moved back to Jackson, where I attended junior high and high school, I began playing ball with guys who could drive. We'd drive to Ann Arbor or East Lansing (both about a half hour away) to play at the intramural buildings at the University of Michigan and Michigan State. During that time, I formed a lot of friendships with guys I would later play against in high school. When I got old enough to drive, I'd go anywhere I could find an open court and a game.

It was during this time that I became friends with Bob Elliott from Ann Arbor, who later played center for the

University of Arizona and the New Jersey Nets. He'd call the house with a cryptic message—"They're playing in Romulus (Michigan, home of Detroit Metro Airport, an hour from Jackson)" or "Meet me at the MSU IM (the Michigan State intramural building)"—and I'd tell my mom I was going to play as I headed out the door. She always gave her blessing. She never thought I'd get into trouble; as the cheerleading adviser, she watched all the high school basketball games, so she knew most of the guys I was playing with.

In the summer before our senior year, Bob put a team together, and we played in the high school division of the summer league—the most competitive of its kind—at St. Cecilia Catholic Church in Detroit. A different division, open to players at every level, including the NBA, played later on. Those of us playing in the earlier games stayed to watch the likes of Dave Bing (who played in the NBA for twelve years), George Gervin, and others. Gervin was at Eastern Michigan at the time, and while most teams were pretty loaded with all-star lineups, he had surrounded himself with his high school buddies. But he carried them to wins most nights by scoring fifty or sixty points himself. When you're the "Iceman" and go on to be third all-time in NBA season scoring titles, you can surround yourself with just about anyone, I suppose, and still win.

Bob Elliott and I have remained great friends ever since those days of barnstorming any and every game we could find. But in today's world, I can't picture allowing my high school son, Eric, to drive from our home in Indianapolis to Lafayette or Bloomington by himself. I don't think he'd even ask. Times were different then, which was good for a gym rat like me.

As a kid, I wasn't too much of a discipline problem, though I did end up sitting on the couch, not allowed to go out and play, more often than I would have liked. For me, that was much worse than a spanking. Usually my mom and dad were calm and gave us the whys and hows of the situation before they took away privileges.

All four Dungy kids were disciplined in different ways. My folks knew that certain things would change my behavior but not Linden's. So even though I'd moan about it, they did whatever they thought would work best with each child. My parents always looked at every situation individually, regardless of what seemed fair to us. That's something that took me a while to appreciate, but learning to view each situation by itself has helped me in coaching. I know that I can have blanket rules, but blanket rules don't always fit every individual. I need to treat everybody fairly, but *fair* doesn't always mean *equal*.

I apply that lesson quite frequently with players. Some guys can handle more responsibility, while some aren't ready. A rookie might simply get an explanation from me, while a veteran making the same mistake might get "torched." The veteran should know better, while the rookie is just learning.

To whom much is given, much is required—whether it's privileges, responsibilities, or material items. And if God has given you a lot of ability, I believe you should be held to a higher level of expectation.

It's hard to overestimate the importance of the lessons my parents taught me—lessons that have molded and shaped me. The necessity of persistence, the value of education, the fun of athletics, and the importance of living up to your potential. However, there is one gift they bestowed that I would place above all the others: faith.

My grandfather on my dad's side was a minister who occasionally taught courses at Detroit Bible College. Two of my father's brothers became ministers as well.

As a kid, I understood that Sundays meant good eating.

When I was three, my grandparents moved from Jackson to a two-story home in Detroit. Their church of about one hundred and fifty met on the first floor, while my grandparents lived above the church on the second floor. Each Sunday, about halfway through the service, we could smell the dinner that my grandmother was cooking upstairs. We'd wait for the service to end and then slip up the side entrance to their rooms for Sunday dinner. My grandmother always greeted us with excuses ready: "I couldn't find my best knife" or "I couldn't find my shortening, so I used something else" or "This rhubarb pie has been in the freezer for two weeks, but we'll try it." Regardless of the excuses, Sunday dinner was always good.

My mother's side of the family also gave me plenty of godly heritage. Her parents were God-fearing people of high integrity who died before I was ten. My mother was a phenomenal storyteller, and from her I learned the importance of illustrating a lesson with a word picture. She taught Sunday school every week, and usually, as with her Jackson High lessons, she practiced her Sunday school lessons on us Thursday or Friday night. I knew a ton of Bible stories before I could even read a Bible—a rich heritage.

As far back as I can remember, I understood who Jesus was, that He died because of the things I had done wrong, and that I could go to heaven if I asked Him into my life. I'm guessing I was about five when I first learned that. Despite the Christian lifestyle my parents modeled for me, a real understanding of what it means to make Jesus the Lord of my life—number one in my life—wouldn't hit home until many years later, when I was in the NFL in Pittsburgh.

I can't place a value on the lessons I learned and on the faith my parents imparted day after day after day.

Actually, I can; the value is eternal.

A BLACK QUARTERBACK

CHAPTER THREE

The LORD doesn't see things the way you see them. People judge by outward appearance, but the LORD looks at the heart.

I SAMUEL 16:7

I WANTED TO BE A SPARTAN. My dad may have been a Wolverine when he was an undergrad, but after my parents finished earning their graduate degrees in East Lansing, I returned to Jackson as a huge Michigan State fan.

Both as a sophomore and as a junior, I started at quarterback on the Parkside High School varsity football team, and I had very good seasons both years. As a team, we were fairly good, although when I was in tenth grade, we lost our last game of the year to Jackson High School, my mom's school. We remedied that loss by beating them my junior year.

Although basketball was my favorite sport and I hadn't given much thought to playing football in college, it wasn't out of the question. And if I ever did play in college, I knew it would be for Duffy Daugherty at Michigan State.

But then, following our win against Jackson at the end of my junior season, I quit the high school football team. I was seventeen years old and pretty sure I knew more than my high school football coach, and I was prepared to take a stand.

Quitting wasn't a devastating blow for me. After all, basketball was my primary sport, and we were having a great season. Besides, sometimes making a statement means personal sacrifice, and I was prepared to make mine by quitting the football team.

Today I have a tremendous relationship with Dave Driscoll, my high school football coach. But it wasn't always that way. And if it weren't for an assistant principal who took an interest in me, I'm sure my life would have unfolded quite differently.

Leroy Rocquemore was an African American administrator at our predominately white junior high school. Although he took a personal interest in all the kids, he seemed to pay special attention to the African American boys. He wanted to make sure that we grew as people, not just as athletes. He often took us to basketball games and to movies, or sometimes he simply had lunch with us. Many times he brought us into his office to talk about things other than school. In short, he cared. For two years at Frost Junior High School, I got to know Mr. Rocquemore as more than just an administrator. He was a friend, and when I moved up to Parkside High, he continued to keep tabs on my friends and me.

One of my closest buddies was Bobby Burton, a receiver. The two of us had been starters on the varsity team since our sophomore season and were the leading offensive players on the team. We had just finished the football season of our junior year at Parkside, and it had been a pretty good year, all in all.

Coach Driscoll's policy was for the team to vote for the following year's captains at the end of the season. The winners would be announced at the fall sports banquet in November. That year, I was elected as a team captain. Bobby wasn't.

I just couldn't understand this. It seemed obvious to me that both of us should have been the captains. I could only think of one explanation: for some reason the school didn't want two black captains. It seems impossible now, but at the time it didn't. Parkside's football team had never had two black captains, and no one could convince me that those votes had been counted correctly.

I was hurt and felt certain that a race-based injustice had been done. Reacting to the hurt I felt for Bobby—as well as for myself and for all of the black players—I quit the team. I told Coach Driscoll that I was just going to play basketball my senior year. Basketball was my favorite sport anyway.

Of course, I was a fairly good player, a popular student, a newly elected captain, and the quarterback, so the other African American players decided they were going to quit the football team too. I hadn't really thought about that possibility when I decided I wasn't going to play, but it didn't bother me at the time. I figured everybody had to make his own decision.

My dad, of course, said I had to do what I thought was best. But, as he always did, he wanted to know what I was going to do to improve the situation. He wanted to know what I could do to make things better, rather than just reacting. But I was seventeen, and I didn't care if the situation got better or not. My feelings were hurt. Bobby's feelings were hurt. And I was so focused on playing basketball in college that I didn't think I would miss football in the least.

The player walkout began after the postseason banquet in November and continued through the rest of the school year. At the end of the summer, when the team was preparing to go back to practice, Mr. Rocquemore invited me to his house. He had already talked to me a couple of times about my decision to quit football, but I think he wanted to give me one more chance to reconsider.

"Tony, you enjoy playing football, and these other guys enjoy playing football. You should have your senior year to play, and so should they. At the end of the day, what are you really upset about, anyway?"

I began to answer, but he continued, talking over me without waiting for a response. I hadn't realized his question was rhetorical. "Even if the issues are that important, should they spoil the fun that all of you should be having playing football as seniors? Thirty years from now, you don't want to look back and say that you missed out on something you really loved doing." Then he asked the question he really wanted me to answer. "Why would you let *anything* stop you from doing what you have the ability to do?"

Although by then I was convinced he was right, I had always had quite a temper, and my pride just wouldn't allow me to back down. Practically speaking, I could understand Mr. Rocquemore's point, but from a moral standpoint, I was still pretty sure I was in the right. Plus, at seventeen (and even at fifty-one) pride and hurt feelings can be pretty overwhelming emotions.

Mr. Rocquemore knew I would have trouble asking Coach Driscoll if I could return, so he said he would talk with him and do his best to smooth everything over. "I'll tell him you want to play and make everything all right. Don't worry about it."

After he spoke with Coach Driscoll, Mr. Rocquemore arranged for the three of us to meet. Coach was a very principled guy, and he set the tone for the meeting.

"Tony, you can come back, but you've missed winter conditioning, and you've missed our summer workouts. So you guys"—he knew if I came back, the others would also come back—"are going to have to do some extra stuff to earn your way back." He mentioned extra running, washing the dishes at camp, and so forth, as his requirements "if I'm going to let you back."

When he had finished, I think the only thing I had heard was, "if I'm going to let you back." I was getting mad, thinking, If *he's going to let me back?* I started to get visibly upset, and Mr. Rocquemore gave me a look—it was the same look I would later give John Lynch during a press conference before the 1999 NFC Championship Game in St. Louis—that kept me quiet and in my seat. But all the while, even Mr. Rocquemore was thinking, *Now why did Coach have to go* there?

After the meeting, he took me aside and said, "Coach is the coach, and you're the player, and there are times in life when you're going to have to do certain things. That's just how it goes. That's a lesson you're going to have to learn to get through life."

In the end, we all went back and worked our way back onto the team. It was a great year—we only lost one game, the de facto state championship game (they didn't have play-offs in those days). Even more important, today I have a great relationship with Coach Driscoll. In fact, he came to Super Bowl XLI to see me, and we shared an emotional hug at our Saturday practice before the game.

I see now what I couldn't as a strong-willed teenager, thanks to the firm hand of Coach Driscoll and the gentle guidance of Mr. Rocquemore. If Mr. Rocquemore hadn't taken that interest in me—not merely as an athlete and a student but as a friend—everything would have been different for me.

When my friends and I left him and went to high school, he didn't stop caring about us. If he had, I wouldn't have played football my senior year, and many doors never would have opened for me later in life. He took a step he didn't have to take, and I listened to him based largely on the relationship he had worked to develop with me. I use this principle all the time now that I'm coaching.

That experience also taught me about the downside of making quick decisions. To this day, I'm very deliberate—probably too deliberate at times—when I can afford to take the time to sort through a decision-making process.

Something got in the way of my vision of playing football for Duffy Daugherty at Michigan State: he retired. But his retirement opened up a number of possibilities in my mind. I considered playing basketball at Duke or Arizona, where my friend Bob Elliott was headed. I also thought about the University of Southern California for football. I had gotten to know a number of players on different recruiting trips, including Gary Jeter, a high school All-American from Ohio. Wayne Fontes, who was then a USC assistant coach as well as their national recruiter, invited me—along with Gary Jeter and Marvin Powell, another future star—to spend a weekend at Southern Cal.

Although I couldn't make the trip to USC, the visit really impressed the other guys, who called me during the weekend. "Tony, you've gotta come here!" Gary said. "You won't believe it—they're gonna put us in the movies, in Hollywood! They took us over to the Sunset Strip. This place is really something!"

The pitch worked for them. They ended up at USC but didn't have time for the movies, since Gary and Marvin kept busy with football in college and then went on to play in the NFL for thirteen and eleven years, respectively.

Meanwhile, another coach had warned me about Southern Cal. "You'll never play quarterback," he said. "Their quarterback lived with the coach. You can't possibly beat him out." I initially chalked this up to negative recruiting. But sure enough, when I did some research, I found that Pat Haden, USC's sophomore quarterback, had lived with head coach John McKay's family while he was in high school. I scratched USC off my list.

Cal Stoll, the second-year head coach at the University of Minnesota, actually presented the most intriguing opportunity for me. Cal had coached the wide receivers at Michigan State under Coach Daugherty, and I saw joining his program at Minnesota as the closest thing to playing at Michigan State. Plus, two coaches I really liked—Woody Widenhofer and Tom Moore—were doggedly recruiting me to Minnesota.

Minneapolis was closer to Jackson than Southern Cal—but not too close. And the city seemed to be home to a large number of Fortune 500 companies. Although I wasn't sure what line of work I would end up in, I figured that an education, plus summers spent working for some of those companies, would yield lifelong dividends.

At Minnesota, I could play both basketball and football, which wasn't possible at most of the other schools I was looking at. Playing more than one sport was a fairly new thing at the time, although Quinn Buckner had done it at Indiana University during my senior year of high school. He had been named the Chicago High School Player of the Year in both football and basketball, and he continued in both sports at IU. I thought I would like to play both as well, and Minnesota was one of the few schools that was open to the idea of their quarterback also playing basketball.

Woody Widenhofer was the best recruiter I had ever seen. He attended almost every one of my basketball games my senior year, and we became lifelong friends. But shortly after I signed with Minnesota, Coach Widenhofer resigned and joined the Pittsburgh Steelers. Tom Moore stayed at Minnesota as the quarterbacks coach, and it was from him that I learned the same offense we run together in Indianapolis today. It was a perfect fit for me and my skills because it allowed me to call much of the game and think while I was out on the field.

Coach Cal Stoll at Minnesota was one of the first CEO-type coaches. Most of the coaches I had seen previously, such as Coach Driscoll, coached either the offense or the defense in addition to performing the duties of a head coach. Coach Stoll did not. He wasn't one of those tower-type coaches like Bear Bryant at Alabama, who was far removed from the field. Coach Stoll, like Coach Daugherty had done at Michigan State, hired great teachers as his assistants and then gave them the latitude to coach. He set the vision and direction, motivated the team, and then let the assistant coaches do the coaching.

Coach Stoll held a meeting with the freshmen every year. During the course of our meeting, he asked, "Every one of you thinks you are going to play in the NFL, right?" Every head in the room nodded. He pulled out a photograph of the freshman team from five years prior. The guys who made it to the NFL were circled.

"Him. And him," he said, pointing to the picture. "Two of them made it. Out of thirty-two, thirty-three, thirty-five, whatever we've got this year, one of you will go on to play in the NFL. Or if you're lucky, two. You're going to have to outwork everybody in this room and then catch a break in order to make your living in the NFL."

Of course, we each thought we were going to be that one, but I must admit, this did make an impression. Coach Stoll went on to talk about our education and preparing for the rest of our lives—lives without football. Since I was just days removed from my parents' home, that message resonated with me.

He continued, "Success is uncommon and not to be enjoyed by the common man. I'm looking for uncommon people because we want to be successful, not average."

Listening to Coach Stoll, I knew I had a greater chance of becoming uncommon by my efforts than I did by my natural gifts. Some players are uncommon because of their God-given natural abilities, like being blessed with the height of Yao Ming or the vertical jump of Michael Jordan. Others have to work to become uncommon. Steve Kerr of the Chicago Bulls shot five hundred free throws a day to make himself uncommon.

The truth is that most people have a better chance to be uncommon by effort than by natural gifts. Anyone *could* give that effort in his or her chosen endeavor, but the typical person doesn't, choosing to do only enough to get by.

That lesson was still fresh in my mind a few weeks later when we took the field in Columbus for Minnesota's season opener against Ohio State. As we warmed up, Coach Stoll assured us that we could win even though we were heavy underdogs. After a few minutes, the Ohio State players emerged to a big roar from the crowd. I turned to Larry Powell, a highly touted freshman running back, and proclaimed, "Powell, we can get these guys. Look at 'em. They're not as big as I thought they'd be."

Five minutes later, Ohio State's offensive and defensive linemen came out of the tunnel to join the rest of the team, and I realized that those initial fifty guys were only their skill-position players.

Larry turned to me and spoke slowly, drawing out every word. "Tony . . . I don't know how we're going to do today."

The halftime score was 35–7, on the way to a final of 56–7, Ohio State. Coach Stoll calmly confessed after the game that he didn't have a speech for that situation.

So much for my spectacular introduction to college football.

I did get in the game for a few plays toward the end, but most people were watching an Ohio State sophomore running back who started making history that day. Archie Griffin began his thirty-one-game streak with at least one hundred yards rushing in each game. Incidentally, his last game in that streak also came against us, in 1975—my junior year.

I got hurt late in my sophomore year of football, and that caused me to give up basketball after only one season. It was actually a good decision; the demands of playing both sports at a high level while keeping up academically were really more than I could handle.

Although most of my college football memories are positive, some of the clearest include close losses in games that we had a chance to win—later games against Ohio State and Michigan immediately come to mind. In addition, it was during these years that I realized I needed to make some decisions about my own personal values.

Like most underclassmen, I wanted to fit in. Many of the guys I played football with went out for a few beers at night or went to campus parties, which always included drugs and alcohol. Throughout high school I had never known anyone—anyone, that is, who was an athlete or serious about taking care of his body—who drank, smoked, or took drugs. No one I respected, anyway.

That changed at the University of Minnesota. There, guys who were performing at very high levels athletically also drank, smoked, and used various illegal drugs. Some coaches from other sports knew about it and even encouraged players to take their recruits to area bars.

At that point, I was forced to rethink my stance on drinking and drugs and make a decision that wasn't necessarily performance based. Up until then, my primary reason for not drinking and doing drugs was that it would hurt my performance—my dad's slides of those cigarette-smoking lab rats had never left my mind. Once the decision moved to a moral ground, however, I still came out at the same place.

What would my mom and dad think? always went through my mind whenever I had the opportunity to take a drink or smoke a cigarette. I had been taught that smoking and drinking were not right for us as a family, and illegal drugs—well, they were illegal. Therefore, they were not for me. But this was a test, because I saw that great athletes could drink and do drugs and get away with it—for a while.

I still hung out with all the guys and went to parties, but I never did smoke, drink, or take any drugs. And the more I was around those things, the more I understood why my decision was a smart one.

Wisconsin is a big rival for Minnesota. Even today, Big Ten alums in our Colts locker room laugh about the rivalry games in the conference. It seems that each week, the teams are playing for something: the Old Oaken Bucket (Purdue–Indiana), the Little Brown Jug (Minnesota–Michigan), the Illibuck (Illinois–Ohio State), the Governor's Victory Bell (Minnesota–Penn State), the Heartland Trophy (Iowa–Wisconsin), the Paul Bunyan Governor's Trophy (Michigan–Michigan State), or a bronze pig called the Floyd of Rosedale (Minnesota–Iowa). If somebody's not handing something over after a game, it just doesn't seem like a Big Ten game. The Minnesota–Wisconsin game is the longest-running rivalry game, dating back to 1890. The winner gets Paul Bunyan's Axe.

My junior year, we were playing Wisconsin at home in Minneapolis. The weather all week had been awful, with heavy snow in the middle of the week. I told my folks not to bother trying to make the trip, but by Saturday the weather was perfect, with clear blue skies and the bracing Minnesota cold of late November. It was around thirty degrees, and the snow that had been cleared off the field was piled four feet high along the benches. Wisconsin had trounced us the year before in Madison, and we had some guys from Madison on our team who badly wanted to win. In addition, this was our last game of the year, and we wanted to send our seniors out with a victory. It was an emotional game for us.

As we got into the game, we found we could run at will against them. From the opening kickoff, we could just *feel* that we were going to win. On the opening drive, we took the ball and gashed their defense all the way down the field with our running game. But I knew I only needed one touchdown pass to set the Big Ten record. So on first down and goal from their seven yard line, I changed the play at the line of scrimmage from a run to a pass. As I was releasing the ball, my arm got hit, and my pass was intercepted in the end zone. When I came off the field, our offensive line coach, Roger French, was there to meet me. "I am so mad," he shouted at me. "If I had a gun, I would shoot you right now!"

I was glad he was unarmed.

Coach French later went to Brigham Young University and coordinated some explosive passing offenses, but that day—understandably—he wanted to run the ball. Thankfully, our running backs stayed hot, the offensive line controlled the line of scrimmage, and we dominated Wisconsin with the run, winning 24–3. I even threw that touchdown pass to set the record. And we were happy to have Wisconsin hand over Paul Bunyan's Axe.

When I arrived in Minneapolis in the summer of 1973, I was eager to start learning the no-huddle offense from Coach Tom

Moore as soon as possible. I also wanted to familiarize myself with the campus and begin a summer job.

The school lined me up with a position at a meatpacking plant called Feinberg's. It was within walking distance from where I was living—about fifteen blocks—which was ideal because I didn't have a car. My shift started at 6 a.m., which gave me time in the afternoon to work out and spend time learning the offense with Tom.

There were two minor difficulties with the meatpacking job. First, I had never worked so hard in my life, before or since. Second, I always seemed to have stray dogs following me from work to the university's football offices. I didn't feel like I was in danger of being attacked, but it took me about three days to figure out what was attracting them—the smell of pastrami.

I stuck with that job all summer, remembering what my dad had taught me about learning from every experience. I definitely learned one thing—I never wanted to work in a meatpacking plant again. It made me value my football scholarship and free college education much more. After that summer, I found jobs on my own, without the university's assistance. No more meatpacking.

The summer after my freshman year, I had a great job working for Cargill on a research farm in Elk River, just north of Minneapolis. I would pick up three inner-city high school boys and drive them to the farm, where we helped with some of the research projects. Despite the early schedule—we had to be there at 7 a.m., meaning we left around 6 a.m.—I really enjoyed it. The farm tested different types of animal feeds. We would measure the amount of food that was given and what was left over (in the troughs, thankfully) and weigh the animals periodically, among other tasks. We all found it fascinating. I got to know the high school boys through our conversations on the way *to* the farm since we were usually too tired to talk on the way back. It was one of the first times I really understood that not everyone had a dad at home.

In my third year, I hit the jackpot, landing one of those office jobs I had always heard about—an internship with General Mills. Our team was introducing a new cereal, Golden Grahams, into the national market by testing it in three or four cities and creating an advertising campaign. It was like being on *The Apprentice*—without the worry of getting fired. I finally felt like I was putting my business courses to good use. But I also realized that neckties and I were not compatible. I still get a headache if I wear a tie for more than fifteen minutes.

By my senior year, my reputation as a football player was building, and the jobs were a little easier to find. I was much better at avoiding early mornings, farm animals, meat-rending machines, and ties. That summer I worked in the sporting goods department of Dayton Hudson's flagship department store in downtown Minneapolis. Right before the season started, the *Minneapolis Tribune* ran a preseason Big Ten section with a story about me, along with my photo. With my huge afro and suit, I looked as if I had just walked off the stage from a Sly and the Family Stone gig. The caption asked, "Would you buy a tennis racket from this man?"

Probably a fair question.

In the end, I carved out a pretty nice college football career under Coaches Stoll and Moore at Minnesota. I graduated as fourth all-time in total offense in the Big Ten, a two-time team Most Valuable Player, and captain my senior year. I was also a two-time Academic All–Big Ten, all the while having a blast running our innovative offense.

We played Illinois my senior year, and they executed

very sophisticated schemes on defense, requiring me to make adjustments during the game: "If you see this alignment, we're getting into this formation," and so forth, as Tom Moore had instructed me. We won the game, 29–14, and afterward, their head coach, Bob Blackman, congratulated me for the work I had done orchestrating our offense. That meant a lot to me coming from him, because the intricacies of their defense were specifically designed to confuse the quarterback.

As a result of my on-field performance in college, there was no doubt in my mind that I would be drafted and go on to a career as a quarterback in the NFL. I had worked out for scouts and coaches from a number of teams, including the Washington Redskins, who said they would be looking for a third quarterback and that I fit the bill. Some friends thought I might go to the Vikings since my style was so similar to that of Fran Tarkenton, their quarterback at the time.

I shared a fairly small apartment in Minneapolis with my teammate, wide receiver Mike Jones. Mike was from Detroit Central High School and was terrifically talented. Terrell Owens reminds me of Mike—a tall, sleek, fast guy who can run, catch, and jump. Mike had hurt his Achilles tendon our junior year and was never quite the same after the injury, but he was hoping to be drafted as well.

Back then, the NFL draft wasn't televised over the weekend. That year, 1977, the draft was held on a Tuesday and Wednesday, and it lasted twelve rounds. Three of the guys Wayne Fontes had recruited to USC four years earlier turned out to be as good as advertised. Ricky Bell went to the Buccaneers as the first pick overall, Marvin Powell went fourth to the New York Jets, and Gary Jeter went fifth to the New York Giants.

My only goal was to go somewhere in the remaining 330 picks.

Mike and I waited by the phone all day Tuesday, then

started our vigil again Wednesday morning. The phone finally rang Wednesday afternoon. The Giants were on the line in the tenth round—and wanted to speak with Mike. So Mike was the 255th pick, following our defensive back, George Adzick, who had gone to Seattle in the ninth round. I hoped Coach Stoll hadn't been right when he said only two guys would go to the NFL. We celebrated Mike's selection for a while and then turned our attention back to the phone to wait for my call.

The phone didn't ring again. And while I didn't know it at the time, it wouldn't be the last time I waited by the phone for a call that never came. That evening, around eight o'clock, we called a buddy who was with the Associated Press.

"Is the draft over?" I asked.

"Yeah, it's over," he confirmed. We hung up.

"Hmmm. Nobody called me. That doesn't seem like a good sign. . . ."

It wasn't. The phone did ring a short while later, though, as NFL clubs tried to fill out their rosters, much as they do today. Starting toward the end of the draft, clubs begin to get an idea of the positions they still need to fill for training camp. If they're not able to draft enough players at a position to fill out their roster, the scouts begin working the phones, trying to find the highest-rated nondrafted players who might agree to come to camp as free agents.

I had a number of opportunities during the course of those telephone calls to play defensive back or wide receiver, but I didn't receive a single offer to play quarterback in the NFL.

I was crushed.

PUTTING GOD FIRST

CHAPTER FOUR

Seek ye first the kingdom of God, and his righteousness; and all these things shall be added unto you.
    MATTHEW 6:33 (KJV)

I WAS IN SHOCK after not being drafted into the NFL. Something about this didn't seem fair. It didn't seem right. I was numb. Devastated. I prayed, *God, I can't believe it. Help me figure out what I'm supposed to do now.*

I did have one opportunity to play quarterback, but it was in Canada. The Montreal Alouettes held my rights in the Canadian Football League, and their coach, Marv Levy, had spoken with me a number of times before the draft.

"See what happens in the draft, but keep your mind open to coming here," he said. "You'd be perfect for this game with your style. You'll be in this league for a long time."

Looking back, I think the National Football League couldn't figure out what to do with a black quarterback who wasn't a prototypical drop-back, passing quarterback. The following year, 1978, Doug Williams came out of Grambling State and was drafted in the first round by the Buccaneers. Doug, however, had tools I didn't have: he was about three inches taller than my six-foot-one frame, had about thirty pounds more than my 180, and was a pocket passer with a cannon for an arm. I was more like Warren Moon, who came out of the University of Washington the same year. Warren wasn't drafted either, and he started his career in the Canadian Football League.

A number of the NFL free-agent calls were offering me between $1,000 and $1,500 as a signing bonus. By contrast, Montreal was offering me a bonus of $50,000. However, I had always had my sights set on the NFL; I wanted to compete against the players I felt were the very best. I was hoping for a divine signal that would make my decision clear, even if it meant signing to play a totally new position.

Lord, I'd really like to play in the NFL, but it doesn't appear to make a whole lot of sense right now. I've pretty much got a guarantee to make the team as the quarterback in Montreal for more money, but I really want to try the NFL, even though it'll be at a position I've never played. Please help me figure out what to do. I prayed that prayer—and others like it—repeatedly over the next few days.

It would have been helpful to have a clear sign as to the direction the Lord wanted me to go—maybe something plastered on a billboard on the side of the road or flashed on a scoreboard at a stadium or written clearly in the clouds with a divine finger. I have to admit that I looked in all those places, just in case.

At that moment, even a powerful wind, earthquake, or fire similar to what Elijah had experienced would have been helpful—although, as it turned out, the Lord didn't appear to Elijah in any of those. Instead, it was a gentle whisper—a still, small voice—in which Elijah heard the Lord speaking. How did Elijah do that? I have always felt I needed a loud voice or a clear sign to help me make decisions in times like that.

I didn't hear the audible voice, but in my heart I still felt led to the NFL. I talked with Tom Sherman of the Buffalo Bills, who wanted to play me at free safety. I was ready to head up there to play when Tom Moore, my college coach, entered the picture again.

Tom had left the University of Minnesota after my senior season and joined Woody Widenhofer as a wide receivers coach with the Pittsburgh Steelers. Tom and Woody had spoken with the Steelers head coach, Chuck Noll, and told him that I was a bright guy who could fit somewhere within their organization. They didn't need another quarterback—they'd taken Cliff Stoudt in the fifth round—but Tom told me he was sure I could help the Steelers in some way. I updated him on the Bills situation, letting him know that Tom Sherman was mailing a contract to me the next morning. Tom Moore hopped on a flight and brought the Steelers contract with him, ensuring he arrived before the mail.

I called Tom Sherman and explained that I knew several coaches with the Steelers and felt that was the better opportunity. Then I signed with the Pittsburgh Steelers for a bonus of $2,200, plus another $20,000 in salary if I made the team. I was so excited and sure that was where God wanted me to go—until I started telling my friends.

"Are you nuts? What position do you think you're going to play?" The Steelers had just missed going to their third straight Super Bowl in 1976. "You think you're going to play receiver? Ever heard of John Stallworth? Well, even he doesn't start at receiver for them. And eight of the defensive guys—*eight* of them—just went to the Pro Bowl, plus three guys from the offense. Eleven guys in the Pro Bowl! Donnie Shell and Jimmy Allen are the backup DBs. Where do you think you're gonna play? How are you even gonna make the team?"

"Well, uh, I don't know. I want to play with the best, and

these guys are the best." Signing with the Steelers had seemed like the right thing to do immediately after the draft, but I found myself second-guessing my decision for about a week afterward.

I was just walking in faith—faith in God and faith in what Tom had told me: "You're a smart guy, so you're going to have chances to make it with us in Pittsburgh somewhere. And since we're already good, it's not like we need to give the veterans much work in the preseason. We won't need to worry about playing our first-string offense to see how they're going to function as a unit. We know how they're going to function. Coach Noll wants to give the young guys lots of chances to play in the preseason games, so you'll get a chance to show what you can do on the field, to come in and make an impression—whenever we figure out where to put you."

The more I thought about it, it didn't really seem like a logical decision at all, but I *had* prayed about it, and joining the Steelers just seemed to be the right thing to do. Over and over in life, I've looked for that moment captured by Cecil B. DeMille in *The Ten Commandments,* when I could hear that same voice of God so clearly heard by Moses at the edge of the Red Sea: "Go this way, and I'll part the waters for you." But there has been no such moment. I have yet to hear God's audible voice, although I have often felt led by God in more subtle ways. My dad always believed that God uses the logic and the passion He's given us to help direct us, and I believe that too. This must be the "gentle whisper" thing. The "still, small voice."

So I headed off to Pittsburgh with no idea what God had in store for me—either personally or professionally—in that city.

It turned out that I was a wide receiver in the NFL . . . for about two months. I went through the minicamps and about two weeks of training camp; then, because of some injuries to other players, the Steelers moved me across the line of scrimmage to the defense, at safety.

I loved the challenge of learning a new position, and it was great to be in with Mel Blount, Donnie Shell, Jimmy Allen, and the rest of those guys. Fortunately for me, they were all willing to help, and our defensive coordinator, Bud Carson, was a genius. I absorbed everything I could from him. In fact, I was so busy studying and watching game films that the coaches let me borrow a 16mm projector so I could watch them in my room. Unfortunately, the projector somehow interfered with the television reception—causing "snow" on the veteran players' TV screen.

In addition to many great players, that team included some really solid Christians. Because of our physical and rough style of play, we weren't necessarily seen as a group of believers. But even head coach Chuck Noll, who was a devout Catholic, often used Bible verses to inspire us. When Mark Brunell, Tony Boselli, Kyle Brady, and other Jacksonville Jaguars players were criticized in the late 1990s for not being tough enough on the football field because they were Christians, I could only think of our Steelers teams of the 1970s and smile.

Larry Brown, Jon Kolb, Donnie Shell, and John Stallworth all really worked hard to put God first in everything they did, every day. "What would Jesus do?" they asked, well before bracelets and bumper stickers made that phrase popular. Donnie, in particular, was one of the most fired-up Christians I had ever met. He was the captain of the special teams when I arrived, and he was determined to become a starter on defense, even with the great players the Steelers had then. He and John Stallworth were best friends, and both were great examples for me.

Jon Kolb and Larry Brown, two of the biggest, strongest linemen I knew, both had mild, gentle spirits. When I arrived in Pittsburgh, they were still known as the Steel Curtain and had a tough, somewhat negative image. Once I stepped inside the circle, I realized how far from the truth that perception was. It was refreshing to see how different these guys were from any other group I had ever been around.

+ + +

As I alluded to earlier, I had always had a problem with my temper. I often earned technical fouls in my high school basketball games and was known to lose my cool in football games as well. In high school and college, I was a perfectionist, usually riding my teammates rather than encouraging them.

"Venting," I called it.

"Dumb," my dad called it.

Our exchanges usually ran something like this:

"Did you change the referee's call?"

"No."

"Did it make the situation better?"

"No, but I felt better, and then I could focus."

"Well, you might have felt better faster if you were thinking about the next play instead of taking three or four or ten plays to 'vent.' You waste a lot of emotion and energy in venting or in worrying about an injustice or something you can't do anything about."

That was excellent advice from my dad, but I wasn't ready to listen. It wasn't until those Steelers invited me into their Bible study that I really began to change. There I was exposed to guys I respected who were constantly in God's Word— always praying and reading their Bibles together. These professional players were not the weak and the meek; they were some of the biggest, toughest guys I had ever met. And yet they were drawing their strength and purpose from God.

I had known from a young age that I was going to heaven, but I had never fully engaged God and let Him direct my life moment by moment until I saw those guys doing it. I had been a good kid, by and large; I stayed out of trouble, was usually polite, and stood up for my values. Yet the concept of putting God first in *everything* I did hadn't been my primary focus. Finally I understood, and I started to move from being a casual Christian to a fully committed follower of Jesus.

My crash course in playing safety must have worked, because I was still on the team as we headed into the final cuts before the regular season. Some of my success resulted from my efforts to absorb the defensive scheme by asking questions and watching film on my own, but a good bit of it stemmed from the fact that I bought into Coach Noll's approach so quickly.

At the Steelers minicamp, shortly after the draft, I had taken to heart Coach Noll's words about what it took to win in the National Football League.

"Champions don't beat themselves," he told us. "If you want to win, do the ordinary things better than anyone else does—day in and day out. We're not going to fool people or outscheme them. We're just going to outplay them. Because we'll know what we're doing. When we get into a critical situation, we won't have to think. We'll play fast and fundamentally sound."

Chuck Noll developed much of his coaching philosophy from the legendary Paul Brown, and I got mine from Chuck. I tell people that I'm from the Paul Brown school of football.

It was the summer of 1977, and I still hadn't made the team.

In those days, the relationship of the football clubs and

the media was different. Local reporters traveled on the team charter to games. I vividly recall Dwight White, our Pro Bowl defensive end, sitting in the back of the plane, blowing cigar smoke rings while talking with Vito Stellino, one of Pittsburgh's beat writers at the time. Vito always had good information, in part because he was good at what he did and in part because he sat in the back of the plane with Dwight White.

After training camp, we stayed at the historic William Penn Hotel in downtown Pittsburgh. Coach Noll made the rookie room assignments alphabetically, so my roommate was linebacker Robin Cole, the first-round draft choice from the University of New Mexico. I had met Robin at a college all-star game our senior year, so we were pretty good friends by then.

We played our last preseason game on a Friday night and had the weekend off until Monday's team meeting. The last cut would be made on Saturday or Sunday, whenever the coaching staff made their decision. On Saturday morning, I picked up a paper and immediately turned to Vito Stellino's article detailing which guys were going to get cut. My name was on Vito's list. I figured that if the story was in the paper, Vito must have gotten his information from the coaches, Dwight, or some other "reliable source."

I decided not to leave the hotel all weekend. I didn't want to miss that phone call. The last thing I wanted was to walk into Monday morning's team meeting and get cut in front of a roomful of guys. Meanwhile, my roommate, Robin, was gone for much of the weekend. He was relaxing—coming and going from the hotel with the confident swagger of a first-round draft pick.

For the second time in four months, I sat for two solid days beside a phone that never rang. I kept calling down to the front desk. "Are you sure there aren't any calls for my room?"

Monday rolled around. It was a hot, steamy September morning in Pittsburgh. I drove to the facility with Robin, sneaking into the back of the locker room so nobody could see me. They had left my stuff in my locker. I was just about to take my personal belongings when I saw my name plate on my locker—it was still there. Suddenly I realized, *I've made the team.* I played it cool, making sure everything was hung up neatly, acting as if I had just been doing a bit of rearranging.

I don't think Coach Noll even realizes what an important lesson I learned that weekend. It was an unforgettable and excruciating experience, that entire weekend of sitting and waiting. To this day, I make sure to tell our guys exactly when cuts are coming, and I try to give them a one-hour time window to stay by their phones.

Early in that first season, the issue of drinking and drugs—something I thought I'd already dealt with—finally came to a climax for me. During my first road trip as a Steeler, everyone was given two beers as we boarded the flight home after the game. I certainly wasn't prepared for this, and I wasn't sure what I should do.

I definitely wanted to fit in and be like everyone else. But I also knew that if I drank the beer, I probably wouldn't be able to drive once we landed in Pittsburgh. Fortunately, I saw a few of the other guys give their beer away, and that little nudge of positive peer pressure helped me not to give in to something I didn't really want to do.

That year, 1977, I had a fair amount of playing time at the safety position, and I ended up intercepting three passes for the season. One of those interceptions came in a game that was remarkable, at least from my point of view.

Back in May, when I had been anxiously sitting by my phone during the NFL draft, the Steelers had selected a quarterback named Cliff Stoudt from Youngstown State University in the fifth round. Now, in an October game at Houston, both starting quarterback Terry Bradshaw and backup Mike Kruczek were knocked out of the game with injuries. Cliff was on the inactive roster that day, so I was brought in at quarterback to finish up the fourth quarter.

I played terribly. I fumbled a snap, and Rocky Bleier and I fumbled a handoff. I didn't realize the backs took the ball differently at Pittsburgh than they had done in college. To make matters worse, I threw two interceptions near the end of our 27–10 loss. In the process, I became the last player in NFL history to intercept a pass *and* throw an interception in the same game.

I felt awful about my performance because I knew I had cost us the game. Despite my disappointment, however, I realized that I had done something very few people would ever do. I took snaps from Mike Webster, handed off to Franco Harris, and threw passes to Lynn Swann and John Stallworth—all during a regular-season NFL game. If I had practiced with the offense at all, the fumbles wouldn't have occurred. However, I once again began focusing on how I could continue to improve as an NFL safety.

Monday was an off-day for players, but that day, while I was watching TV, the phone rang. It was Coach Noll's secretary; the coach wanted to see me right away.

When I arrived in his office, Coach Noll updated me on the situation: Bradshaw was getting his wrist X-rayed, and Kruczek would be out for an extended period of time. They were in the process of trying to locate Neil Graff, a quarterback who had been with us during training camp and was now somewhere in Canada on a hunting trip. In the meantime,

Coach Noll told me to attend the quarterbacks meeting that afternoon.

I immediately wondered about Cliff Stoudt. After all, Coach Noll had drafted him, not me. Cliff might have struggled in the preseason, but I had been playing defense and hadn't practiced one minute at quarterback.

Coach Noll answered before I could even ask my question. As always, his assessment was brief and to the point: "We have some questions at quarterback right now. As the week goes on, we'll have a better idea about Terry, Neil, and Cliff. We'll see who gives us the best chance to win. If you do, you're going to play. If we have another option that gives us a better chance, you'll go back to safety."

After the quarterbacks meeting, I raced home and began calling my buddies. "I might be starting on Monday Night Football against Cincinnati . . . *at quarterback*."

The next day they did locate Neil Graff, and Terry Bradshaw checked out healthy enough to play with a cast. I was back at safety. But even so, in the days and years to follow, I drew great satisfaction from knowing that Coach Noll had had confidence that I could go in and play quarterback—and direct all of those future Hall of Famers.

Some people had suggested to me that I wasn't drafted as a quarterback because of my race. At first, I didn't agree; I just figured that playing quarterback in the NFL was completely different from playing in college. But after talking with coaches and scouts that first year, I grew less certain. A number of them said they had passed on me in the draft because of quantifiable characteristics such as my height and arm strength. Later in the season, however, when we played guys like Bob Griese, Joe Ferguson, and Fran Tarkenton, I would deliberately walk by, look them in the eye, and measure my height against theirs. I was as tall as each one of them. I began to wonder if race had indeed played a role. To make matters worse, when I saw the backup QBs . . . now *that* was really frustrating. A lot of them just weren't very good. I continued to wonder.

During that week in the middle of the 1977 season, I realized that quarterbacking in the NFL was ultimately no different from playing quarterback at any other level. I believe I could have done it, given the opportunity. But I didn't get that opportunity, and whether it was because of my race or because of some legitimate factor, it was time to move on.

In the following off-season, I was able to work out regularly at the stadium. I added about eight pounds to my frame, reaching 188 pounds. Back then, the Steelers and the Pirates shared Pittsburgh's Three Rivers Stadium, so I tried to schedule my off-season workouts—which fell during the Pirates' regular season—for the middle of the day. I often wrapped up my workout and headed next door to the Pirates clubhouse just in time to see guys like John Candelaria, Bert Blyleven, Dave Parker, Phil Garner, Rennie Stennett, and Omar Moreno.

The Pirates clubhouse was noisy, worlds apart from the silence and anxiety of a football locker room on game day. The baseball players were frying chicken and playing cards, yelling back and forth, answering mail, and listening to radios. In the middle of the bedlam, I saw my first Spanish-language Bible as Manny Sanguillen sat in his locker—as I learned he always did—quietly reading.

The next season, when the Pirates had added Bill Madlock and Tim Foli and were on their way to a World Series win with their "We Are Family" theme, I asked Willie Stargell about the noisy atmosphere in the clubhouse on game day. "Isn't it a little distracting?"

Willie flashed that broad smile of his and then laughed as he decided the question was funnier than he first thought. He looked at the wiry, twenty-four-year-old Steeler in front of him and spoke thoughtfully. "I've been playing baseball for a long time, Tony. When I look over in your locker room on game day, I can't believe how tight everybody is. As for me, every time I've ever heard the umpire get ready to start a game, he always says, 'Play ball!' I've never once heard him say, 'Work ball!' I think that's something you football guys have forgotten."

I filed that away, not realizing how often I would draw on that thought later when I had teams of my own to guide through a pregame setting.

I had gained those eight pounds by lifting and running and preparing in ways I had never had to as a quarterback. I was headed into the 1978 training camp with a year of playing defense under my belt. I was still watching as much film as possible and absorbing everything I could from Woody Widenhofer and the guys on the defense. Physically and mentally, I knew it was going to be a much better year for me.

But then I started dragging a little, feeling a little tired as camp approached. I headed over to camp a couple of days early, and the team doctor checked me out. Mononucleosis. If you had known me and my dating habits back then, you'd know that mono isn't always the kissing disease. I was focused on my career as much as anything, but I was also pretty shy. I did know a few girls, and I enjoyed being around them, but before I got too involved with someone, I wanted to be sure she was someone I could see myself marrying. Because of that, I never really had a serious girlfriend. I was probably looking for someone like my mom. Up to then, I hadn't found her.

The doctor put me on antibiotics, just in case I had some other infection in addition to mono, and told me he would check on me every few days. I would be allowed to take the field when my white blood cell count dropped back to normal levels.

I started to improve quickly, but day after day . . . after day after day . . . my white blood cell count was still too high. After missing three weeks (preseason lasted just about forever back then), I was really frustrated and was getting difficult to be around.

Late one evening in our room, I told Donnie Shell, "I don't know that I'm going to make this team. By the time I get back, my conditioning level will be down, and there are other new guys who are looking to do what I did last year—take somebody's spot. This is just not going according to plan."

"Tony, I think you're at a crossroads," Donnie said. "You know what life is all about. You profess to be a Christian, and you tell everybody that God has first place in your life. Now, when your career looks like it's teetering, we're getting a chance to see what *really* is in first place for you."

I thought about that all day and then came back to the conversation with Donnie.

"You're probably right," I told him. "I feel like I've been learning from you guys and growing, and I'm feeling better about my faith and thinking that I trust the Lord. I'm trying to understand what you guys have. But all of a sudden, I come to a crisis point, and I begin to panic. My thoughts turn to 'What am *I* going to do?'"

Donnie paused and measured me squarely. "All the Lord is trying to do is find out what's in first place in your life, and right now, it looks like football is." I immediately knew

Donnie was right, and I felt convicted. I think that was the point at which I really began to understand what it means to be a Christian, and I began making an effort to start changing and growing as a person. It was the first time I was able to look at football as something that God was allowing me to do, not something that should define me. I couldn't take my identity from this sport; I had to consciously make sure that God was in first place. Now that I'm older and have gone through many much more difficult crises than those three weeks of mono, I look back at that time as key to my maturity as a Christian.

Several days later, I still wasn't better, but I had begun to simply pray that whether I sat out the entire year, came back immediately, or was cut, I would keep God first. About two weeks later, as we were getting ready for our first preseason game, I was finally able to start practicing again.

It was one of those miracle years. I was healthy, and it seemed like every time I took the field, the ball was headed my way. We went 14–2 and won the Super Bowl over Dallas, 35–31. I led the team in interceptions and was tied for tenth in the NFL. I was one interception behind Herm Edwards, who would coach with me years later (though I think he would gladly trade that interception for being able to fish as well as I can).

Despite all the good things that occurred that year, I can still look back and say that 1978 was the first season in my life in which sports weren't the most important thing to me. I finally realized that how I lived on earth was just as important as my salvation. God had me here for a reason, and it wasn't just to play ball. It was then that the words of Matthew 16:26 really started to sink in: *"And what do you benefit if you gain the whole world but lose your own soul?"*

LEADING TO LAUREN

CHAPTER FIVE

There are only two kinds of people in the end: those who say to God, "Thy will be done," and those to whom God says, in the end, "Thy will be done."

C. S. Lewis

AFTER WE WON THE SUPER BOWL in Miami, the summer of 1979 was much the same as the one before. I was lifting and running, hanging out with Steelers and Pirates, and growing in my faith. That fall, I arrived at camp in fantastic shape. I was healthy, too—no mono, thank goodness. I breezed through the initial cuts and reached the weekend of the biggest cut of camp.

All the cuts had been made but one—the coaching staff still had to get rid of one more player in order to reach the required number. We were hanging out in Joe Greene's dorm room—Donnie Shell, Mel Blount, Franco Harris, Terry Bradshaw, Joe, and I—trying to figure out what the coaches were going to do. It was apparent that the coaches were having difficulty deciding or working out a trade, because it was taking longer than usual. Finally, there came a knock on the door.

I looked around the room: Shell, Blount, Harris, Bradshaw, Greene . . . and Dungy.

I stood up. "Well, it's got to be me," I said, laughing as I left the room.

As it turned out, I had not been cut, but I had been traded—from the best team in football to the worst. I was headed to the San Francisco 49ers. And in spite of my attempt at humor, I was sorry to go. After doing so well in 1978, I had fully expected to be with the Steelers for many years. I had even bought a house during that off-season, so this move was a shock. But this was the NFL; trades and cuts were always a possibility.

The previous year had really shaped my attitude, though. If this had happened even one year earlier, I probably would have been devastated. Now, however—as would happen many more times in my future—I saw it as God moving me to where He wanted me to go.

I had really enjoyed my time in Pittsburgh. More than being the best team in the NFL, the Steelers were a great organization in which to grow up as a player and a person and, as it turned out, to grow in my faith.

Art Rooney, the Steelers' owner, was unlike any other owner I would ever meet again. If people were visiting the club and he was around, they would have no idea that he owned the team. He didn't put on airs or expect recognition. He walked to work every day from his home near downtown Pittsburgh, and even when the neighborhood changed for the worse, he refused to move out.

I only played for the Steelers for two years and was never more than a backup when I was there. But when I was traded, Mr. Rooney wrote a letter to my parents, telling them how much he had enjoyed my playing for him and his getting to meet them when they came to games. He wrote that I had been a big part of their Super Bowl win and asked them to continue to come back to Steelers games any time they were in the area.

Mr. Rooney saw everyone who came through his organization as one of his kids. Everything about the Steelers was first-class and all about integrity. In that respect, Mr. Rooney set the tone for the entire organization. He cultivated an environment of caring and closeness, and Chuck Noll reinforced that with his coaching.

With those benefits, however, came responsibility. When new guys arrived, Mr. Rooney always brought them in and explained that they were now Steelers and that they were going to win and have a great time. But then he would continue. "We have a great group of guys here. But you have to understand that this is Pittsburgh. It's a tight-knit community, and you are now *Pittsburgh* Steelers. Wherever you go, you're going to represent us as a team and as a community, so govern yourselves accordingly."

He was the most supportive man I could imagine. When we won, he would come into the locker room and shake everyone's hand until he had moved all the way through the ranks. When we lost, he'd come into the locker room and sit down and talk with us for a while. He was even known to give cigars to Joe Greene and other guys who smoked them and to shoot the breeze with Terry Bradshaw about horses.

It had been a privilege to play for Mr. Rooney, and I knew I would miss my time in Pittsburgh.

I played the 1979 season in San Francisco. In the meantime, the Steelers represented Pittsburgh just fine on the field, doing the ordinary things better than anyone else and winning their fourth Super Bowl in six years.

In San Francisco, we went 2–14. We opened the year with a seven-game losing streak, beat Atlanta, and then ended our second long streak of the year—six consecutive losses—by drilling the Buccaneers 23–7.

While San Francisco was a different environment from Pittsburgh, it was no less valuable for my career development. It was Bill Walsh's first year as head coach, and he was beginning to lay the foundation for the Super Bowl teams he would eventually field there. Joe Montana was in his rookie season at quarterback, and other pieces were being added in order to build the team. Years later, I would often draw on Coach Walsh's teachings as I tried to build the Buccaneers.

Even a 2–14 team wouldn't have me, though, and I was traded before the 1980 season to the New York Giants. I was traded along with Mike Hogan in exchange for Ray Rhodes and Jimmy Robinson, a trade that would soon launch several coaching careers. Within a couple of seasons, Ray and Jimmy were out of the league as players and into coaching.

As for me, I lasted for most of training camp with the Giants before being released. Three teams in two years. The end of the line for me as an NFL player had obviously arrived. Now I had to figure out what I wanted to do next.

Giants head coach Ray Perkins spoke to me as I was leaving training camp in New York.

"Tony, you're very smart, and you have a good approach to the game. I think you'd make a very good coach someday." I figured that was his way of getting me out the door without too much conversation, but later I would learn that Coach Perkins just wasn't the type to make small talk.

I had spent parts of summers working at various Pittsburgh businesses, like Mellon Bank and Heinz, but I hadn't found anything that I loved. So I headed back to the University of

Minnesota to work out and stay in shape in case another team called, volunteering as a defensive backs coach for the Golden Gophers for the rest of the 1980 season. Finally the Denver Broncos called, late in the year, but I had missed so many games by then that I figured I wouldn't do anyone any good. I declined and effectively ended my playing career.

Immediately after the season, Coach Perkins followed through on his earlier comments, calling to offer me a coaching position. I was very interested, and after talking with him, I figured I was destined to go to New York. In the meantime, Wellington Mara, the owner of the Giants, mentioned to his close friend Art Rooney of the Steelers, that it looked as though they would be hiring a former Steeler—me—as one of their coaches.

Mr. Rooney called Coach Noll, who called me. "If you're really interested in coaching, I think we can create something for you right here," he said. I accepted the offer and became a Steeler once more.

In taking that job with the Steelers at the age of twenty-five, I became the youngest coach in the NFL. The situation could have been a disaster, but the Steelers made it easy for me to break in as a coach. Even though I was younger than most of the players, and they had seen me come in just three years earlier not knowing anything about defense, those guys were professionals. So many of them were locked into the idea of living for Christ that it didn't matter who was coaching them. They worked hard and honored God through it because that's just what they did. Before I knew it, I was doing odd jobs, breaking down film, and essentially acting as an assistant to the head coach.

Chuck Noll always reminded us that "Football is what you are doing right now, but it's not your life's work. You've got to continue to prepare for your life's work." Occasionally it occurred to us that he had been in football for such a long time that it certainly seemed to be *his* life's work, but I don't think anybody ever had the guts to say it.

Chuck often preached the importance of time away from the office, and we knew it wasn't just lip service. Chuck lived out his message. He loved to cook, drive boats, and fly planes. He never wanted to just hang around the office, especially if the work was done. His philosophy was "Get the work done so you can enjoy the other parts of your life." I was single at the time, so the other parts of my life in Pittsburgh did not include family. But the Steelers organization was certainly a great place for me to learn and to shape a philosophy.

Even though I never did work for Coach Perkins, I have always been grateful for the encouragement and direction he planted in my mind. He had been around me for only a few weeks of camp, so for him to say what he did carried a great deal of weight, despite the fact that he was cutting me at the time. As a coach with the Steelers, I looked forward to going to work my second day on a job—for the first time ever.

It was Father's Day weekend of 1981, my first year coaching with the Steelers. The phone rang late on Friday night, June 19. It was our chaplain, Hollis Haff, who told me he needed a last-minute speaker for the father-and-son breakfast at St. Stephen's Episcopal Church in Sewickley, just outside of Pittsburgh. Each year, one of the Steelers players or coaches spoke, but this year's speaker, lineman Ted Petersen, had gotten sick.

I didn't feel like getting up early—I had just walked in from an all-day, out-of-town football clinic. I think Hollis could read my mind. "I know it's a lot to ask, but we've done this every year, and they're really counting on us to have someone there. Ted's sick, and I wouldn't even ask, except . . ."

I told Hollis I'd do it as a favor to him.

The next morning I showed up at St. Stephen's to meet with the senior pastor, Dr. John Guest. I made the appropriate apologies on behalf of Ted and the Steelers, and Dr. Guest asked if he could sit with me during the meal. "I've got a bio prepared on Ted, but I'm afraid I don't know anything about you," he said. "At least if we sit together while we eat, I could put together a reasonable introduction."

During breakfast, I shared with Dr. Guest what I planned to say to the group. Thanks to my mom's training, I never have been afraid to speak in public, and at that point, I was always ready to talk about my faith. Because it was an event for father and sons and I didn't have any children of my own, I talked about a subject I knew something about and that most boys are interested in: athletics. In these types of settings, I often used 1 Corinthians 9:24-27 as my starting point. In that passage, Paul talks about competing and running to win. I told the group that we always have to be sure the prize we're after is worthwhile. I explained that while the Super Bowl is a great goal, if it's all we're after, we'll be disappointed when we get there.

When I finished speaking, Dr. Guest approached me again. "I'm not sure how to say this, but there's a girl in my congregation here that you've really got to meet. I know this sounds strange since I've only been with you for an hour, but I think you two would be perfect for each other."

I did my best to gently blow him off. "Hmmm, that's interesting. Maybe . . . sure, we could do that sometime. Okay. Thanks."

As I left, Dr. Guest could tell that I wasn't taking him seriously. He called Hollis Haff later to get my phone number.

"Tony, I know you think this is crazy, but I'm serious," he said when he called. "You really ought to meet this girl."

I was thinking, *This church has five thousand people, and there are no single guys she can get attached to? What must she look like?*

Dr. Guest called me three or four more times over the next couple of weeks, asking if he could simply introduce me to this girl. "That's all I want to do. I'm just so certain that you will click and this will be perfect."

Meanwhile, I was not quite so certain. "Maybe you could just give me her number," I suggested. I thought that would get him to quit calling me and make all this go away.

"I'm sorry, Tony, but she's not the type to take kindly to you calling her directly. I really need to do it this way—to introduce you."

All the while, Dr. Guest was apparently trying the same tactics with the girl he wanted me to meet, and he wasn't getting any further with her. I later learned that she was even less interested than I was. She was thinking, *Here's a guy who played for the Steelers and now coaches with the Steelers, and he can't get a date in Pittsburgh? What kind of a nerd must he be?*

She was closer to the truth than I was. I was quiet and shy, and I wasn't particularly interested in dating. I was more interested in finding a woman I could marry, and I figured that day wouldn't come for a while yet.

After weeks of putting Dr. Guest off, I finally agreed to meet the girl. The Steelers were leaving to begin training camp on July 20, so I told him I would only be free the following day, Saturday, July 18. Dr. Guest then called the girl and pitched the idea that I would like to come by and meet her. She reluctantly agreed.

When I got to her house and she opened the door, I was stunned. Lauren Harris was *beautiful*. She reminded me of the way my mom looked when I was a young boy. She had a pretty smile and a thin, athletic build. I couldn't believe she wasn't already dating someone. She was dressed conservatively, like a schoolteacher, although at the time she was actually taking summer classes herself.

Lauren was pretty reserved, at least at first, not yet knowing this man the minister had sent to her door. And I was *nervous.* Her parents were both there, and her dad, Leonard, was gregarious and very friendly to me right from the start. He seemed to be moving a hundred miles an hour as he raced around, trying to get to work. I would later learn that this was par for the course for him. Her mom, Doris, looked as if she could have been Lauren's older sister. She sat down in the kitchen with us, and we talked for a while, getting acquainted.

On his way out the door, Leonard asked me to share a little football advice with Chuck Noll. Then he was gone. As Lauren and her mom and I continued to talk, I became a little more comfortable and started to relax. Lauren was so genuine. She wasn't trying to impress me; nor was she impressed that I was an NFL coach. In fact, not only was she *not* impressed that I was a coach with the Steelers, my job was actually a mark against me in her book. Her brothers had played football, and she didn't care for the way girls had chased them all throughout high school simply because they were athletes.

We talked about her teaching—she taught sixth grade—and her involvement at her church. Right away I knew there was a gentle, caring side to this girl.

After only about twenty minutes, Lauren stood to leave. She had to get to her class, and I needed to head for work. At the end of that first meeting, I already knew there was something different about her. In the past, whenever I had met a girl, I immediately began to think about how I was going to tell her that I wasn't interested in getting serious. With Lauren, however, I was trying to figure out a way to see her again. All of a sudden, this whole thing that I had been pushing away seemed to be a really good idea. I told her we'd be leaving soon for training camp but that Chuck always gave us Sundays off; maybe we could do something on the weekends. She said that would be fine.

We went to breakfast and church together the next Sunday and had a really nice time. We talked about things we each liked to do, and I learned that Lauren liked tennis. I dropped her back at her house, and . . . here's where Lauren's story diverges from mine. Since I'm the one telling the story, you'll hear my version first, and then, to be fair, I'll also give you her version—the *wrong* version.

As I dropped her off, I said, "I'm headed back to training camp, and I'll be gone for the week, but if you wouldn't mind giving me your number, *I'll call you, and maybe we can play tennis sometime.*"

She heard—and swears to this day that I said—". . . give me your number, and *maybe I'll call you,* and we can play tennis sometime." I can only assume she was too nervous to have heard me correctly. Or maybe—and I'm sure this is not the case—I was too nervous to have articulated my request correctly.

So there we were at her doorstep. I was thinking this was going well, while it turns out that she was mad and put off by my attitude. Although she thought I might be one of those guys who had a lot of girlfriends, she grudgingly gave me her number. I did in fact call that week from the hall phone in the dorm at camp. After that, we started to see each other more often. We went out every Saturday night during camp, and we also attended church together every Sunday morning in Pittsburgh. Lauren had been raised Catholic but was now attending that Episcopal church pastored by John Guest. After we went to church, we'd often have breakfast together in Sewickley, then try to do something fun before I had to head back to camp. We even played some tennis, with each of us winning our share of games.

We often spent time just talking, especially about Dr. Guest's sermons and the lessons we had each taken from them. We also discussed Christian philosophy at length, which helped me see the world from Lauren's perspective. Lauren's faith was clearly very important to her.

In spite of the fact that I had been an athlete and was still involved in football, Lauren was beginning to fall for me just as I was for her. In fact, she was actually becoming a football fan for the first time.

Although I felt an immediate connection with Lauren, I remained a little cautious. Dating her had not been the result of a spontaneous decision. In fact, I had thought and prayed about it a lot before I ever called her after our first meeting. As I said, I never wanted to get too involved with someone I couldn't see myself marrying. She was so pretty and seemed to be everything I was looking for in a woman, but I wanted to be sure it wasn't just physical attraction.

Once I returned from camp, we began to see each other a little more during the season. But even so, our times together were infrequent and precious. The more time we spent together, however, the more certain I was that she was the one. Like many other times in my life, there was no booming voice from God or one defining moment when I realized that I wanted to marry Lauren. Somehow, I just knew God had led me to the right person.

It really didn't take me long to see that Dr. Guest had been right about the two of us. By the fall of that year, I was ready to propose, although I'll admit that proposing to Lauren was not my finest hour. One night that November, just four months after we met, we were sitting on her parents' couch, and I began talking in general terms about the kind of woman I wanted to marry. I said I was looking for a woman who loved the Lord and wanted to use biblical principles to raise a family, someone who was generous and caring, and so on.

Of course, I was describing Lauren and leading into my proposal. But I later learned that as I was saying all these things, I hadn't made this clear at all, and Lauren assumed I was asking for advice about somebody else. Until this point, we had never referred to ourselves as dating, we were just "hanging out." A lot. Finally, I said I thought she fit all of those qualities I'd been looking for in a godly woman and that I thought we should get married. Still sitting, I began fishing in my left front pocket for the ring I had purchased for her.

She said yes, despite my failure to be eloquent—or to even get down on one knee. I was very excited and looking forward to married life, although I'm not sure Lauren could truly envision everything she was getting into.

The initial rapture of married life lasted well into the first day. Well, maybe *well into* is stretching it a little. We had waited until June to get married because Lauren wanted to spend her wedding night outside of Pittsburgh. She had visions of getting married and boarding a flight that day, so we had to wait until school was out. Since I had played football in San Francisco, we decided to start our honeymoon there before flying to Hawaii a few days later. I had pushed for staying the first night in the Pittsburgh Hilton, but my arguments fell on deaf ears. We set the ceremony for 1 p.m. so we could catch a flight for the West Coast that afternoon.

We planned a very small wedding because between Lauren's teaching colleagues and Steelers coaches, players, and staff, we knew we'd never be able to cut the guest list without hurting someone's feelings. We were married by John Guest in a lovely, intimate ceremony in Lauren's church. Donnie Shell was my best man.

We left for San Francisco at 5 p.m., but since no direct flights were available, we arrived very late in the evening. We were exhausted from the long day and long flights even before we touched down. I had arranged to borrow a car from Paul Hofer, a former 49ers teammate. Paul and his wife met us at the airport and sent us on our way—in their convertible.

Lauren and I were beyond exhausted by this time, as it was now approaching midnight. I stopped at a convenience store on the way to the hotel, and things might have been fine had I not broken the car key off in the door. We found a pay phone and called Paul so he could bring us a spare key. By now it was late. Very late.

Barely functioning, we arrived at the hotel at 1 a.m., fifteen hours—with the time change—after our wedding ceremony had begun. Completely wiped out, we both tried valiantly to hang in there, finally stepping off the elevator on the eleventh floor. We looked at each other and smiled; we had survived the trip.

At that moment, the power in the hotel went out. Someone had cut a cable outside the building, and we were plunged into darkness. We felt our way down the hallway, finally finding our room. It had been a very long journey to this point, and I've often said that it's all about the journey.

Not on June 19, 1982, it wasn't.

Two days later, however, we were sitting blissfully on the beach in Hawaii, excited once again about our marriage and our life together under God's watchful care. Any talk of "If we had just stayed the night at the *Pittsburgh Hilton* . . ." or "Even *borrowing* a car instead of renting one wouldn't have been a problem if someone knew how to *work a car key* . . ." seemed like distant memories.

To this day, I tell Ted Petersen that if he hadn't gotten sick, I'd still be single—and probably dateless.

LEARNING TO LEAD

CHAPTER SIX

Whoever wants to be a leader among you must be your servant, and whoever wants to be first among you must become your slave.
MATTHEW 20:26–27

IT WAS 1984, and a new kid on the block and would-be competitor to the NFL, the United States Football League, had just been formed. Our defensive coordinator, Woody Widenhofer, left the Steelers to become the head coach of the USFL's Oklahoma Outlaws. Woody was our defensive staff's second loss in two years. George Perles, our assistant head coach, had gone to the Michigan State Spartans as their new head coach in '82.

Although I was only twenty-eight at the time and recognized I was awfully young, I also knew I was the coach who knew our defense the best. I hoped I was next in line for the Steelers' defensive coordinator position. A few days after Woody left, we were in New Orleans for the NFL Scouting Combine, an event where guys who will be in that year's draft gather for workouts while NFL scouts watch. Chuck Noll asked if I wanted to go with him to Preservation Hall. I had no idea what or where that was, but I figured he must be getting ready to talk to me about becoming the defensive coordinator.

We met after dinner in the hotel lobby and walked out into the cool Crescent City evening. Chuck always was a fascinating conversationalist. He spoke of the 1974 Super Bowl the Steelers had been part of in New Orleans, and then he talked about a number of other topics, all unrelated to football. We arrived at Preservation Hall, a little hole in the wall with great New Orleans jazz. We kept talking while listening to a guy play the piano for about forty-five minutes, and then Chuck got up to leave.

"Wasn't that great?" he remarked. I agreed, and we headed out into the chilly night air once again. Chuck began talking about jazz and its origins and how New Orleans jazz was distinctive. I can't say that I learned a whole lot about jazz that night. The whole time we were together, I was trying to figure out if I should say something about the defensive coordinator position or just let the conversation play out, figuring he'd get to it soon enough.

He never did, though, and as we returned to the hotel, I realized that I must not be Chuck's choice for the position. When I got home to Pittsburgh, I informed Lauren, who wasn't as ready as I was to accept this decision. She was convinced that I should at least talk with Chuck and ask him why he seemed headed in a different direction. After going back and forth with her for about four days, I finally did just that.

"Coach, have you given any thought to what you're going to do with the defensive coordinator position?"

He looked startled. "Of course, Tony. Nobody knows as much about our defense as you do. That's always been my thought process since Woody left. You're our defensive coordinator."

I blew out a breath and gave a rueful laugh, a mixture of relief and exasperation evident on my face.

"Were you ever going to *tell* me that?"

"Tony, you're our defensive coordinator."

That was just the way Chuck was. Like when I went in at quarterback in 1977—I was the next man in line, even though I didn't know it. Things just kept moving along as planned—at least in his mind.

The off-season of 1984 also brought us our first child, Tiara. We were in a position financially to allow Lauren to give up teaching and become a full-time mom. Up to this point, Lauren had always been firm in her resolve to keep teaching for a while before having children. But now, only two and a half years after the wedding, we found ourselves with a baby daughter and a single income: God apparently had a different schedule for us than we had thought.

Almost immediately Lauren and Tiara began to develop the same closeness I had seen Lauren share with her own mom. Being our first child and a girl, Tiara received the royal treatment—from us, from both sets of grandparents, and from everyone at our church. And not only did she receive attention, she also received *clothes.* I never realized just how much moms enjoy dressing up their little girls until Tiara came along. She was really a joy, and she got me thinking about the responsibilities of being a father. Up until this point, I had played a lot of golf in the off-season with Bill Nunn, one of the Steelers scouts. But after Tiara was born, I began to play fewer and fewer rounds, just feeling the need to be home as much as I could. Today, I hardly play golf at all.

Tiara was the sole recipient of our parental attention until 1987, when Jamie was born. He cut into her territory a little, but she didn't seem to mind. Jamie, of course, set off those thoughts in my mind that I'm sure every father of a boy must have. *Will he follow in my footsteps? Will I get to play ball with him like my dad did with me? Will he enjoy going to my office as much as I liked going with my father?*

I was very fortunate to be working for Chuck at this point. We had settled nicely into our coaching routine and never spent needless time at work. He was very family oriented, and I never worried that coaching football and raising a family might clash.

Looking back, I can see it was no accident that I felt led to choose a $2,200 signing bonus to play an unfamiliar position with the Steelers rather than take whatever the Bills or Alouettes had offered. In Pittsburgh I met Lauren, was surrounded by guys who were serious about their faith, won a Super Bowl, and started my coaching career. However, in spite of all these good things, God eventually kicked me out of the Pittsburgh nest.

In the spring of 1987, we drafted a very good defensive class—Rod Woodson, Delton Hall, Thomas Everett, Hardy Nickerson, and Greg Lloyd. Those guys all played some in 1987, and we anticipated that they would play even more in 1988. However, as we headed into the 1988 season, we lost some significant leadership. Both Donnie Shell and John Stallworth retired, and Mike Merriweather, the player we had counted on to be the cornerstone of our defense, became embroiled in a contract dispute and sat out the entire season. That was a big loss that we hadn't anticipated, especially in light of the fact that we had let some other veteran leaders go to allow for the development of the 1987 draft class.

We went 5–11 in 1988, missing the playoffs for the fourth

straight year. Chuck was under a lot of heat and asked me to step down as coordinator but to stay on staff as the defensive backs coach. I told him I would rather move on, so I resigned and started looking for a job. We were a long way from 1982, when Chuck had told a Pittsburgh paper that my coaching future was unlimited, that "[Tony could] go as far as he wants." Now I was going much farther than I wanted—out of town.

Lauren and I certainly wouldn't have left the Steelers if we hadn't had to. This was the first time she had ever even thought about leaving her hometown of Pittsburgh. It was also the first time she got a feel for the tougher side of the NFL. Now I see that it was the Lord's way of getting us to a different place, just like when I was traded to San Francisco in 1979.

At that time, there was no doubt in my mind that I was to continue coaching. I just didn't know where. I was fortunate to get a lot of calls in the days after I resigned. Four options stood out from the others: Cincinnati, Kansas City, the New York Giants, and San Francisco.

My first choice was to go to Cincinnati. The Steelers played them twice a year, and I had known Coach Sam Wyche from my year playing for the 49ers when he was on Bill Walsh's staff. Sam called me before Super Bowl XXIII and said he was probably going to lose his defensive line coach. He wanted to know if I'd be interested. I liked Sam a lot, the Bengals had a good team, and Cincinnati was a medium-sized city close to Pittsburgh. Although I didn't know many of their players, I had become good friends with Anthony Muñoz while doing some camps with him for Athletes in Action. All in all, it seemed to be a good fit for us. Lauren and I rooted for the Bengals to beat the 49ers in the Super Bowl that year, all the time thinking we'd be working for the Super Bowl champs in 1989. They lost to the 49ers in the last minute of the game.

After getting back to Cincinnati, Sam called me with bad news. Mike Brown, who had taken over the ownership of the Bengals from his dad, Paul Brown, felt I was really a defensive backs coach rather than a line coach. He was also worried that I would not be content as a position coach and that I would probably be looking to move on if a coordinator position became available elsewhere. Sam concluded by reluctantly confessing that he couldn't hire me.

Shortly following the conversation with Sam, the other participant in Super Bowl XXIII called. Bill Walsh told me he was retiring after their Super Bowl win and that George Seifert was going to take over as head coach of the 49ers. Denny Green had taken the Stanford head coaching job right before the Super Bowl, so Bill wanted me to coach the 49ers running backs. Although Bill was going to work in the front office, he obviously was not taking a hands-off role when it came to hiring a staff for George. While I had played for him in San Francisco only that one year, Bill Walsh and I had talked a great deal after I got into coaching, and he was definitely someone with whom I had a great relationship. He told me he felt I had a great chance to be a head coach and that I could make myself an even stronger candidate by moving over to offense and joining a championship-caliber team.

At the same time, an opportunity with the Giants was on the table. Although Bill Parcells was still in his early days as head coach of the New York Giants, he had already won one Super Bowl. The Giants had a cornerback on their roster, Harvey Clayton, whom I had coached for three years in Pittsburgh. Bill thought Harvey was well trained and brought me in to interview, which turned out to be great fun—considering it was a job interview. He already had Bill Belichick and Romeo Crennel on staff, and the four of us would have talked defensive football philosophy all day if the weather had cooperated. But a snowstorm was blowing into the New York area that evening, and Bill wanted to get me out before I got stranded. I wanted to get home too, although being stranded with those three wouldn't have been a bad alternative.

Meanwhile, Marty Schottenheimer had just gotten the head coaching job in Kansas City after leaving the Cleveland Browns in a dispute over assistant coaches. Marty interviewed me for the Chiefs' defensive coordinator position, but he had already decided he was going to run the system he had used in Cleveland and hire Bill Cowher as the coordinator. He wanted me to come as defensive backs coach. Marty said that part of his reason in hiring Cowher over me was that he couldn't promote someone from the outside over someone from within. I appreciated his candor as well as that philosophy.

As I went through this decision-making process, I was surprised by the pay scale of these NFL teams—it was unlike anything I'd seen in Pittsburgh. Each of these teams offered me more to be a position coach than I had been making as a coordinator in Pittsburgh.

I liked all three situations, and once again there was no booming voice from the sky clearly telling me which way to go. I knew Bill Walsh, but he wouldn't be my direct boss. I hadn't known Bill Parcells at all but had come to really like him in the little time I had spent with him. Both the Giants and 49ers were definitely Super Bowl–caliber teams, but in the end, I just didn't feel comfortable taking four-year-old Tiara and two-year-old Jamie to either of those two big cities. So after talking and praying about it, Lauren and I decided on Kansas City.

Although Lauren was initially worried about leaving her parents and siblings, Kansas City turned out to be a place of great growth for our marriage and for Lauren personally. She developed many new friendships and finally had her own home to set up and furnish, since she had simply moved into my place after we were married.

In some ways, life in Kansas City was easier for Lauren than it had been in Pittsburgh. In Kansas City, more of the coaches were closer to our age, which made their wives her peers. In Pittsburgh, the next youngest coach had been in his forties, with teenage children. I was so young when I was hired by the Steelers that we were closer in age to the players and their wives than we were to the coaches, which was somewhat awkward. In the space of two years, I had gone from being one of the guys to being management. Lauren had become close with Paulette Shell and Flo Stallworth, which was terrific for her but still a bit awkward since I was technically Donnie Shell's boss. Those issues didn't exist in Kansas City.

Working for the Chiefs continued to mold my coaching philosophy and reinforced my desire to maintain a balance between work and the rest of my life. Up to this point, we hadn't realized the number of hours that some NFL coaching staffs were required to work. In Pittsburgh, I had been home nearly every night for dinner. That all changed in Kansas City.

I met Herman Edwards back in 1977 at the Hula Bowl and again at the Japan Bowl, both college all-star games. A cornerback out of San Diego State, Herm played on the West teams in each game, while I played on the East teams. He always reminds me that I was driving for the winning score in Japan—on my way to the game's MVP award, according to him—when I threw an interception at the end of the game. To Herm. For some reason, we hit it off anyway and stayed friends as we both came into the NFL as undrafted free agents. We played at opposite ends of Pennsylvania—Herm with the Eagles, and I with the Steelers.

Many people who remember Herm's playing career don't remember him by name. Instead, they remember him as the hero of the "Miracle in the Meadowlands." This play got the Giants coach fired and created a new formation. In the Victory formation, the quarterback takes the snap from the center and, rather than handing the ball off to a running back, merely drops to one knee while another player stands several yards behind as a safety measure. This ends the play while the clock keeps running.

Herm's heroics came late in the 1978 season, with the Eagles needing a win to stay in the playoff chase. The Giants were leading 17–12 and merely needed to run the last thirty-one seconds off the clock. Their quarterback, Joe Pisarcik, took the snap but stumbled as he attempted to hand the ball off to the running back, Larry Csonka. Csonka never got the hand-off cleanly. The ball hit the hard turf of Giants Stadium and bounced right up to thigh level in front of a hard-charging Herm. Herm scooped up the ball and ran it twenty-six yards into the end zone, giving the Eagles the win. After that, coaches everywhere began using the Victory formation to eliminate the possibility of last-minute disaster from games that should be already won.

Herm and I continued to stay close even after I went into coaching and he kept playing. When his playing career ended, Herm headed to San Jose State to become their defensive backs coach. Then in 1989, my first year as defensive backs coach with the Kansas City Chiefs, Herm and I spent more time together when he joined us as an intern for training camp.

Chiefs head coach Marty Schottenheimer had the disconcerting trait, at least in my mind, of not needing much sleep, often working late into the night. And back then, he was also a micromanager who wanted to be on top of *everything* that took place on the practice field and in the assistant coaches' meetings.

Many an evening "concluded" with Marty pulling out the film from that day's camp practices to watch individual drills one more time. Usually this was at eleven or eleven-thirty at night, which meant we wouldn't finish the day until two or three o'clock in the morning. Whenever Marty started one of these sessions, Herm would cut a glance at me, shrug, and go off to fix popcorn. This late-night routine continued into the regular season.

Although I always longed to get home to Lauren and our children, there was never a question for me that I was born to coach, even as I endured Marty's hours in the office.

Even though in Kansas City I sometimes found myself on the job at three o'clock in the morning watching film with Marty, I still enjoyed coaching more than anything else I had done. After those crazy hours, however, Herm and I vowed that if we ever had the chance to make the schedule ourselves, we wouldn't spend, or allow our assistants to spend, that much time in the office. With Chuck Noll, I had seen firsthand that it was possible to work fewer hours and still be successful. I didn't like the burden my absence in the evenings placed on Lauren, who was at home alone with the kids.

Bill Parcells and the Giants won the Super Bowl that year, and San Francisco went on to win two titles under George Seifert. As for the Chiefs, the 1989 season in Kansas City couldn't have been more perfect. Working for Lamar Hunt was just as good as working for Mr. Rooney, and I also came to appreciate the approach of the other owners in that bunch, Mr. Mara of the Giants and Eddie DeBartolo of the 49ers. Lauren and I knew we had made the right decision to come to Kansas City. I learned a lot about taking care of details from working with Marty Schottenheimer, and I really enjoyed working with Bill Cowher.

It also didn't hurt that I was coaching a tremendous group of defensive backs. All four starters were Pro Bowlers at some point in their careers. I still consider those three years, when I was responsible for eight players rather than the whole defense, to be my favorite years of pure coaching. Not only was I able to focus my attention on details that would make them better players, I got the opportunity to really know them as people.

After I had been with the Chiefs for three seasons, Chuck Noll retired from the Steelers, and Bill Cowher left Kansas City to replace him as head coach. The Chiefs lost to the Buffalo Bills in the playoffs in January of 1992. A week later, Lauren and I watched the Buffalo-Denver AFC Championship Game from the hospital while waiting for Eric to be born. Losing to Buffalo the week before was actually a bit of a blessing for me personally. If we had won, I would have had to make a tough decision. Would I have gone to Denver with my team for the championship game or stayed in Kansas City with Lauren, who was almost ready to deliver? I'm glad I didn't have to make that choice. I like to think I would have made the right one, though.

I soon faced another choice, however, that was no less daunting, at least in Lauren's eyes. Marty had previously told me that if Bill Cowher ever left, I would be his new defensive coordinator. Just as Bill was taking the Pittsburgh job, Denny

Green left Stanford to become head coach of the Minnesota Vikings. Denny contacted me and asked me to become his defensive coordinator. I had gotten to know and like Denny when I played in San Francisco, where he was part of the 49ers coaching staff under Bill Walsh. But since I fully anticipated becoming the defensive coordinator in Kansas City, I planned to decline Denny's offer.

Then Marty suggested that I go check out the Minnesota job. As it turned out, he had already decided to hire Dave Adolph of the Raiders as his new defensive coordinator. Dave and Marty were close friends, and Dave had been Marty's defensive coordinator in Cleveland. Marty hadn't yet told me of his decision to hire Dave, but Lauren sensed something was different with the Schottenheimers. Hiring Dave Adolph didn't sit well with me, based on Marty's assurance that I would be the next coordinator. I reminded Marty of the conversation we'd had three years earlier when he told me that he couldn't hire someone from the outside over guys who had been within the organization. He did remember our conversation, but he said this was a special circumstance he couldn't have anticipated.

Lauren wanted me to stay on as the Chiefs defensive backs coach, but I didn't feel like that was a good option for me anymore, given the way things had played out. I knew I wouldn't be able to put my heart into my work—a crucial ingredient for success. Lauren was suspicious that I had orchestrated the whole thing just to get back to Minnesota. But while I was really looking forward to working with Denny Green, my decision actually had more to do with my need to leave the Chiefs than with where we were headed. It wasn't that I was mad at Marty Schottenheimer. I know he felt bad about going back on a promise, but he had never anticipated the opportunity to be reunited with Dave Adolph. I looked at it, once again, as God moving me in a situation where I would never have chosen to move myself. This wouldn't be the last time it would happen.

After I became a head coach, I had much more empathy for Marty's position. Things do happen that you can't anticipate. As a result, I've learned not to make many promises to players or coaches, and Marty and I remain good friends to this day.

Lauren, for good reasons, did not want to move, since she had just given birth to Eric, our third child, the very week Denny contacted me. But Denny is pretty savvy; he knew he needed to recruit Lauren, not just me. Minnesota in January can be intimidating, with average highs around twenty-two degrees. Kansas City isn't particularly balmy at that time of year either, but Lauren had a full support system there. So when Denny invited me to interview in Minneapolis, he invited Lauren for the interview as well.

We brought Eric, who was only eight days old when we traveled to Minnesota for our visit. Kirsten Lindbergh, Denny's secretary, took care of the baby the whole time we visited with Denny. Of course, being back in Minnesota was like being home for me, even though the weather was painfully cold. Lauren wasn't looking forward to leaving Kansas City at all. And given that she didn't yet know the full details of what was going on behind the scenes with the Chiefs, she was understandably not very open to the possibility. I believe her exact words were, "You're dragging me and a one-week-old baby into this subzero arctic."

Unlike our move from Pittsburgh, where after praying about it we both felt the change was right, Lauren just didn't want to leave Kansas City. However, she understood that if we stayed, though I might be able to make it work, I would not be in the right frame of mind. Reluctantly, she agreed to support me, and we survived the move.

✢   ✢   ✢

Although it was difficult for us to leave Kansas City in 1992, working for the Minnesota Vikings gave me the preparation I still needed to be effective as a head coach. During those four years in Minnesota, I grew as a coach and as a leader. Denny Green imparted wisdom I have drawn upon every year since then in my head coaching career.

Denny was very concerned with the efficient use of time and sticking with a schedule. In the process, he made certain that his assistant coaches spent time with their families. He reinforced the idea of head coach as CEO, a model I had seen in Coach Stoll and Coach Noll. Denny trusted his assistant coaches and knew the importance of not spending too much time on just one side of the ball.

In addition, Denny always ran the scout teams. The scout teams are the backup players who simulate the opponent's offense and defense in practice. Having the head coach direct the scout teams served two purposes. First, it made everybody realize the importance of the scout team and made the scout players pay attention. Second, it gave Denny a great opportunity to get a firsthand look at his young players and backups. That's why years later, after the 1999 season, Denny was able to release two outstanding quarterbacks, Jeff George and Randall Cunningham, with confidence. Denny had seen Daunte Culpepper's talent on the scout team, even though Daunte hadn't taken any game snaps during his rookie year in 1999.

Denny also believed that his assistant coaches should interact with the media. Being under the media microscope is an acquired skill. I knew how important it was for me to articulate my thoughts and help the media do their jobs without giving away information the club needed to keep private. There's a strong trend around the league these days toward silencing assistants, with various clubs having a "One Voice" doctrine. I can appreciate that to some extent; it makes it easier for a head coach to craft a message and keep everyone on the same page. At the same time, however, league rules mandate that we give the media access to our players, so the reality is that information is flowing from various sources within the organization anyway. At the end of the day, the only people a One Voice doctrine silences are those who should be the most loyal—the assistant coaches. If people really want to leak something to the press, they can and will do so—with or without a strict media policy.

The major consideration for me today, as it was for Denny then, is the development of assistant coaches in a league environment in which the media are increasingly hungry. In the course of any given week, the head coach holds a postgame press conference immediately following the game, a post-mortem press conference the following day, a midweek conference call with the opponent's local media, various other interviews, a "production meeting" the day before the game with network announcers who will broadcast the game, plus any game-day interviews for the team's local radio partner. And that's just for a routine regular-season game.

For each of these interviews, the coach had better not slip. All NFL coaches have, at one time or another, said something without thinking through all the ramifications. In this era with so much sports-related media, every comment by the head coach is likely to be dissected and discussed at length, and anyone can express an opinion in an online blog. This places a tremendous pressure on the head coach to say exactly what needs to be said at every moment.

As I allow my assistant coaches to interact with the media, they take some of the media pressure off of me. More important, their work with the media allows them to develop these skills during their tenure with me. Their promotion at some point to a head coaching position will carry enough shock, and dealing with the media is guaranteed to be one of the most difficult transitions. I want to help prepare them. An assistant coach who becomes a head coach should not have to go from having no interaction with the media whatsoever to being the lead voice of the team. It's too much to expect someone to master that skill without some on-the-job experience. I owe a great deal to Denny for helping me develop my media-relations skills, and I, in turn, want to do the same for my assistants.

Denny Green supported his assistant coaches' families. He allowed our children to be at training camp and scheduled days off so we could get home. Chuck Noll was like this too, although no one on our Pittsburgh staff had young children at the time. When I started coaching in Minnesota, Tiara was seven, Jamie was five, and Eric was just an infant, so I went home often. During the regular season, we usually finished our day's work before nine o'clock in the evening.

In the meantime, Herm Edwards had taken my old job as defensive backs coach at Kansas City and was working those exhausting hours with Marty. More often than not, Herm would come out of his first evening staff meeting and find a voice-mail message from me on his office phone before he headed into the second, late staff meeting.

"Hey, Herm, just checking in. It's about eight-thirty right now, and Jamie's sitting here preparing my instruction cards for practice tomorrow while I look over some notes. Remember to go find some popcorn, and you'll be done in six, seven hours, tops. Look, I don't want to stay on the phone too long, 'cause I'm about to head to bed. Catch you later."

It may not have been the kindest thing to do, but Herm

and I still share a good laugh over it. And I'm sure he deserved it as retaliation for something.

I'm not entirely certain why Denny Green chose me over the many other coaches on the Vikings staff he could have mentored. The staff had some tremendous minds—including Brian Billick, Tyrone Willingham, and Tom Moore—who would move on to other great things. Denny knew me from having been my special teams coach during the year I played in San Francisco. During my time in Minnesota, as my name gained momentum in league circles, much of my success was due to Denny's mentoring. Maybe he figured it was only a matter of time before I was a head coach.

Denny made sure that he involved me in the decision-making loop whenever possible. When it wasn't possible, he talked with me afterward to explain the factors that had been involved in making the decision. He didn't necessarily care if I agreed with him, but he did want me to start thinking in ways that would develop my decision-making ability.

For instance, in 1992 Denny wrestled with the decision to bench Rich Gannon in favor of Sean Salisbury. As he worked through the process, Denny let me know what he was thinking. In part, he needed my assistance in selling such a dramatic change to the defensive players. But he went beyond that to explain why he thought the change was important and what the pros and cons were for the switch. He wasn't asking for my opinion; he was challenging me to think through the situation as if I were the head coach.

Normally, as the defensive coordinator, I would not have even thought about decisions like that. But these were the types of decisions I would have to make when I became a head coach and saw even more variables. I'm thankful Denny gave me so many trial runs behind the scenes.

I have always viewed myself as loyal, even if it meant being somewhat stubborn. By my last year in Minnesota, I was growing increasingly popular with the media. Denny had never been a media favorite, even though we were winning. At one point, speculation was circulating that Denny was on a short leash. A good friend asked me if I would take the head coaching job if the Vikings fired Denny.

"No."

My friend pressed the point. From his perspective, if Denny were no longer the coach, the position would be empty—I wouldn't really be replacing him. So he asked again if I would take the job.

"No. Dennis Green gave me this job as defensive coordinator. I will not take his job."

My friend's logic was probably more solid than mine, but I stuck by my answer. There are certain bridges that are not worth crossing, no matter what others think. Loyalty and relationships are important. On a more practical note, I was also thinking about Lauren. She was more anxious than anyone for me to get a head coaching job in another city so we could escape the Minnesota winters.

Although it seemed at the time that I might never get a head coaching job, the Lord already had one picked out for me.

AN UNLIKELY OPENING

CHAPTER SEVEN

Commit your actions to the LORD, and your plans will succeed.
  PROVERBS 16:3

GOD WORKED through Denny Green to shape me as a coach and prepare me for advancement. The Lord also brought Tom Lamphere into my life in Minnesota. Tom was with Athletes in Action, a ministry of Campus Crusade for Christ. Athletes in Action focuses on the spiritual needs of athletes, encouraging and equipping them to use their platforms for Christ. Tom had been the Vikings' chaplain since the early 1980s.

Ever since I was traded in 1979, one of the first things I did whenever I moved to a new team was to connect with the team's chaplain. Many team chaplains are on staff with Athletes in Action, so a lot of them know each other and know when they are getting a Christian coach or player from another team. When I moved to Minnesota, I was looking forward to meeting Tom, and he had done his homework on me by contacting Mike Lusardi, the chaplain in Kansas City. By the time I joined the Vikings, Tom already knew of my faith.

Tom claims that others had told him I had a "great football

mind." As a result, he was convinced that someday I would become a head coach and gain an even greater platform. Although he didn't share his thoughts with me right away, Tom made it his mission to help me grow in my faith and in my leadership abilities. He wanted to help equip me to use that greater platform when I got it.

I liked Tom right away. I saw his sincere heart for people. Tom had heard that I liked to fish, especially when there's no hook in my hand. We made plans to get together for a day-long fishing trip in June, a few months after my arrival in Minnesota.

June arrived, and the two of us headed out for a day of walleye fishing. Until I get to know someone, I'm somewhat quiet and reserved, but Tom was the exact opposite. He asked me point-blank where I stood spiritually. Because Tom is often asked to refer players and coaches for speaking events, he wants the people he recommends to be solid people of faith. He then told me a little about the spiritual climate of the organization, and he described areas in which I might have an impact.

When Tom dropped me off at my house, Lauren met us at the door. "Did Tony talk at all?" she asked. Tom assured her that I had.

After that, Tom and I started meeting together regularly, and after about a year, he recommended we spend some regular time together studying the Old Testament book of Nehemiah. Nehemiah is only thirteen chapters long and often doesn't get as much attention as some of the other books of the Bible. But Nehemiah contains significant lessons about godly leadership. Tom wanted me to not just read Nehemiah but study it and begin to apply some of those leadership lessons in my daily life.

Tom and I spent a year reading, studying, and discussing those thirteen chapters, meeting every Thursday morning for breakfast at 6 a.m. at Jerry's Market. I often brought two-year-old Eric with me. Eric loved pancakes, and he would eat while Tom and I discussed Nehemiah. During that year, Tom told me he believed the Lord had bigger things for me and that when the time came, I would need to be a strong leader and a strong Christian. He reasoned—correctly—that when I did get a head coaching job, it would be because a change would be needed, and I would face many challenges. Through the course of our study, Tom pointed out that most of the failings of biblical leaders were spiritual rather than tactical. I needed to be prepared as much spiritually as I was in the Xs and Os.

I learned three key truths from Nehemiah. First, Nehemiah's opportunity came in God's time, not his own. Second, Nehemiah diligently prepared his mind and his heart so he would be ready when God's time arrived. Third, Nehemiah needed to be prepared to take on the problems, doubt, and adversity that would come his way both from the outside and from within.

During my tenure in Minnesota, I increased my football knowledge, tactics, and strategies. In addition to all that Denny was exposing me to, Chris Foerster, our offensive line coach, and I often talked about big-picture things. Whenever Denny went through mock drafts with the coaches, Chris and I would spend hours afterward replaying the draft scenarios and talking about whom we would have chosen, when we would have tried to trade, and so forth. We also talked about training camp schedules, practice plans, and game management. More than anything else, we talked about how to win consistently in the NFL. I tried to force myself to think in terms of the big picture in preparation for the day when I would need to think about an entire football team, balancing short-term success and long-term stability.

✛　✛　✛

I had had two head coaching interviews before I even went to Minnesota, although neither job was right for me. The first interview was in Philadelphia in 1986, when Buddy Ryan got the job as the Eagles head coach. The following year, 1987, I was interviewed in Green Bay for the Packers' head coaching position. That was an interesting interview. I sat across the table from Tom Braatz, vice president of football operations for the Packers, and we talked for about two hours. Finally, I asked him what the Packers were looking for in a head coach. Without batting an eye, Tom said, "Number one, we want a guy with head coaching experience. And number two, we want a real creative offensive guy." Since I was a defensive coach who had never been a head coach before, I obviously was not hired for the job. I wondered why I had even been invited for the interview.

I had only two other interviews over the next eight years—in Jacksonville, when I finished second to Tom Coughlin, and again in Philadelphia, when I finished second to Ray Rhodes. I really felt as if I had been close on both, which made not getting the jobs that much more disappointing. Lauren was especially disappointed. She believed deeply in my abilities, and she was still looking for a place where she could thaw out.

In 1993, the Vikings had the number one defense in the NFL. Although there were seven head coach openings that year, not only did I not get an interview, I never even got a phone call indicating I was on a team's list of candidates. That was a tough pill to swallow. I began to think that if God did have a head coaching job lined up for us, it might be a fairly long wait. Lauren was probably thinking the same thing, but Tom Lamphere wasn't. He was always quick to remind me that God had already selected the team I would be coaching. I just needed to do my current job well, keep preparing, and wait on God's timing. I needed to trust His leadership rather than try to force an outcome I wanted.

Two years later, after the 1995 season, there were two openings. I still had interviewed only twice during those eight years and four times overall. I didn't know anyone at either team—the Miami Dolphins and the Tampa Bay Buccaneers. I told Lauren not to expect this to be the year that anything happened. It was well documented that Jimmy Johnson was the top choice of both clubs. Johnson had resigned from the Dallas Cowboys and would likely have his pick of the two teams. If Johnson went to Miami, Steve Spurrier from the University of Florida would be Tampa Bay's top choice.

We figured the only way I might have any chance at all was if Jimmy took the Tampa Bay job, since then there would be no clear front-runner in Miami. But Jimmy signed with the Miami Dolphins, saying he had a better chance of getting to the Super Bowl with Miami's future hall-of-fame quarterback, Dan Marino, than with Tampa's quarterback, Trent Dilfer. A friend of mine got word that the coaches at the University of Florida were packing to move two hours south to Tampa, so I never gave the Tampa job another moment's thought. It was time for me to start concentrating on next year's Vikings defense, doing my level best to trust God for the future.

Jerry Angelo, who was the Buccaneers' director of player personnel (and is now the general manager of the Chicago Bears), called me just before the East-West Shrine Game, a college all-star game, to see if I would be there. Rich McKay, the Buccaneers' general manager, wanted to meet with me. I had planned to be at the game, so we arranged a meeting. I still wasn't getting my hopes up, though, so I warned Lauren that this interview was a real long shot. I knew how disappointed she had been when my previous interviews hadn't gone the way we wanted.

As I arrived at the Santa Clara Marriott to meet with Rich, the little screw came out of one of the hinges on my glasses. I had never had a problem with my glasses before, so it had never occurred to me to have a backup pair. At this point, however, my glasses were in two pieces. I tried to hold the lenses in front of my eyes as I squatted down in the hotel driveway to look for the screw. I searched desperately all over the ground and finally found it—three minutes before the meeting was scheduled to begin.

I entered the hotel and said to the bell captain, "This is an emergency: I have a screw loose." I held up my glasses. "Do you have one of those really small screwdrivers?"

He stared at me and then started to look around the stand for a screwdriver we both knew wasn't there.

I was on the verge of being late and couldn't wait any longer. I was about to head to the meeting when the bell captain told me of a nearby optical center that could fix the glasses.

A dilemma—should I call Rich and tell him I would be late? Or should I be on time for the meeting but not be able to see him? If Rich were to ask me to diagram a play, or if he showed me something and asked me to respond, I'd have no shot.

I finally figured that being on time was more important than being able to see, so I headed for the meeting, all the while kicking myself for being too cheap—I mean *frugal*—to own a second pair of glasses. I arrived at the meeting room right on time. I wondered if I should wear the glasses, even though they would only be hanging on one ear. I'd have to hold them up with my hand—nice—but at least I'd be able to see. Or I could not wear the glasses and hope that I wouldn't trip over a chair. Neither option was good, but at least I wasn't late. I decided to pocket the glasses. I took some comfort in knowing that this interview was only a formality, since Steve Spurrier would be taking the job anyway.

Rich introduced himself, and I told him this would be one of his more interesting interviews:

"I can't see you at all right now because, although I ordinarily wear glasses, they broke just as I arrived at the hotel." I told Rich my story, and he commiserated with me since he also wore glasses. I finally decided to put them on, then sat through the interview with my head tilted to one side to keep the glasses from falling off. About halfway through, Rich said he wasn't going to ask me to review anything, and I was welcome to take the glasses off. He was gracious throughout, but I felt like an idiot.

Most of my prior interviews had gone well, but this one had not. When I reported back to Lauren, I told her I was pretty sure I had blown any slim chance I might have had at getting the job.

"It's just as well that Spurrier is taking this job, because I have no shot," I said. "Usually I tell you that I'm close, right? Well, I'm not close. We can forget this job."

The interview with Rich was enjoyable, however, because we had talked very little about football. This surprised me because Rich was John McKay's son and had played football at Princeton. Instead, we spent almost the entire time talking about winning, developing chemistry and a winning atmosphere, and relating positively to players. During the interview, Rich asked why I believed I had come in second or third in all those other head coaching searches. I informed him that it hadn't happened all that many times. I listed my actual interviews—a low number compared to the number of times the media had mentioned my name as a candidate. Rich was surprised.

Three days later, I had pretty much put Tampa out of my mind when Jerry Angelo called back to arrange a second meeting between Rich and me, this time at the Senior Bowl. I began to see a faint ray of hope. Then I heard that the Gainesville coaches had stopped packing because Spurrier was undecided.

I bought a second pair of glasses.

Before my second meeting with Rich, I read an article by Hubert Mizell, longtime columnist of the *St. Petersburg Times.* According to his inside sources, I wasn't being considered seriously among the candidates for the Bucs job. I was only a "minority interview," brought in to demonstrate the Bucs' commitment to diversity.

I was crushed. Nobody had more inside sources in Tampa than Hubert Mizell. I found myself questioning God's plan and timing.

However, I still had a glimmer of hope. Not only had Rich and I developed a good rapport, but Jerry, whom I had known only casually before this process, was calling me every two or three days to tell me not to worry about what I might be hearing or reading. He said the Buccaneers were simply being very diligent and weren't conducting the search through the media.

I met with Rich again at the Senior Bowl in Mobile, Alabama. We met for dinner at Roussos Restaurant, and we still didn't talk many football specifics. Instead, Rich began asking me about the Buccaneers' current players. We didn't get into too much detail but instead talked generally about how I thought certain players might fit into *my* plans for the club.

I returned to Minnesota and Lauren. The next day at the

office, I couldn't focus on the simplest of tasks because of my excitement over the possibility in Tampa. Lauren seemed to be having the same problem at home.

Jerry called two days later. "Rich needs to know the name of your agent."

"May I ask why?"

"He wants to begin discussing a contract." I hung up and contacted Ray Anderson, who represented Denny Green and Ty Willingham. I asked Ray to contact Rich. Then I went home to tell Lauren that things looked promising.

"You'd better not be kidding me, Tony! You'd better not be kidding me!" Lauren had been on this roller coaster before, when I had interviewed in Jacksonville and their president had called me to say I was one of the last two candidates. She didn't want to get her hopes up unless it was a sure thing, especially on days like this one, when it was twenty degrees below zero outside. I swore Lauren to secrecy for a couple of days until Ray could work things out with Rich.

The team flew us to Tampa so we could meet with the Glazers, the Bucs' owners. They made arrangements for us to stay at the Tampa Airport Marriott, where Rich said he would meet us. As Lauren walked off the plane and into that warm Jetway, I could tell from her gait and the angle of her shoulders that she already didn't want to return to Minnesota—ever—except to get Tiara, Jamie, and Eric.

Rich met us in the hotel lobby. As we stepped onto the elevator to head to the parking garage, some cameramen spotted us, and the chase was on. Once we were buckled in, Rich sped off, winding through the parking garage and out of the airport, driving like he was in *Starsky and Hutch*. He used the back streets of Tampa, and by the time we arrived at Bern's Steak House, Rich had left the press far behind. Or so we thought.

Even on an ordinary night, Bern's is an experience unlike

any other. The restaurant has red velvet walls with gold trim, which added to the storybook feeling of the evening. We had a great meal and an enjoyable conversation with the Glazers. I wanted to be sure they knew how important my faith was to me. Given that they were Jewish, I wasn't sure how that would be received. As it turned out, the Glazers were wonderful people of faith. They seemed accepting, open, and welcoming of my approach to coaching, faith, and life. As we wrapped up our three-hour dinner and headed upstairs to Bern's famous dessert room, someone suggested we turn on the television.

The station we turned to was broadcasting live from outside of Bern's. About five hundred people appeared in the background of the camera shot from Bern's parking lot.

Then I heard the reporter. "We believe that Rich McKay is inside with the new coach of the Buccaneers, and we're waiting for them to come out."

It was a surreal experience to watch our situation unfold on television.

A moment later, Mr. Glazer said, "Let's go out. Don't you think we should introduce them to the next coach of the Tampa Bay Buccaneers?"

It was official. Lauren was finally done with Minnesota winters. We were headed to sunny Tampa, Florida.

In the process, I had once again learned a valuable lesson. God's plans don't always follow human logic. I was finally a head coach, but it had happened in a setting and through a process that had made me believe I had no chance. We often can't see what God is doing in our lives, but God sees the whole picture and His plan for us clearly.

BUILDING THE FACULTY

CHAPTER EIGHT

Good teachers help all their students earn an A.
DR. WIL DUNGY

HEAD COACH of the Tampa Bay Buccaneers. I couldn't believe I'd actually gotten the job. I was especially humbled when I thought about all the times I had fallen short and all the other African American coaches who had gone before me but had never gotten this chance. I realized that the one thing I could do to help them—and the coaches who followed behind us—was to win. Actions speak louder than words. Winning would create greater potential for change than talk alone.

When I arrived in Tampa in 1996, the Buccaneers hadn't been particularly successful on the field. I hoped that losing history would make the players more receptive to my new ideas. And despite that history, I was convinced we would win right away.

My first order of business was to assemble a coaching staff. The prior year's Buccaneers staff included some terrific coaches, and I was tempted to have some of them stay on. I was good friends with George Stewart, the Buccaneers special teams coach, and I really wanted to keep him. But while the Bucs were deciding on me, George had accepted a job with San Francisco. At that point, I decided to start fresh with an entirely new staff. The Buccaneers weren't just any club that I had the chance to rebuild. This was one of the least successful franchises in professional sports. While it pained me to do it, I let the assistant coaches go. I was thankful that those guys quickly found jobs elsewhere. I believe they understood.

Herm Edwards had left coaching and was scouting for the Chiefs, evaluating players from around the league. He was convinced that his best bet for advancement in the NFL was to continue on his current path in personnel and hope to become a general manager someday. But I knew how much he loved coaching, and when I was named head coach of the Bucs, I immediately turned to Herm, thinking we would form a natural partnership. I wanted him to be my assistant head coach and to coach the defensive backs. He was a good teacher of fundamentals. Even more than that, he knew how to work hard, and he knew how to win. To my surprise, however, Herm wasn't interested. At least not right away.

At first glance, Herm and I seem to be almost polar opposites. He is emotional and talkative, while I'm more analytical and reserved. But he was exactly the type of guy that I wanted for that staff. I wanted teachers more than tacticians, smart coaches who were driven to accomplish our goals and could get those goals across. I also wanted coaches like Herm who would encourage players to maximize their talents. This was a group of players that was going to require a great deal of quality instruction and encouragement. While I was in Pittsburgh observing Coach Noll, I had learned that you need all types of personalities on a staff. The last thing I should do was surround myself with fifteen clones of me. Herm certainly met that requirement.

At the core, however, Herm and I are actually very much alike. We're both old-school types. We came into the league in the same way—as undrafted free agents. We learned to focus on fundamentals and making sure things are done the right way. Herm is a mentally tough guy whose father was in the military. In addition, he is expressive, animated, and a great motivator. Most important, he has the same personal values that I have. I knew he would be a perfect complement to my coaching style. He would also help me turn around the mindset of our team; he had done it before. The Eagles had been struggling when Herm began playing for them, but over time, they became winners. That's what we had to do in Tampa—change a culture, in a team and in a city, that had been losing for a long time.

But no matter what I did to persuade him, Herm wasn't ready to leave Kansas City. I interviewed other guys and tried to keep an open mind. None was quite the right fit. In the meantime, I continued to build the rest of my staff.

Monte Kiffin and I had been on the Vikings defensive staff together during my first three seasons in Minnesota. Monte had left in 1995 to become defensive coordinator for the New Orleans Saints. Jim Mora, the head coach of the Saints at the time, got along well with Monte, and Monte's defense had performed very well. I interviewed Jim Haslett, whom Monte had tutored in New Orleans, but Jim didn't want to leave New Orleans for family reasons. When Jim Haslett decided to stay, Jim Mora gave me permission to hire Monte as my defensive coordinator. I still don't know how that happened.

Shortly thereafter, Joe Marciano, also of New Orleans

contacted me. I knew Joe from my time in Kansas City and Minnesota, when we had practiced against New Orleans during training camp. I had seen firsthand how good Joe was at coaching special teams. I told Joe, however, that I was sure Jim Mora wouldn't let him leave, especially since he had just given up Monte. Joe said that Jim would let him go if he could find a suitable replacement. He asked me to hold the position open for him, and I did.

Clyde Christensen, Charlie Williams, Tony Nathan, Chris Foerster, and Ricky Porter made up the offensive staff. I hired Mike Shula as my offensive coordinator because Mike's offense in Chicago had always given us trouble in Minnesota. Although we were going to build up the defense first, I knew Mike would have the patience to lead the offense as we built it.

Other than Monte, I had to work a little harder to find coaches to fit our defensive scheme. I felt a little like Coach Noll, who never wanted to bring in players or coaches from other organizations because he didn't want to have to overcome a prior way of doing things. He wanted everyone to immediately buy into the Steelers way, and he didn't want any other influences to trickle in. That's why, when he traded me to San Francisco, he didn't trade for a player but rather for a draft pick. I knew exactly what I wanted to do on defense, and Monte was the perfect person to do it. I didn't want other coaches to bring in other philosophies. I needed people who would teach what Monte wanted done.

I hired my staff with a few basic thoughts in mind. First, they had to be men of character and integrity. While I admire Christian faith, that was not a prerequisite. Integrity, however, is paramount with me. Second, they had to be good teachers; otherwise I wouldn't consider them. I wanted men alongside me who recognized that as coaches and teachers—just like as parents—we are entrusted with the lives of others. We are responsible to help mold them into all they were created to be—as football players, teammates, role models, and productive members of society. Third, I was looking to create opportunities for African Americans who weren't already in the NFL. Finally, I was hoping for guys who would make a long-term commitment to the Bucs.

The Buccaneers had become a way station for coaches. A coach would land in Tampa when he was looking for a job, then leave for a "better job" whenever a position became available. We needed Tampa to *become* that better job. I wanted the Buccaneers to become a place where coaches—and players— aspired to be.

Not everyone I contacted wanted to come. I spoke with Ron Brown, the receivers coach at the University of Nebraska, about joining us in Tampa. I had known Ron for years and thought he would be a perfect fit in light of his character and his coaching style and teaching philosophy. Ron asked me to give him a week to pray about my offer.

"What? Ron, I've got to put together a staff. I don't know if I can wait that long."

Ron was adamant, and I agreed to wait for him. We were both glad that he took his time. A week later, he called me back to decline. He said he would love to coach in the NFL and be a part of what we were creating in Tampa, but he believed the Lord wanted him to stay at Nebraska, where he was involved with a number of outreach opportunities.

"I know He'll find somebody else to do His work if I go, but I really believe this is where I'm supposed to be right now." Of course, I respected Ron's decision and how he came to it.

Several of our college scouts recommended that I speak with Lovie Smith, the defensive backs coach from Ohio State.

At the same time, they were also suggesting Rod Marinelli, the defensive line coach at Southern Cal. I had never met either one, but after interviewing them, I knew they would both be a perfect fit. I hired them both. All the qualities I was looking for—strong character, mental toughness, strength, passion, and a commitment to teaching fundamentals—were true of both Lovie and Rod.

Joe Marciano called again, asking me to continue holding the special teams job. I kept the promise intact. I wouldn't fill it—yet—but time was becoming a factor.

Herm was still not interested in coming to Tampa. To this day, I have a written phone message from Herm that reminds me of the complete lack of urgency he felt to leave Kansas City to join me in Tampa: "Herm Edwards. Says he'll be at home in California."

Monte, Rod, and Lovie were all on board at One Buc and ready to get to work. I didn't let them meet as a staff for the first month, though, because we still didn't have a defensive backs coach, and I wanted the defensive staff to be complete before they started meeting together. Rich McKay started coming by a little more frequently, with an increasing sense of urgency about the status of my staff. In the NFL, there's a tremendous amount of pressure to hire a staff quickly. The concern is that the longer you wait, the greater the chance that the best coaches will be under contract somewhere else. I was bound and determined to have the right staff, but I wasn't pleased with the delay either.

After this went on for a month, I knew I had to push Herm. I played my last card by appealing to the one thing I knew would get him—his passion. I told Herm that this was what we had always talked about, starting with a clean slate and doing it our way. This was our chance. Our chance to show the NFL how to win.

Herm remembers it differently. He claims that I finally called and said, "You owe me."

Either way, he came. What he may have owed me I'm not sure, but I'm glad one of those approaches worked. Herm became my assistant head coach and defensive backs coach. He also became our resident bad cop, a role I think he enjoyed.

Finally Joe Marciano called back. He had lined up a suitable replacement for himself in New Orleans, and Jim Mora had agreed to let him come to Tampa. I couldn't believe it, but it was worth the wait. In fact, the whole situation was remarkable. Two coordinators, Monte and Joe, had been under contract to the same club, which allowed both of them to make lateral moves (not promotions) to the same opposing club in the same conference. I've never heard of another such thing, before or since.

Looking back, I truly believe the Lord brought that staff together. Since that time, all those guys have gone on to do some terrific things in the NFL and elsewhere. People have given me far too much credit for their success. There is no other way to explain the way this staff came together except to say that God orchestrated the process.

Herm had been one of the final pieces of the staffing puzzle for the Tampa Bay Buccaneers. To celebrate his arrival, we went to lunch. Herm swears it was Miami Subs—and he's still miffed that he had to pay. He says I'm cheap.

I'm not really cheap, although I did learn the value of a dollar from my dad. Once, when he was shopping for a television, my dad must have driven to every electronics store in Jackson, East Lansing, Ann Arbor, and Detroit. I finally pointed out that the twenty dollars he was going to save by his comparison shopping was more than consumed by the value of his time and the gas he used shuttling around southern Michigan. My words fell on deaf ears. And that wasn't the only time he did that. Although we had cars that were new to our family, they were never truly new, always used. I think because my dad grew up during the Depression, he was conscious of carefully stewarding his resources. My dad did not waste anything, including money. Therefore, he was careful not to waste the things with which he had been entrusted.

As for me, I'm fairly frugal, just like my dad.

The fact that Herm ended up buying his own lunch at Miami Subs on his first day as the Bucs assistant head coach was simply because the establishment that he picked was cash only, and I usually didn't carry cash. We ordered, and when I stepped to the counter to pay, I realized that I couldn't use my credit card. I began feeling my pockets, even though I knew I wouldn't find any cash in them. Herm had to pay for his own lunch.

And my lunch too. He's never let me forget it.

Despite my excitement at being head coach of the Bucs, the team's headquarters at One Buccaneer Place quickly brought me back down to earth. For the first two or three days, One Buc looked great to me because I was so excited to be a head coach. But after a couple of days, when I started really looking around and trying to figure out where I would put coaches and hold meetings—well, it was a letdown. In the words of Bucs defensive tackle Warren Sapp, One Buc was "its own third-world country."

One Buc was a low, one-story stucco building. It had been

built in 1976 just outside the flight path at Tampa International Airport. It was only several hundred yards from runway 18L/36R, one of the two main runways for the hundreds of flights in and out of Tampa every day. Its location was both a blessing and a curse. Being so close to the airport was very convenient for our scouts, for visiting free agents, and for our whole team when we traveled to away games. But the noise of flights taking off and banking in our direction was sometimes deafening. I guess there was one positive side effect of the noise: we never had to pipe in crowd noise when practicing for away games. However, the acrid smell of jet fuel that often blew into our building made us all certain we were shaving years off our lives.

We had no parking lot for visitors . . . or players. Some players used the small parking lot that belonged to an old public golf course across the street, but most opted to park in the grass beside the road in front of the building. They took their chances with traffic and occasional tickets from the airport police. Every so often we'd hear the screech of tires—too late—as a car unsuccessfully navigating the two-lane road sideswiped one of our parked cars. A small, wooden guard shack stood next to the sidewalk leading into the main entrance.

Inside, One Buc had a reception area for the few visitors we did have. The greeting area was relatively large—relative to the size of any other room in the building, anyway. Beyond that reception area, however, the uniqueness of One Buccaneer Place could be found. I was one of only two coaches whose office did not also serve as a meeting room. As the assistant head coach, Herm merited his own office. Actually, that wasn't the reason. There just wasn't room in his meeting room for a desk, so we cleaned out the tiny storage closet in the back of the meeting room and somehow wedged a desk and filing cabinet within its walls. However, his unique closet-office mandated an open-door policy, as the door could not be closed unless the desk chair was removed.

Frankly, I was never particularly bothered by One Buc. Once Herm got the grounds staff to strategically place rat-traps behind our desks—and to check and empty them as necessary—One Buc seemed fairly hygienic as well. I often thought of my dad teaching in the "separate but equal" days. He always told us it didn't matter what his building looked like; his job was to help his students learn just as much as the students in the other building were learning. Herm and I vowed that we would win a championship in that building. There were already enough excuses for the losing culture at One Buc, and we were determined to change that. We had to. That's the nature of the business if you want to be around for any length of time.

DO WHAT WE DO

CHAPTER NINE

Champions are champions not because they do anything extraordinary but because they do the ordinary things better than anyone else.
CHUCK NOLL

"I DON'T YELL A LOT. In fact, yelling will be rare," I told the Buccaneers at our first team meeting. In addition to the change in coaching staff, I felt the culture of One Buc needed an infusion of fresh ideas. With that in mind, I believed this opening team meeting would be critical to setting the tone.

"When I get mad," I continued, "I usually talk at the same volume I'm talking now. And when I get really mad"—I paused—"I *whisper.* So if my voice at this level won't get your attention, and you believe you need someone to yell at you to correct you or motivate you, then we'll probably need to find you another team to play for so that you can play your best."

In that first meeting, I outlined several basic tenets that would become our hallmarks:

- Top 5 in the NFL in giveaway/takeaway ratio
- Top 5 in the NFL in fewest penalties
- Top 5 in overall special teams
- Make big plays
- Don't give up big plays

These basic tenets were not exactly rocket science; in fact, they are exactly the same principles I would later use with the Colts. Some people think of me as a defense-minded coach, or they think I somehow changed who I was as a coach when I went to Indianapolis. But the reality is, I'm a former college quarterback who played defense in the NFL and coached under Chuck Noll, Marty Schottenheimer, and Denny Green. I learned that it doesn't matter how you win. You play to your team's strength, whether it's offense, defense, or special teams. I believe the best way to achieve success in each of these three areas is by attention to detail and a commitment to the fundamentals—doing the ordinary things better than anyone else.

I then began to talk about our future. Going back to something Mr. Rooney had always taught us in Pittsburgh, I said, "We expect to win a Super Bowl. But if that's all we do, it will be pretty shallow. We need to not only win but win with players who positively impact the Tampa Bay area."

I told them that I expected our team to live and play by the concept "Whatever it takes," then ended with a second basic phrase, which I posted in our locker room: "No excuses, no explanations."

Overall, I thought it was a good, positive meeting that clearly outlined the frame of mind we needed to embrace for the future of the organization and for the future of our lives.

When the meeting was finished, Herm felt the need to make sure everything was even more clear, so he selected some of the team leaders, including John Lynch, Warren Sapp, and Derrick Brooks, and then he read them the riot act, reiterating everything I had just said, but in a much more animated manner. It was his first act as bad cop. Herm was so good in that role that I'm sure I never even knew about some of the issues faced by our team. Herm was my first line of defense. I've heard that he was known to tell guys, "We can either resolve this now and get it behind us, or we can get Tony involved. I don't think any of us want that." Very few things hit my desk.

When I was in Minnesota, Denny Green had been a big proponent of creating what I call "artificial adversity," making things tougher on the players than they had to be. He believed this was an essential foundation for handling the turbulence of a season or game. As coaches and as players, he wanted us all to be comfortable enough with our routine to know what to expect and when. When we would have an upcoming Monday night game—and thereby an extra day available to practice and plan the game—he often gave us that extra day off or had us work on something that turned our attention away from our opponent.

"After all," he reasoned, "if the coaches and players start to think that we need an extra day to prepare for a big game, what happens when we hit the playoffs and only have the usual number of days or, worse yet, a short week?" If players got too comfortable in their routine, what would happen when that routine was disrupted? "Players might begin to wonder, 'Can we win a big game without an extra day?' Sure we can—if we're efficient and disciplined."

Denny knew that football, like life, is unpredictable, but it was our job to train the team to remain disciplined even in unusual situations. As I thought about how to prepare the Bucs to handle any situation we might face, I went back to some of Denny's tactics. Once we had become locked in on a schedule, he often created a disruption to that schedule just to see how guys would respond. During the preseason of my first year with the Vikings, Denny announced that we were going to Cleveland on the day of the game. He said we would get off the plane, head to the stadium, and play. This was unusual; most teams travel to an away game at least a day before the game— sometimes arriving even two days early if it's an especially long trip. But Denny wanted to see how the players would adjust—who would adapt and who couldn't. His larger point was that there were always going to be moments of adversity and confusion during a game or a season, and players either adjusted or they crumbled. He wanted to know as much as possible ahead of time about the innate character of his team. On that occasion, the players grumbled a little, then flew into Cleveland and beat the Browns 51–3.

✣   ✣   ✣

During our first training camp in Tampa, we were headed to Jacksonville for a morning scrimmage with the Jaguars. Taking a lesson from Denny Green's playbook, I told Herm I wanted to disrupt the schedule and bus our guys to Jacksonville.

"Herm, the guys might think that we're just looking to save some money by driving up there"—the Glazers were still trying to shed the frugal reputation the team had gotten from the prior owner—"so I'll need your help. I want every-one to understand that I think it'll be good to disrupt their schedules."

"I think that's smart."

"Good. We'll leave at five o'clock."

"Five? You don't want to meet at the hotel that night? Just get up there, have dinner at the hotel, and then do bed checks?"

"I mean five *in the morning*. We'll have a wakeup call at four, leave at five, roll in there, and scrimmage with Jacksonville."

Herm didn't mind. He usually gets up at 4:30 anyway. But the players hated it. We emerged from the buses a little on the groggy side, just as I thought we would, and were destroyed by the Jaguars during the first practice of the morning. We were beaten physically and mentally. We got a little better in the afternoon. I told our players that I liked our improvement, but we could have done better. The players couldn't believe it. They thought they had done well—*under the circumstances.* But that was my point. We couldn't let circumstances matter. If things got unusually tough, for whatever reason, we still had to function and get the job done.

No excuses, no explanations.

As a team, we got some lasting benefit from that experience. For the next several years, when we'd get into crunch time in a game, I'd occasionally hear a player call out, "Come on, guys! It's time for a five o'clock bus ride!"

Whatever it takes.

That first year, we definitely inherited some talent. In 1995, the Bucs had two first-round draft picks and came out with a terrific haul—Warren Sapp and Derrick Brooks. When I got there in 1996, we had two more first-round picks, and we added to our defensive line again with both picks—Regan Upshaw and Marcus Jones. In the defensive scheme we planned to run, defensive linemen would be critical. Rod Marinelli loved coaching in our system because of the spotlight it placed on his defensive linemen.

My goal was to add to our core through the draft and then continue to add strategically through free agency. We wanted guys who had been productive in college, and we made it a point to pick performance over potential. Because the salary cap limits each team's total payroll, we only wanted to pay significant sums to keep truly special players. We decided we would let others leave for greener pastures in free agency, even if it meant taking a slight step backward while we groomed a successor.

After emphasizing defense in the first round of the 1996 draft, we turned our attention to getting a big-play guy on offense in the second round. The Jets had the first pick in each round that year (they took Keyshawn Johnson first overall). We wanted Leeland McElroy, a running back out of Texas A&M, but we doubted he would still be available when our number five pick came in the second round. So Tim Ruskell, our director of player personnel, lined up a trade with the Jets if McElroy was still available when their pick arrived. He got on the phone with Jets assistant general manager James "Shack" Harris, working out the particulars of the trade. I heard Tim conclude the conversation with, "But if our player is still on the board, we have a deal, right? Good."

The Redskins made their pick at the end of the first round, and McElroy was still on the board. We were ecstatic, and Tim had Shack on speed dial. Before Shack answered, however, the Jets' pick came in: Alex Van Dyke from Nevada—the Jets' second wide receiver in two rounds. They hadn't kept their part of our deal.

Tim was not happy when Shack picked up the phone and said, "Tim, I'm so sorry. When Van Dyke was still there, the coaches just went ahead and took him right away."

We were thrown for a loop and began frantically working the phones to try again to move up from our pick. We called the three remaining teams in front of us, sure that one of them would take McElroy. We were offering picks, players, our children . . . but the Arizona Cardinals took McElroy with the next pick.

The Jets, as it turned out, had been our only hope.

We were disappointed and frustrated, but we had only two picks in which to gather ourselves and decide whom we wanted next. We had been so focused on McElroy that we needed time to turn our attention to others—time we didn't have. Even though we needed a great, game-changing back, we decided our best option was to make do with the next player on our board—a battering-ram, short-yardage running back.

Mike Alstott.

Of course, after the pick, we knew we would need to meet with the media and say how thrilled we were to have Mike. But as we gave our separate interviews, I know we were all extremely disappointed at how close we had been to getting McElroy. Years later, we came out looking like geniuses for having picked Alstott. He went on to become the second-leading rusher in Buccaneers history and to score almost twice as many touchdowns as any other player in the history of the franchise. I'm a firm believer that the Lord sometimes has to short-circuit even our best plans for our benefit.

We had two picks in that second round, and we were pre-pared to trade our second pick. Rich had told me during the week that Bobby Beathard of San Diego would probably call and offer us their first-round pick in 1997 for our second-rounder this year. Given that we had so many needs, we figured that was the way to go. *If* he called.

When that pick was approaching, I was starting to have second thoughts. We still hadn't fully recovered from the McElroy/Alstott pick, and I was focused on Donnie Abraham. Donnie would fit our scheme perfectly; he was a solid person, exactly the kind of guy Monte and Herm would like to add to our defense. While we knew that building for the future with an extra first-rounder next year made sense, our previous pick hadn't gone well, and we wanted to walk out of there with a second-rounder we liked.

When we were on the clock to make our pick, the phone rang. I'm still amazed that Bobby called, just like Rich had said he would. Rich told him we would call him back. We debated and finally decided to trade.

Donnie Abraham was still there when we picked in the third round, making our 1996 draft a nice combination of preparation and God's providence.

By the way, two years later, we added Leeland McElroy to our roster when Arizona cut him. Although he was a good player and a great person, he couldn't make our team. Funny how things work out.

As we were adding players through the draft and free agency to improve our level of talent, we had to continue working on the mind-set of a group that had lived so many years within a negative culture. I thought back to the things Tom Lamphere and I had talked about. Nehemiah also inherited a defeated group and had to change their culture and attitude so they could move forward. Nehemiah kept his people focused on their task of rebuilding the wall around Jerusalem. Rather than dividing their attention and focusing on the external threat that sought to destroy them, they stayed ready with their swords by their sides while they continued to work on the wall. Each person and family worked to build the portion of the wall in front of where they lived.

The Buccaneers were a group in need of remaining on task, focusing on what was before them. I knew that my job was to keep the guys focused on the things they could control, not on outside noises from media and fans or other things they couldn't control.

It's hard enough to be successful in this league—and in life—without hauling around the extra baggage of distractions. Right off the bat, we discussed how to deal with the media. "Negative will sell," I told the team. "But so will the positive. So let's always be positive. Whether you like them or not, the media will always be present in the NFL. It's a fact of life, so you have to deal with it and make it as positive as possible. If

As a baby in 1956, I had no idea what a big part phone calls would play in my NFL career.

↑ ABOVE

A nine-year-old at Michigan State University. My dad was teaching and working on his PhD but still found time to play catch with me.

RIGHT →

A big rivalry existed between my high school, Parkside, and Jackson High— but not in this case. My mom, who taught at Jackson, was also my biggest fan.

Basketball was my favorite sport in high school. This was taken during my senior year with Bobby Burton (my best friend and a central figure in a football crisis our junior year), Shelby Hathorn, and Coach Ben Sierra.

← LEFT
University of Minnesota Coach Cal Stoll and me.

RIGHT →
At a 1978 charity event with Pittsburgh Steelers future Hall of Famer Franco Harris and teammate Rocky Bleier. The veterans taught us early the importance of getting involved in the community.

Hanging with Dennis Winston and Donnie Shell at training camp during my first year in the NFL. Donnie (far right) tutored me spiritually, as well as on the field, and would eventually be the best man in my wedding.

Chuck Noll and me at a Steelers practice. I couldn't have had a better mentor for my first job as an assistant coach in the NFL.

During the 1978 playoffs with the Steelers, on our way to Super Bowl XIII.

. . . TO COACH

↑ **ABOVE**
On June 19, 1982, Lauren Harris
joined the Dungy family . . .

RIGHT →
. . . and she is as beautiful today
as she was the day we met.

Another benefit of coming to Tampa—
great fishing in the Bay! I enjoyed this day
with tight end Dave Moore, the Bucs' best
fisherman, especially when I caught this
beautiful permit.

FOOTBALL ISN'T EVERYTHING

It was a real joy to have my parents, Wilbur and CleoMae Dungy, by my side when I got
my first head coaching job with the Tampa Bay Buccaneers in 1996.

*Eric with me on the field for the
pregame warm-up—his reward
for a week of good grades.*

Just after the team prayer following my first win as head coach of the Bucs. It was a terrific feeling, even though it took almost two months to get there.

Dungy's Mentors for Life was a program I started in Tampa to encourage people to invest in the youth of the Bay area. Two hours prior to kickoff, the Bucs would join the kids and their mentors on the field.

Speaking to a group of kids for Family First, the organization that launched All Pro Dad in 1998. All Pro Dad was designed to help men improve as fathers and learn better ways to interact with their children.

*Three of the Dungy boys with actor/director Spike Lee on opening day of the Bucs
2000 season. Spike became a Bucs fan after we traded for Keyshawn Johnson.*

Eric with defense tackle Warren Sapp at a Bucs game in 1999. I always remind our players that kids like Eric are watching everything they do.

Lauren and me watching Jamie and Eric's baptism at Idlewild Baptist Church in Tampa. Knowing that Jamie had accepted Christ and would be in heaven would definitely comfort us later on.

My introduction as the Indianapolis Colts head coach in January 2002 after flying into the Colts complex on Jim Irsay's private helicopter.

Thanksgiving Day against Detroit in 2004 with Eric and James. I grew up just one hour from Detroit, and watching the Lions play on Thanksgiving was a family tradition. We had over a hundred family members there that day.

I don't often lose my cool with officials. Whenever I start, I usually hear my dad's voice asking me, "Will it make the situation better?" I've learned that while it may feel good to vent, it's better to listen to my dad's wisdom and rely on quiet strength instead.

When I first met Peyton Manning in 1997, neither of us dreamed that we'd one day take the field together as part of a Super Bowl–winning team. This photo was taken right after Peyton broke the record with his 49th touchdown pass in 2004.

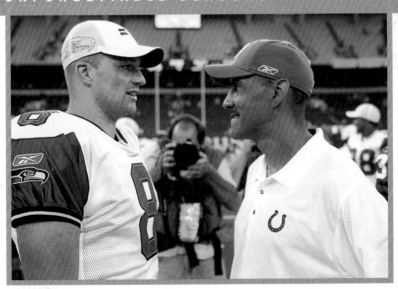

After a game against the Seattle Seahawks in 2006, I'm thanking Seahawks quarterback Matt Hasselbeck for a card he had sent to our family when James died. It was one of thousands from all over the country that we will never forget.

My assistant Jackie Cook brought the Basket of Hope program to the Colts. We take the baskets to kids at Riley Hospital for Children to brighten their stay—but it's even more fun for us than it is for the kids.

Lauren and me with Dr. Ben Carson and his wife, Candy, at a fund-raiser for the Carson Scholars Fund, a wonderful foundation that awards scholarships to kids from all around the country. In 2005, Lauren and I teamed up with the Colts to open an Indianapolis chapter.

← LEFT

Tiara and our niece, Lisa Harris (daughter of Lauren's twin brother, Loren). They usually prefer to stay in the background, but on this occasion, after the Colts won the 2006 AFC Championship Game, everyone was too excited. After twenty-six years in coaching, we were finally headed to the Super Bowl!

↓ BELOW

It's not always fun dealing with the media, but I see it as an opportunity to tell the world about how my Christian faith affects the way I coach, win or lose. I did enjoy this interview with CBS's Jim Nantz after the AFC Championship Game.

↑ **ABOVE**

Making history in the Super Bowl with Lovie Smith. This photo marks the first time opposing coaches were photographed together with the Vince Lombardi Trophy before the game.

BELOW ↓

Hoisting the elusive Lombardi Trophy on the winner's platform with a group of special people, including Lauren, Colts owner Jim Irsay and his wife, Meg, and Peyton Manning.

After our Super Bowl victory, we set the trophy off to the side and focused on what was really important.

Football sometimes takes away from our family being together, but this time it provided a special moment—flying back to Indianapolis after Super Bowl XLI.

One of our Dungy traditions, led by Lauren, is dressing alike for a Christmas picture. This one is from 2006.

they hate you, they won't suddenly disappear. They'll just make your life miserable. So don't give them reason to hate you."

We then discussed body language and the importance of nonverbal cues. "Make eye contact when you're answering the media. Don't act like a loser, even when you've lost. Don't blame anybody else." We had to make sure that we were together in this project.

We needed to let the media do their jobs, but we also needed to be proactive about getting the message out rather than letting them dictate the stories. I always tried to be very cordial with the media, and my goal was always to be sure that my responses were well thought out. I never wanted to antagonize anyone, but I planned to answer the questions in a way that emphasized the positives without giving away too much information. I think the media appreciated our treating them professionally and with respect, although winning probably improved the tone of their stories more than anything else.

No excuses, no explanations.

Talent at Tampa Bay wasn't a major issue. The Vikings had played the Bucs twice a year, so I already knew the talent level was good. The Bucs had also been drafting many of the guys that we had wanted for the Vikings—Sapp, Brooks, and John Lynch among them—so I knew the Bucs had been drafting the right guys, at least on defense. When I arrived in Tampa, the talent was there. It was the culture that had to change.

When I was in Minnesota, we knew that if we could get the Bucs down early, they would give up, and we could win easily. But if they started well, they would be competitive with us to the end. It seemed that the team had cultivated a fragile mind-set that had infected their play for years. They always expected something to go wrong, and it usually did.

When I arrived in Tampa, I began meeting with the players who lived there, trying to understand from them what needed to be fixed. Although all the issues were relatively minor, they contributed to the team's second-class, defeatist, excuse-laden mentality. I began to sell the philosophy that we are responsible for what happens to us, not anyone or anything else.

No excuses, no explanations.

At the same time, I started to address some of the issues the players were bringing to my attention. I realized that by addressing minor issues we could bring about a major culture shift. The Bucs' previous owner had been known for his frugality, and in order to save a few dollars, the team often stayed in inconvenient locations when they were on the road. When I came on board, we began to stay downtown at Marriotts, Wyndhams, and Ritz-Carltons. It was a small change but part of a bigger shift I wanted us to make.

The players also complained that they were often treated with a lack of respect. For example, the equipment manager was very concerned about the cost of replacing lost towels. He felt that players might be tempted to take towels home to wash their cars or dogs or whatever. He was right—the cost of towels certainly can add up. But his solution was to assign each guy a towel with his name attached to it by a clothespin. This way, he could inventory the towels and know who had taken one. We told the guys we were going to treat them like adults and leave the towels out in a stack. If they could not be trusted with the towels, we would go back to assigning one towel per player. As time went on, we never needed to do that. It was another small change but part of a bigger cultural shift.

One of the things I couldn't change was the location of our training camp at the University of Tampa. The University of Tampa had been founded more than sixty years earlier in a hotel Henry Plant had built in the late 1800s along the banks of the Hillsborough River. Originally intended as a getaway for vacationing northerners, it has since been turned into a very pretty school. As a training camp, however, it had seen too many lousy Bucs teams wander through its halls and grounds. I wanted a new, fresh place to train, someplace without any connection to losing. But we simply didn't have another feasible option.

I thought of my dad's advice to focus on the job, not the surroundings, and decided to embrace the situation rather than try to change it. I told the guys we didn't *want* to leave the University of Tampa. We wanted our team to become tough, so we wanted camp to be tough. We wanted the grass on the field to give out during the first thunderstorm. We wanted the dorm rooms to be spartan. It was a mind-set shift, and the guys accepted it.

No excuses, no explanations.

As for One Buc, I knew it needed countless improvements—a team meeting room, offices separate from meeting rooms, a room big enough to house all of the weights so some weren't out on the patio, a third practice field, and so on. But as I told the guys, the Pittsburgh Steelers practiced every day on a sixty-yard Astroturf field . . . and had won four Super Bowls.

No excuses, no explanations.

At a team meeting, I ran through a laundry list of excuses our players could easily hang a poor season on if they chose to:

- We have a new coaching staff.
- We have to learn a new system on both offense and defense.
- We have sub-par facilities.
- We have a young quarterback.
- We never get the benefit of the doubt from officials.

- We have distractions over a stadium, and we might move cities.
- We never win in the cold.

Those were all great excuses, and we could have used any and all of them. However, our goal was to win football games, and excuses were not an option. Instead, I told them we expected several things of them:

- Be a pro.
- Act like a champion.
- Respond to adversity; don't react.
- Be on time. Being late means either it's not important to you or you can't be relied upon.
- Execute. Do what you're supposed to do when you're supposed to do it. Not almost. All the way. Not most of the time. All of the time.
- Take ownership.

Whatever it takes.
No excuses, no explanations.

One of the first articles written in the local newspaper after we took to the practice fields in Tampa pointed out the fact that almost no profanity was heard at practice anymore. While I choose not to use profanity because of my faith, I have never mandated a certain vocabulary from anyone else. I simply ask players and coaches to be mindful of their language when we have open practices during training camp. I think the fact that so many of our assistant coaches were positive teachers helped that process. I also continued to emphasize the need for our staff to be encouraging and positive in their approach to coaching.

Other changes were a little tougher. I cut out the golf

carts at camp and made the players walk or take shuttle vans; I wanted to make things just a little more difficult than they were used to. We didn't allow any hazing of rookies. In fact, I talked often about being a team and developing the trust and togetherness we would need to help us down the road. I couldn't see any way that hazing could help us to do that. That change probably hurt the veteran players the most since they were now no longer allowed to make the rookies sing during meals at training camp.

The only thing veterans still got were some seniority privileges: signing up for weightlifting times, selecting plane seats, and so forth. I made everyone share a room with another player, so veteran players no longer enjoyed single rooms. I've since shifted my thinking on this a bit. We can all learn and adapt even though our principles remain intact, right? Now I allow players to have single rooms on the night before games if they so choose. They've convinced me that sleeping patterns can be dramatically different, and too many guys were complaining that their sleep was being disrupted. I do still require roommates at camp, however.

After all the changes to the roster and the beginnings of change to the team's attitude, we hit the ground running. We were facing the Green Bay Packers in the season opener on the first day of September 1996, in Tampa, and our guys were excited and ready to play. We felt like we were much better than previous Bucs teams mentally, physically, and emotionally, and we embraced the challenge of facing the team that had won our division the year before. I had given the team a talk at the end of the preseason to remind them of the players' responsibilities and to point out that it might take some time to get the team turned around:

"Coaches can't tell you everything—if they could, we would need fifty-three coaches. It has to come from you. We *will* get it—eventually. Probably not this year, but we're going to get the details covered." But we all believed that the effects of our efforts would be noticed immediately on the field against the Packers.

By halftime we were down 24–3 on our way to a 34–3 loss. Herm turned to me in the locker room and said, "This may be a *little* tougher than we thought."

There was no doubt about that. After dropping the opener, we headed off to Detroit, where we lost. Then we went to Denver and lost again. The Denver game was one we should have won but for a mistake here and a mistake there. The following week I gave a speech at a United Way rally in Tampa, using the following notes:

"We won't panic. There won't be wholesale changes. [We will] *do what we do* because it's good. Because it's right. Also, we can't and won't let anything from the outside split us up."

We hung in there as a unit and returned home to face the Seattle Seahawks. The announced crowd was just over thirty thousand, but there couldn't have been twenty-five thousand in the stands. I kept a video of the beginning of that game, because it had a shot of the crowd at kickoff. That crowd certainly didn't look "crowded" up there to me. We lost 17–13, squandering a big lead in the fourth quarter. As we walked off the field, a fan hung over the opening, yelling that we stank and that he was never coming back. I remember thinking that day that we really needed to show these people something positive, some progress. I knew it would happen—but when?

The following day I opened the team meeting by showing the game video and telling the team to have faith.

"There is going to be a time soon when fans won't be able

to get a ticket to come to these games. Just hang in there and do what we do, and it will take care of itself."

We were at home again the following week against Detroit. (As further proof of what a small world it is, Wayne Fontes—the Southern Cal recruiting coordinator who had talked Marvin Powell and Gary Jeter and countless others into playing football for Rich McKay's dad—manned the other sideline as Detroit's head coach.) The Lions shut us out and won big. Another debacle. I was thankful that we had a bye the next week and a chance for the guys to get away from football for a while. At this point we were 0–5 with two close losses and three that weren't so close. We all needed a little time to regroup.

During our bye week, Bryan and Joel Glazer took me to lunch. As Mr. Glazer's sons, they were in day-to-day control of the team. I was certain they were going to offer suggestions or at least point out that the Buccaneers had been better than this in 1995. But instead of giving advice, they assured me that they were in it for the long haul. They understood that my plan might take time to implement, and they were willing to wait.

"Whatever it is you need to do, you have our complete support."

This was a very special moment for me, and it remains a wonderful memory. I was so encouraged to have their backing at that low point in my first season with the Bucs.

I brought the coaches in for a meeting that week and gave them the same message, this time coming from me. "We're going to get this turned around soon," I told them. "You guys have been great, and the players are buying into what you're teaching. We don't have any wins to show for it yet, but we are playing better, and I can see little improvements, even if the rest of the world doesn't. So hang in there. You have my complete support."

I called Coach Noll and asked his advice. "Don't change what you believe in," he told me. "My first year we won our first game but then lost thirteen in a row. The next year we lost our first four games. Stick with what you want to do, even though it's not always going to be easy." Similarly, another experienced NFL coach, Dick Vermeil, called to tell me to stick with my plan. He said it looked to him like we were making progress.

Do what we do.

I never doubted we were heading in the right direction, but it was affirming and important to have the owners' and my coaching peers' encouragement. Today, whenever I notice other coaches who might need a word of encouragement, I always try to offer it.

We came off our bye week to face Minnesota. Chris Foerster and I had a pretty good idea about their talent and schemes, which probably gave the players a little more confidence. They needed it. After all, Minnesota had the best record in the NFL at 5–1, while we were 0–5. And all the while we were telling our guys that our plan was working. We tried to make sure that our Wednesday team meeting was upbeat.

"This is a perfect setup to get our first win," I told them. "We've had a good week of practice, and we're the healthiest we've been all season. They're the best team in the NFL, but we're getting better each week. Our plan is solid, but this won't be a 'game-plan game.' It will be a passion game. Execution. Attitude. Protect the ball. Have a little swagger."

We took the field and did all of those things. We trailed 7–0 at halftime. In the second half we scored three touchdowns, including an amazing play by Mike Alstott. Not only was he the battering ram we were expecting on that play, he pushed two guys backward from the five yard line and extended the ball gracefully into the end zone just as he was knocked out of bounds—touchdown. Once we had the lead, Warren Sapp sacked Warren Moon and caused a fumble, which our Chidi Ahanotu recovered. All of a sudden we realized, *We're going to win.* I can still remember the excitement and relief we felt as the clock wound down and we wrapped up our victory, 24–13.

We gathered for a postgame prayer. We always prayed, as a lot of teams do, both before and after the game. This particular prayer still stands out—not for what was said, which I can't remember, but because I hoped the guys now realized we were going to give thanks in all circumstances. We had already prayed together following our five losses. I wanted them to know that a great win would not change our core values. We would thank God both as gracious losers and as grateful winners.

Although we had a chance to get on a roll then, we didn't. In fact, we began another slide as we dropped three more games in a row and fell to 1–8. One of the three, however, was the Packers again, this time up in Green Bay. We lost 13–7, but it was better than being crushed as we had during our first game against those guys. Green Bay was a playoff team, and we had significantly closed the gap. The plan was slowly working.

Do what we do.

Whatever it takes.

No excuses, no explanations.

I pointed to the evidence and made sure the team knew that we had improved, but I also let them know I expected more from them. I said I would continue to treat them as adults—the way I would want to be treated—but I reminded them that there was an alternative.

"A lot of people say I've got to make you afraid—afraid of being cut, afraid of me. I don't believe that's true." I have always believed that if you tell people what needs to be done, they will do it—if they believe you and your motives for telling them. I knew these guys would see through manipulation but would respond to motivation.

I also told the team that, despite my soft-spoken approach, I would hold each of them accountable.

"There are three possible options to correct this and get where we need to be. One solution is for me to change, to decide I'm wrong, to change my vision for this team. That one is not going to happen. Another option is for you to change—put in more time, go harder, pay more attention to details. As a final option, we'll simply have to go find other guys. Your choice."

Dave Moore, one of our tight ends, later told me that he had expected me to blow up at the team that night. "I was always waiting for you to blow up in practice, at halftime, in a Monday game-film review," he said. "With all the near misses that were resulting from guys just not paying attention to the details, I figured at some point you were going to lose it. But you never did. I don't know how you did it, but I think that's why we finally got the message."

Dave forgot one incident, however.

I felt good about laying out those options for our team. I had let them know where I stood, and now I was ready to move on, turning my attention to our game the following week against the Raiders. But the next time we met at the facility, I completely lost my composure.

It was Wednesday before our game against the Raiders, and I was angry. My anger had nothing to do with football or our losing streak, however. I was upset because two players had missed personal appearances. Errict Rhett didn't miss his appearance completely but was thirty minutes late for an autograph session at a car dealership. Regan Upshaw, on the other hand, completely missed a visit to a fourth-grade class. Making matters worse, this was the second time Regan had missed a visit to that class. This appearance was to have been the makeup that the teacher rescheduled after Regan missed the first. On Wednesday morning I had received a letter from that fourth-grade teacher, and it was painful to read. She was understandably upset, and what made it worse was the fact that she had explained Regan's first absence to the class as a misunderstanding. Now, reading about the class's disappointment when he didn't show up for the second time, I was beside myself.

I began the Wednesday morning team meeting by telling the guys that we were not going to talk football—at all. Instead, I informed them of the incidents involving Rhett and Upshaw. "I don't care about the Raiders," I told them, "and I'm not going to talk about the Raiders. We need to focus on *us,* on changing our own attitudes and accountability. Obviously your word isn't important to you if it doesn't involve the game of football. You don't seem to think being accountable off the field is important. But as far as I'm concerned, we are never going to win consistently until you all get rid of that attitude. The quicker you figure it out, the better."

I told the team that Errict and Regan were not the disease but that they were merely symptoms of a bigger problem. Too many of our guys had the same attitude—they were unwilling to give 100 percent if they didn't personally think it was important.

"What you don't understand is that champions know it's all important," I said. "You have to understand that all the little things your coaches are asking of you really do matter. Knowing I can count on you is just as important to me as your talent. You'll always find excuses for not doing exactly what you're supposed to do. But that's exactly what creates a losing environment."

In 1996, we needed to change that losing environment so we could start doing what we do.

That incident still stands as my biggest blowup in a meeting in eleven years as a head coach. My description of the meeting is far calmer and more coherent than the meeting itself probably was, by the way.

We beat the Raiders that week. We went on to win five of our last seven games, including a game in San Diego in which I believe we grew up as a team. Until then, the Buccaneers hadn't won a game on the West Coast in about ten years. Previous teams had tried all sorts of gimmicks to change their luck. They had gone two days early, gone one day early, kept their watches set to East Coast time, whatever. Anything and everything they could think of. I told our guys that it wasn't complicated. It's a game at one o'clock in San Diego, the same time as a four o'clock game in Tampa. Just do what we do.

We fell behind 14–0 in the first quarter. However, this time our guys stayed the course and played together. For the first time, we encountered adversity and overcame it. We chipped away at the Chargers' lead, played great defense, and won 25–17. John Lynch and I later agreed that that game in San Diego was where our run of success in Tampa began.

As we prepared for the season finale against Chicago, I distributed a handout to the players. I wanted to make sure we kept teaching and encouraging all season long. Here is what I handed them:

> *The first step toward creating an improved future is developing the ability to envision it. VISION will ignite the fire of passion that fuels our commitment*

to do WHATEVER IT TAKES to achieve excel-
lence. Only VISION allows us to transform dreams
of greatness into the reality of achievement through
human action. VISION has no boundaries and
knows no limits. Our VISION is what we become
in life.

Our vision had to be one of excellence, of playing the best that we could play every time we hit the field, whether it was practice, regular season, or the Super Bowl.

"This game won't matter in the standings, and we won't make the playoffs," I said. "But I want you to play as if it were a playoff game. Use this vision to imagine that this game means everything in our season. Show me how you would perform if it did."

We dominated the Bears from start to finish. With the win over Chicago, we finished 6–10, dead last in our division. But we had made great strides and really improved. The Bucs play-ers dumped Gatorade on me after that game. Gary Shelton of the *St. Petersburg Times* wrote an article asking why anyone would throw Gatorade on a 6–10 coach. But he followed up by saying that this year had felt different from past ten-loss seasons in Tampa.

It felt different for us, too. We finally felt as if we had begun to change the mentality around One Buc and were headed in the right direction.

Whatever it takes.

No excuses, no explanations.

Do what we do.

FILLING THE CORNERS

CHAPTER TEN

Do not go where the path may lead; go instead where there is no path and leave a trail.

RALPH WALDO EMERSON

WE REALLY BELIEVED, as we headed into the 1997 off-season, that we were close to reaching the level of success we had been striving to achieve. Even though our 1996 record was 6–10, we had finished the season strong and felt good about our defense. And our offense had shown an ability to control the ball and pound it ahead with our running game. However, we were in dire need of offensive playmakers. We still had trouble making big, momentum-changing plays.

Heading into the 1997 draft, we held two first-round picks—San Diego had traded the second one to us from the 1996 draft. With our two picks, we were focused on getting a receiver with great speed and a running back who "could hit home runs." We believed this combination would give us some offensive threats to stretch opposing defenses.

During the off-season, heading toward the draft, Derrick Brooks became a regular visitor to my office. Derrick was the outside linebacker drafted by the Bucs in 1995. Each day, his message was the same: the Bucs needed to draft his college teammate Warrick Dunn, the running back from Florida State. Over and over again, Derrick came by with that same advice.

At the end of February, the assistant coaches and I headed to the NFL Scouting Combine, which had moved from New Orleans to Indianapolis, to meet some of the top college seniors, including Warrick Dunn. I came away from our initial meeting highly impressed. I was around him for only about twenty minutes, but I left with the feeling that this guy could be something really special in the league. Coach Noll had always said to err on the side of production over looks, and Warrick certainly put that philosophy to the test. At only five-foot-nine and 180 pounds, Warrick was small for Florida State, let alone the pros. I double-checked my impressions with Bobby Bowden, FSU's head coach since 1976. Coach Bowden told me that despite his size, Warrick was the best player he'd *ever* coached at Florida State. Coming from Coach Bowden, that was quite a statement.

As we deliberated the pick, I continued to think about my training under Coach Noll.

"Watch the film, not the stopwatch," he used to say. After all, the point is to select athletes to play football. Some guys test well, either with their foot speed, leaping ability, strength, or other measurable physical traits. But some guys just play well. If given a choice, I'd rather select the guy who did both, of course. But I didn't want to discount a great college player simply because he had suspect physical traits, especially if the guy played high-level competition well. Warrick fit that profile. He was small, but he had been highly successful at FSU, playing in the tough Atlantic Coast Conference.

Conventional wisdom said small running backs could not hold up in the NFL, but I was inclined to follow Coach Noll's advice and go with production over size. Rich McKay, Jerry

Angelo, and Tim Ruskell all agreed with this approach. The year prior to my arrival, the Bucs had selected Warren Sapp and Derrick Brooks. Both players had some physical question marks, but both had performed exceptionally well in college and were off to a good start in the NFL. Rich was focused primarily on not "missing" with our picks as some former Bucs teams had done. He believed we could minimize our risk by focusing on a player's production against top competition.

Warrick Dunn had made many big plays for the Seminoles, and we desperately needed such a playmaker. In addition, Warrick was the kind of guy who would do other things that might not always be noticed by the fans. He picked up blitzes without fear, even if it meant blocking much bigger players. He had soft hands and caught the ball well coming out of the backfield. And if his quarterback threw an interception, he always hustled to get into the play and make the tackle.

We didn't know whether Warrick could hold up physically for an entire season as the every-down running back, but *he* believed he could. In the meantime, we were sure he could be a play-making running back. We believed big things would happen if we gave Warrick "touches"—chances to get the ball through rushing attempts, pass receptions, and punt and kickoff returns. We all agreed we wanted to draft Warrick Dunn.

Our question then became *where* we would have to select him. Did we need to get him with our first pick at number eight, or could we get him with our second pick? Or, because of his size, could we trade down from our second pick and still get him even later in the first round? When the draft began, we found ourselves in a multi-party trade, with picks flying around everywhere. In the first round, we moved down from eight to twelve, but we also acquired the sixteenth pick.

As for receivers, we were looking at three from the state of Florida: Ike Hilliard and Reidel Anthony from the University of Florida and Yatil Green from Miami. We also liked Rae Carruth of Colorado. All had positive and negative qualities. Hilliard ran excellent routes and had solid hands but didn't have Anthony's speed. Carruth had neither Anthony's speed nor Hilliard's hands but was a nice mix of the two. Green had size and some great tools but didn't seem as polished. After considerable debate, we entered the draft with our focus on Dunn first and then one of the receivers. Hilliard was my favorite, but it wasn't a clear-cut decision for any of us.

The Giants made that decision for us, taking Hilliard at the seventh pick. We still had three receivers we liked on the board, so we decided to shoot for Dunn with our first pick, with Tiki Barber of the University of Virginia as our fallback if Dunn was gone.

Warrick Dunn was still available at twelve, so we immediately sent the pick to our representative at the draft in New York. We were all excited about getting Warrick. Then we saw Yatil Green go to the Dophins at fifteen, so we decided to take Reidel Anthony at sixteen. We were thrilled with our first round, and in subsequent rounds we got some players who became solid starters over the next few years. One of these was our third-round pick, Ronde Barber, Tiki Barber's twin. I still have my draft notes, which show that we had some questions about Ronde's tackling, which turned out to be unfounded, and note that our primary concern was that this would mark the "first time the twins have been split." Both players obviously adjusted just fine during their careers in Tampa and New York despite the separation. As coaches, we all felt good about the 1997 draft.

From the time our newly drafted players first took the field at minicamp, we were excited about the possibilities. It was still hard to see in the preseason what would happen—our offense was still sputtering—but we felt we had significantly improved over 1996.

To this day, that 1997 season remains my favorite in football. I remember every game from that season off the top of my head, in order, almost play-by-play. The 1997 season was everything I had wanted for 1996 on my most optimistic of days. We played well, and the community became energized. We rode a wave of excitement and renewal that crested in a playoff appearance. People waited outside our locker room to call out to us and encourage us. The prior year, only our families had been there.

The entire environment that year was special. I found that while life drags on when you're losing, it marches on when you're winning. I wanted the season to slow down so I could soak it up and enjoy it as long as possible.

Not only was 1997 special for our team, it was a good year for my family as well. Lauren and I were really having fun discovering the Tampa Bay area. Like most of the staff, we rented a home in 1996 because we weren't sure what was going to happen with the old stadium. Now we were told that we could expect a new stadium and that the team would be staying in Tampa, and everyone felt good about putting their roots down in the community. Lauren and I even began to build a home.

In addition to being a great mom to our kids and helping them to develop as students, Lauren found plenty of opportunities to volunteer within the Tampa community. She especially enjoyed reading to kids at local elementary schools. Tiara, now twelve, and Jamie, ten, were adjusting well and making new friends. Eric had just started kindergarten, so Lauren was able to get more involved with the Buccaneers Women's Organization. All in all, our family had really found a home in Tampa.

We opened the season at home against the San Francisco 49ers—Steve Young, Jerry Rice, and company. The stadium was full but not jammed. Al McGuire, the late Marquette basketball coach, said he always used to check the corners of the arena for empty seats to see if a game was sold out. That has become a habit of mine during player introductions. On that day in the old Tampa Stadium, we had a good crowd, but the corners were still slightly empty.

Steve Young left the game early with a concussion. Jerry Rice was injured on a hit by Warren Sapp. Warrick Dunn made a great run to put us in position for the go-ahead score. What a difference a year made. In 1996, we had opened at home against an upper-echelon team and had gotten pounded. A year later we opened against another top-tier team and won 13–6. I could feel confidence permeating our locker room.

Just like the year before, we followed our season opener with two road games. These were both against NFC Central foes in places where the Bucs had historically had trouble winning. We shut down Barry Sanders in Detroit as Warrick Dunn exploded onto the turf in the Pontiac Silverdome and was named the NFC's Offensive Player of the Week.

That game also marked the first game in which I was assisted by my brother-in-law, Loren Harris, my wife's twin. Loren's job was to handle my headset cord. Coaches' headsets hadn't yet gone wireless, and someone had to manage the slack in the cord as a coach moved up and down the sideline.

If my sons Jamie and Eric had finished their schoolwork for the week, I would let them assist me as well. They were usually pretty low-key about being the coach's sons—except for one particular game when the television cameras followed Jamie a lot. In fact, during the broadcast, John Madden even circled him on the Telestrator for viewers. The next day at school, I think Jamie made the most of being a television celebrity.

At the game in Detroit, Loren was standing close behind me, holding the cord. When we scored, I felt a tug. Out of the corner of my eye, I could see that Loren was trying hard to restrain himself from cheering. I had nodded when we scored, but I was already moving on to what was next, and Loren needed to keep up. But I kept feeling the cord pulling my headset.

Running off the field at halftime with a 17–3 lead, I looked at Loren. He was trembling. "Are you all right?" I asked.

He shook his head. "I don't know, Tony. I've got to let it out some!" I laughed and thought, *Just like his twin.* I told Loren it was okay for him to express his feelings during the game . . . as long as he didn't yank my headset off.

The following week, we played in the Metrodome in Minneapolis. Heading into the fourth quarter, we led the Vikings 21–6. On third down with seven yards to go, we gave the ball to Warrick on a draw play. All we needed to do was run down the clock, but that didn't stop Warrick from doing something spectacular. He made about four guys miss tackling him on a fifty-two yard run to the end zone. We were 3–0.

As I walked the seventy-five yards from the visitors' side of the field to the locker room, I thought about what I was going to say to the team. The players would be excited—with good reason. But I didn't want them to lose sight of the consistent, workmanlike habits that had gotten the team to that successful point.

We prayed, as we always did after a game, and then I began. "Gentlemen, great job. But this was a business trip, and winning the game was simply what you were supposed to do. When you talk to the press, I want you to act like you expected this to happen." Suddenly, a phrase popped into my head, one I have continued to use ever since: "We'll celebrate on the plane. But when it lands, we've got to focus on next week."

On the flight home, the whole team felt great. The Bucs

had always struggled to win the big, marquee games, but now we had just won three big games in a row. We had beaten two division opponents on the road, and we had beaten possibly the best team in the NFC, the San Francisco 49ers, at home. What a great start to the season.

We played the Dolphins at home the following week, with the game nationally televised on Sunday Night Football. This time the "corners" of the stadium were completely full. I checked.

One of the employees in the Bucs ticket office said a man walked up to the ticket window shortly before kickoff and was informed that the game was sold out. His jaw dropped and he just stood there, incredulous. "I can't believe it. I've been coming here for years and buying my ticket just before kickoff. It's never been an issue!"

I thought back to my 1996 claim that someday a Bucs game would be sold out. Back then, it had seemed too much to hope for. Now that claim had come true.

Everything was perfect. We were playing against Dan Marino. The stadium was awash in our new team colors, pewter and red. We were on a roll. Due to injuries, we were missing two starters, defensive tackle Warren Sapp and linebacker Rufus Porter. But I told the team it didn't matter that those guys weren't playing. I said we would win if we played solid, fundamental defense. Do what we do.

Warren later told me that I really upset him when I told the defense he was insignificant. He had hoped I would tell the defense they needed to rise up and play above their heads.

"I didn't say you were insignificant, Warren. I'm sorry you didn't play. At the same time, I needed to get a message across. You know our defense is about assignments, being willing to let the other guy make the play while you do your job. I don't want guys thinking in terms of making up for teammates who aren't there. I need the next guy to step in knowing that we have confidence in him."

Everybody played well. The offense carried us with 31 points, as Trent Dilfer and Mike Alstott had big games. I think the fans and some of the players were even more pumped up than they might have been because of Jimmy Johnson. Only a year earlier, he had chosen to coach at Miami rather than at Tampa Bay, in part because he thought he could get to a Super Bowl faster with Dan Marino and the Dolphins than he could with Trent Dilfer and the Buccaneers. With the Bucs' victory, the stadium was rocking.

That game lit the fire of football in Tampa. It was the start of the enduring community support the Buccaneers are still accustomed to today. When I showed the players the tape of the stadium prior to kickoff, every seat was filled. I also showed them the kickoff of the poorly attended Seattle game in 1996 and pointed out what a difference they had made in only one year.

We were scheduled to play Arizona the following week. We were informed by the league that if we beat Arizona, the Fox television network wanted to move the next game, which was against Green Bay, from 1 p.m. to 4 p.m. When setting the schedule, the league places the games of greatest interest—that is, the games between good teams—late Sunday afternoon or on Sunday Night Football or Monday Night Football.

In 1996, we had played every game on Sunday at 1 p.m. In 1997, we played during primetime. The Buccaneers had become a good team.

We beat Arizona to push our record to 5–0, a first for the Buccaneers since 1979 and the days of John McKay and Doug

Williams. Next we traveled to Green Bay to play the Packers at Lambeau Field. Clyde Christensen, who then was our tight ends coach, called my room early Sunday morning. Chapel was always held on Saturday night, so we had some extra time on Sunday before the four o'clock kickoff. Clyde suggested we take a walk through Appleton, Wisconsin, where our team was staying, to enjoy the October scenery. I agreed and thus began a new tradition.

Clyde and I have been going out for game-day walks ever since. I welcome the exercise, but we do it more for the conversation. We've walked together all over the country and have never had a problem with fans. Usually we're not recognized, but even when we are, the comments are either positive or only jokingly hostile. Along the way, Clyde and I get a chance to share topics that are on our minds. Usually we discuss where we are at that time, both literally and with respect to the team's play. We also talk about what the Lord has been doing in our lives.

That day in Wisconsin, we marveled at being 5–0 and playing the Packers, who were 3–2 and therefore two games behind us. We hoped they would be three games behind us by the end of the day. And, like those days out on the Michigan lakes with my dad, we had a chance to reflect on the wonders of creation on that beautiful Wisconsin morning.

Unfortunately, in the game that afternoon, we played more like the 1996 Bucs, which we thought we had left in the past, than like the 5–0 Bucs with the league's best record. We fell behind, battled back in an attempt to escape with a win despite ourselves, but ultimately lost to the Packers, 21–16. The loss was a good reminder that we still weren't where we wanted to be. It was an extremely disappointing realization.

Back in Tampa, we hosted Detroit and Minnesota, the two division rivals we had beaten on the road in consecutive weeks during our five-game winning streak. We lost both home games, scoring only fifteen points total in the two games. During that stretch, Michael Husted, our placekicker, missed several field goals.

Michael's mother was battling cancer in the middle of that season—cancer that ultimately took her life. Michael was a very private person, and while the team knew about his mom, the press and the public were unaware of what he was dealing with. He was getting criticized for missing kicks, and I was getting criticized for not replacing him. It's not unusual—fans seem to think players live in a vacuum, not subject to the same pressures and problems as the rest of us. They boo and yell their displeasure because a player's not playing up to their expectations.

Michael never used his difficult personal problem as an excuse. He pushed ahead and held himself accountable for his performance. Kicking is a difficult task mentally at the best of times, and Michael really had his hands full during those days. Even though he was missing kicks he would ordinarily make, I decided I was not going to replace him. While this was hurting the team in the short run, I thought both Michael and the team would be better if we stuck with him. I was certain that we'd be better as a unit for standing beside one of our own members through a difficult time.

I told the team during a meeting, "Michael is going through some tough times on and off the field. But I don't care how many kicks he misses along the way; he will remain our kicker. If he misses, we'll need to rise up and get the ball back. But before it's all said and done, he's going to make some big kicks for us."

Now that we had lost three games in a row, two of them at home, some of the naysayers understandably became more vocal. They had seen so many lean years in Tampa that as we headed back on the road at 5–3, they were certain we were the same old Bucs. Despite our fast start, they expected us to collapse over the second half of the season.

We traveled to play the Colts in Indianapolis. We were ahead in the third quarter until the Colts scored eleven points to tie the game. Early in the fourth quarter, Mike Alstott fumbled on our own eighteen yard line, and the Colts ran it in for a touchdown. We had already lost three straight games, and now we had given up eighteen straight points and were trailing in the fourth quarter on the road—in a deafening dome.

Trent Dilfer responded by marching us on a long drive for a touchdown to tie the score. Our defense held, and Karl Williams returned the Colts' punt across the fifty yard line. We were able to move the ball closer with our offense. With eleven seconds left, Michael Husted kicked a thirty-six-yard field goal to win the game.

That was an exciting victory and a pivotal moment for our team. Our players started to relax, realizing that we really had changed. We weren't the "same old Bucs." We had faced adversity on the road, and we had done what we needed to do.

In the years since then, Michael has expressed his appreciation for my sticking with him during that time. I didn't do anything special. I just treated him the way I would want to be treated. Even at the time, this made quite an impact on him and on the other players. Michael went on to kick well for the rest of the season.

DEFINING SUCCESS

CHAPTER ELEVEN

I would rather play well and lose than play poorly and win.
CHUCK NOLL

WE DRILLED THE FALCONS, 31–10, in Atlanta the week after our victory against the Colts. Then we hosted the New England Patriots, who had lost to the Green Bay Packers in the Super Bowl the year before. We beat the Patriots 27–7. That game was a good measuring stick for us and boosted our confidence. Just as quickly as we had been counted out, we were now 8–3 and on a three-game winning streak.

We split the next two on the road. We lost at Chicago to a bad Bears team. But then we turned around and beat the New York Giants in the Meadowlands, 20–8. The Giants were en route to winning the NFC East.

Next came our rematch with the defending Super Bowl champions, the Green Bay Packers. We had talked at training camp about setting our sights on the top team in our division—which also happened to be the top team in the NFL—and this was our chance. Despite losing three straight games to Green Bay since my coaching staff had arrived in Tampa in

1996, we were optimistic that the way we were playing, plus playing the Packers in Tampa, would be the difference for us to win. But once again, though we kept the score close, we couldn't make the plays to beat them.

With our record now 9–5, we headed back to the Meadowlands for the second time in three weeks, this time to play the New York Jets. Despite facing some adversity—both Trent Dilfer and Mike Alstott were hurt—we were determined to win this game, which would cement a playoff spot for us. At our team meeting the night before the game, I outlined our plan. We'd be aggressive—throwing passes to the receivers matched up against Otis Smith, whom we perceived to be the Jets' weaker cornerback. We were ready to go out and clinch a playoff berth.

We went out and lost, 31–0. Otis Smith ran two interceptions back for touchdowns.

Guys were quiet on the flight home.

Then the pilot announced over the intercom that the Carolina Panthers had lost to the Packers, putting us into the playoffs. The guys were quietly murmuring, uncertain of whether we could start celebrating or should still be in mourning.

Before I could give it any thought, Brad Culpepper, our defensive tackle out of the University of Florida, picked up the microphone and announced over the PA: "Guys, we're in the playoffs! We haven't been to the playoffs in fifteen years, and we're sure not gonna be sad about it!" I think Brad got it just right.

We finished the regular season against the Chicago Bears in Tampa. Despite the fact that we were already in the playoffs, we had a great deal riding on this game. If we won, we would host the first playoff game in Tampa, something that hadn't happened in fifteen years. If we lost, we would have to travel.

A new stadium was being built for the Buccaneers. It was several hundred yards away from the old stadium and was scheduled to open for the 1998 season. I told the guys on the Wednesday before the Bears game that this was set up perfectly for us. We had a chance to host a playoff game for our fans and make the final game in our old stadium a playoff game. But first we had to focus on the week ahead.

We did focus, and we beat the Bears convincingly, 31–15. In the process, with ten wins, we tied the Buccaneer record for wins in the regular season.

Immediately after our game, we watched the Lions win their game, thereby becoming our opponent for the first round of the playoffs. That year, we had split our two games with the Lions, each of us winning on the road. At the home game in Tampa, in the middle of our three-game losing streak, Barry Sanders had become the first running back in NFL history to have two touchdown runs of more than eighty yards in the same game. He had scored all three of the Lions' touchdowns, absolutely gashing us for big runs and gaining 215 yards on only 24 carries (the NFL record for rushing yardage in a game is 295). Now he was approaching two thousand yards for the season. In fact, Barry's season total for that year is still the third highest season total in the history of the NFL. We had good reason to be concerned about playing the Lions again. But even so, our guys were excited. "Coach, that's exactly who we want to play."

The following day, Monday, Brian and Joel Glazer walked into my office and said they were going over to the stadium to give doughnuts to the fans waiting in line for playoff tickets. They invited me to go with them, and we drove to the stadium, anticipating a short visit. I imagined a line about like what you'd see at a movie box office.

We were in for a surprise. The line stretched down the sidewalk, around the side of the stadium, out to the corner of Dale Mabry Highway, and then continued even farther around. There must have been five thousand people eagerly waiting for a chance to buy a ticket for the game.

That's when the feeling hit me. *Look what we've done. We've done exactly what we hoped to do when we came here—excite the community, win games, and create a team people are proud of and excited about.* I walked around and mingled with the fans, thanking them for waiting all night to get a playoff ticket. It was remarkable.

On Tuesday mornings, I met with several of my fellow coaches for a Bible study. We were working our way through the Bible in a year, something we've continued to do ever since that 1997 season. I still have my notes from our meeting the week before we played Detroit. The Bible portion we looked at that day was fairly convicting for me in light of our excitement over making the playoffs. It was a good reminder of my priorities and my belief that we should maintain our schedule to protect those priorities, regardless of the situation.

The teaching that week was from Ephesians 5:25. We promised to memorize this verse from the New International Version:

> *Husbands, love your wives, just as Christ loved the*
> *church and gave himself for her.*

I have additional notes written beside the verse: "Identify ten specific ways to show love to your wife—formulate them along with her." "Love and don't be harsh," which was my paraphrase of Colossians 3:19—"Husbands, love your wives and never treat them harshly."

Finally, my notes contained this, which makes so much sense theoretically but is always so difficult to balance: "How would your business do if you spent the amount of time on it that you spend on your wife and family?" It's remarkable how, as we worked through the Bible that year, certain verses seemed to come up at particularly appropriate times.

Although we had spent our whole married life in the ultracompetitive world of professional football, Lauren and I had always tried to view it through God's eyes. As much fun as it was to be winning, we tried not to get caught up in it. We knew that our family life and our faith walk were more important. Fortunately, we both had great training from our parents as well as from the pastors and chaplains we had been exposed to over the years. And Lauren has always made it a point to help me see what is really important and to keep my job in the right perspective. I know that's why God brought us together.

The competing views of success in our world often create an interesting tension. Society tends to define success in terms of accomplishments and awards, material possessions, and profit margins. In the football business, winning is the only thing that matters.

God's Word, however, presents a different definition of success—one centered on a relationship with Jesus Christ and a love for God that allows us to love and serve others. God gives each one of us unique gifts, abilities, and passions. How well we use those qualities to have an impact on the world around us determines how "successful" we really are.

If we get caught up in chasing what the world defines as success, we can use our time and talent to do some great things. We might even become famous. But in the end, what will it mean?

What will people remember us for? Are other people's lives better because we lived? Did we make a difference? Did we use to the fullest the gifts and abilities God gave us? Did we give our best effort, and did we do it for the right reasons?

God's definition of success is really one of *significance*—the significant difference our lives can make in the lives of others. This significance doesn't show up in win-loss records, long résumés, or the trophies gathering dust on our mantels. It's found in the hearts and lives of those we've come across who are in some way better because of the way we lived.

I will never forget my first time in the playoffs as a coach. I've gone other times since then, but none of the subsequent trips has been able to duplicate the feeling of that first playoff run. It was a new experience for so many on our team. We had coaches who had come straight from college football and many first- and second-year players. Most of our veterans had never experienced a playoff run. This was all new for the city of Tampa as well; the Buccaneers hadn't been in the playoffs since 1982.

Our first playoff game was also the final game in the old Tampa Stadium. It was an unforgettable evening. Our players were eager to play the Lions again, and they were ready for Barry Sanders. Our defense swarmed all over the field— holding Sanders to sixty-five rushing yards and the Lions to only seventy-eight passing yards. As I looked out onto the field midway through the fourth quarter, I realized that with the way our defense was playing, the Lions wouldn't be able to catch us. The player we had "settled for" in the 1996 draft,

Mike Alstott, carried the ball for a thirty-one-yard touchdown run to ice the game.

We had won the last game in Tampa Stadium. After the game, our players ran around the field with Buccaneers flags. Brad Culpepper and others went up into the stands in full uniform to mingle with the crowd. It was bedlam. After I gave my interviews, Lauren drove us home, although many of the fans hadn't yet left. Others were still in traffic on Dale Mabry Highway. Lauren rolled down our windows and began honking the horn, yelling, "We won! We won a playoff game! We're going to Green Bay!"

I was mortified. "Lauren, stop! I'm the coach—we can't be doing that!"

"I can, and I *will*!" Lauren kept honking and yelling, and even I started waving at the fans, who were nothing short of ecstatic. We all were—it was a great feeling.

Yes, we were headed to Green Bay, the defending Super Bowl champions, for the second round of the playoffs. The Bucs had never won a game in which the temperature at kickoff was less than forty degrees. And we had lost to the Packers four straight times. Considering all this, we certainly were a confident bunch.

When the game got underway, we started slowly. Then Trent Dilfer threw two interceptions, and we rushed for only ninety yards. We lost 21–7. What a disappointment. It was an unsatisfying, empty ending to an otherwise great year. We flew home, still proud at what we had accomplished, but our emotions were in the valley.

When we arrived back at One Buc, there were people everywhere. The Bucs fans had been awaiting our arrival for hours. Our buses actually had to park blocks away, so we walked through the crowd, interacting with our fans. It was the perfect finish to a magical year. It was a good reminder to appreciate the joys of the moment—there would be time later to focus on improvement.

We were obviously building the team the right way and could see our progress. At the end of our first year, the players dumped Gatorade on me after our 6–10 finish. This year, following a playoff loss, the crowd of fans was so large we couldn't get into our facility. We were left to wonder, *What will it look like when we finally win it all?*

The 1998 off-season gave us a chance to continue adding depth to our defense and speed to our offense. We added Jacquez Green out of Florida with our first pick, which was actually in the second round. We picked Brian Kelly from Southern Cal as well. He remains a defensive standout in Tampa to this day.

We also saw an opportunity to build on some of the support we had enjoyed in Tampa ever since we had first arrived. We wanted to benefit our community more intentionally. Our quarterbacks coach, Clyde Christensen, attended church with Mark Merrill, a Tampa attorney who had started an organization called Family First. Clyde and I had both grown up with very involved parents, and we were both sensitive to family issues. A year earlier, Clyde had arranged a meeting between Mark and me so we could discuss ways that NFL coaches could assist people in their most important coaching roles—as parents.

We were meeting in my office just before the start of the 1997 season when I realized it was time for me to pick up ten-year-old Jamie from school. I apologized for cutting the meeting short. Mark later said that seeing me head off to pick up my son was more affirming for him than if we'd met for another hour. To be fair, picking up the kids was not the norm for me. Most days, my job was dropping the kids off at school, and Lauren would pick them up. For whatever reason, however, I had to get Jamie that day—and it was the start of a great partnership with Mark Merrill.

In the summer of 1998, Family First launched a new program called All Pro Dad. Clyde and I promoted the program, and we helped Mark host an event at the Bucs training camp. Fathers brought their children and interacted with them at the camp; then we presented specific principles they could apply to being better dads.

Clyde even helped Mark design a T-shirt for the event. A few years later, Clyde was wearing the T-shirt at the office. Nate Webster, a linebacker out of the University of Miami—a refreshingly candid person—stepped back to read Clyde's shirt. After he had read through the "10 Ways to Be an All Pro Dad," including things like "Love Your Wife," "Be a Role Model," "Show Affection," "Eat Together as a Family," and "Pray and Worship Together," Nate said to Clyde and me, "I need one of those shirts. I don't do *any* of those things with my kids!" He really took the message to heart.

I hope All Pro Dad has touched many fathers and, by extension, their wives and children. I hope we've been faithful in using our platform as professional football coaches to strengthen our community.

If the 1997 season was my favorite, the 1998 season might be the one I found most frustrating.

The year started with great promise. We were coming off the magical 1997 season, and the new Raymond James Stadium was spectacular. Before the season began, I had the privilege of participating in its inaugural event. Even today, one of my favorite memories of my time in Tampa was Bryan Glazer's excited phone call informing me that the stadium's first event had just been scheduled: a Billy Graham crusade. He knew I would be excited too, and I became even more excited when I was asked to share the stage with Dr. Graham and welcome the crusade to Tampa. Hearing Dr. Graham speak was awe-inspiring.

Dr. Graham's messages are always so straightforward and to the point—I think that's why they're so powerful. God's gift to us is free and can't be earned. If you believe that Jesus died for your sins, you can live forever with Him in heaven. No matter what has happened in your past, that free gift is offered to you. That was it. So simple. So clear.

When Dr. Graham finished, he invited everyone in the stadium to come and accept God's free gift of a life-changing relationship with Christ. People began streaming down every stairwell—they kept coming and coming and coming. I had never seen anything like it. Watching what God can do through a simple message shared by such a humble man, I was overwhelmed almost to the point of tears. It wouldn't be the last time that happened to me in that stadium.

As for football, we had improved from 1996 to 1997, and we should have kept improving in 1998. Instead, we finished 8–8 with the most inconsistent playing of any team I've ever fielded. We'd play well one week and badly the next. Our problems weren't only on one side of the ball. Our defense alternated between hot and cold performances. Our offense scored in bunches one week and then suffered through droughts. We had lost to Green Bay six times in a row, then finally broke that streak by causing eight fumbles and sacking Brett Favre eight times. We handed 15–1 Minnesota their only regular-season loss. But we also lost to a 6–10 New Orleans team, twice to Detroit, and to Jacksonville when we blew a fourth-quarter lead.

We headed into the final game with a record of 7–8. If we won at Cincinnati, and if Arizona lost to San Diego, we'd be back in the playoffs—barely. We went on the road and finally put together a complete game, beating the Bengals 35–0. I was proud of our team.

We were now relying on the San Diego Chargers, who had only five wins that season, to get us into the playoffs by beating Arizona. We watched the beginning of the game at the airport on the overhead televisions. Some of the guys clustered around tiny handheld televisions. We hung on every play.

When our plane took off, San Diego was poised for a comeback win after being down 13–3 in the third quarter.

A short time into our flight, the pilot's voice came over the intercom. "Air Traffic Control knows whom I have onboard the aircraft this evening, and they wanted me to tell you con-gratulations on today's game." We all sat breathlessly. "They have also passed along the scores from the late afternoon games, including Arizona, who kicked a field goal on the last play to beat . . ."

I didn't hear the rest, even though our plane was deathly quiet.

What distinguished the 1997 team from the 1998 team was not those two extra wins that put us into the playoffs. The 1997 team was simply a better steward of its opportunities. Every team has its own unique set of dispositions, gifts, talents, and opportunities. What they all have in common, however, is the ability to control what they do with those dispositions, gifts, and talents when the opportunities come along.

The 1997 team was younger, with less depth and game

experience. The 1998 team filled in some of those holes and was a year more ingrained into our system. On paper, the 1998 team was the better team. But our 1997 team stretched itself and achieved its potential; the 1998 team was inconsistent and squandered chances. I still believe what I told the team the day after the finale against Cincinnati: "We have a good team, but we didn't take advantage of the opportunities we were given all year long. That's why we had to rely on someone else. We cannot do that again." The same is also true for each of us as individuals.

That, to me, is where we find the best definition of success. We're not all going to reach the Super Bowl or the top of the corporate ladder, but we each have a chance to walk away from something saying, "I did the ordinary things *as well as I could*. I performed to the full limits of my ability. I achieved success." Under that definition, a 5–11 team might actually be more successful than a 14–2 team.

Someday I might coach another team that needs to win its final game and needs help from another team to get into the playoffs. That won't be a problem for me as long as the team has played to the limits of its abilities and has fulfilled its potential. Our 1997 team played to—and beyond—its potential. Our 1998 team did not.

HURRICANES
AND TORNADOES

CHAPTER TWELVE

Excellence that feels it has to be proclaimed, by the mere fact of its proclamation admits the doubt of its existence.
    CLEOMAE DUNGY

WE WERE DISAPPOINTED that we had missed the play-offs, but we soon found ourselves with an excellent scouting opportunity. In those days, the coaches from two of the teams that just missed the playoffs—one team from each conference—coached one of the all-star squads in the Senior Bowl—the college all-star game held each year in Mobile, Alabama. The Buccaneers were the NFC representative in 1998, so my assistants and I went to Mobile for the Senior Bowl just a few weeks after that flight back from Cincinnati. The coaches are with the players in meetings and on the practice field. This gave us significant opportunities to evaluate each player in a variety of settings. In contrast, coaches from the other clubs are relegated to scouting from the stands and interviewing the all-star players during the evenings at the hotel.

With this firsthand background information, we had an excellent draft. In the first round at number fifteen, we were faced with a choice between the best two defensive linemen in the draft, defensive end Jevon Kearse of the University of Florida and defensive tackle Anthony McFarland of Louisiana State. We already had a solid defensive line, but since our entire defensive philosophy was predicated on pressure from the front four, we wanted to add even more depth to that group.

Both defenders had unusual nicknames. Kearse was called "The Freak" in college because of his extraordinary physical abilities. McFarland had been nicknamed "Booger" as a small child by his mother because of his rambunctious behavior. After considerable debate, we selected McFarland. Even though he was a bit undersized for the position, my assistant coach Rod Marinelli and I were convinced he was a high-motor guy who would make up for any lack of size with his remarkable speed and hustling attitude. We also knew more about McFarland than about Kearse because we had coached him for a full week. Kearse was selected by the Tennessee Titans one pick behind us at sixteen, and they were thrilled to get him. They knew he was an excellent pass rusher from the right side, approaching a right-handed quarterback from his blind side.

In that draft, we took four players we had seen at the Senior Bowl. Booger McFarland, Tulane quarterback Shaun King, and Florida State safety Dexter Jackson had all played for our team; Martin Gramatica, a placekicker from Kansas State, had played for the other team. We caught some criticism for drafting Martin in the third round, which is pretty high for a kicker, but a year later, those critics got off our backs when the Raiders picked a kicker in the first round. That wasn't the only time we picked a player before our critics believed he should have been drafted. However, I always keep two things in mind: First, selecting players is obviously an inexact science, as indicated by the number of "busts" through the years—players who did well in college but poorly in the pros. Second, it's more important to get the player we need when we believe we need him than it is to be concerned about being "right." Despite the criticism we received following the draft, all four players we selected paid immediate dividends for us that season.

Even though Booger McFarland was a great player for us and a critical part of our defense, I'm sure it was tempting for some analysts to play "what if" with our selection, especially when Kearse led the AFC in sacks his rookie year. But I had learned from Coach Noll that there's no value for the coach in second-guessing the picks after the draft. Once a player joins our team, our priority is to *teach him,* not worry about the player we didn't select. We do our homework before every draft. We evaluate our past choices and learn from our experiences. After the draft, we move on and do the best we can to teach whomever we have before us.

My mom and dad would agree with this approach.

By the time the 1999 season arrived, our guys were focused and determined to work toward meeting their potential as individuals and as a unit. The start of the season, however, didn't exactly point toward greatness.

We opened at home against the New York Giants and beat them about as badly as you can beat a team without actually winning the game. Our defense held the Giants to 107 yards of total offense. We allowed them only one first-down conversion out of the fourteen third-down plays they ran. We held them to twenty-seven yards rushing on twenty-four attempts, an average of just 1.1 yards per carry. But with a fumble and an interception return, our offense gave up two touchdowns. So much for our basic tenets of focusing on the giveaway/takeaway margin and not giving up big plays.

That game was the first we played with instant-replay review. In this system, a coach can challenge an official's call he believes to be incorrect. The referee then reviews the video of the play, looking at it from various camera angles. If, after review, the original call is upheld, the team whose coach challenged the call is charged with one time-out. In the last two minutes of each half, the coaches cannot challenge a call. Instead, the replay official in the press box determines whether a play should be reviewed.

I was not a fan of instant replay when it was introduced, and I still do not like it. I think officiating, as in other aspects of the game, should be based on real-time human perceptions. Officials have extensive training and perform to the best of their abilities. An official misses a call now and then, but that's just part of playing the game. Using video and multiple camera angles to review only particular plays—not every play—gives an illusion of precision that is just that: an illusion.

I'm still not in favor of replay, but I do think the challenge system is probably the most effective, constructive means that currently exists to deal with questionable calls.

Because of my Christian witness, I don't lash out or make a scene with the officials. But even if I did do that, I don't think berating the officials would help much. In fact, it actually works *against* your team. If I'm harassing an official all day, when he has a chance to make a decision that is close and could go either way, is he suddenly going to give me the benefit of the doubt, just to get me off his back? I doubt it. Officials are only human. In addition, there is always something going on during a game, and focusing on something that has already happened—which you can't change—is counterproductive. My dad's lesson. There's no time during a game to look back; the play clock is running.

Anyway, in the game against the Giants, I blew two opportunities to challenge, probably because I hadn't allowed myself to become well-versed in the replay review system. The first opportunity occurred in the first quarter, when Trent Dilfer was sacked and fumbled the ball, which the Giants recovered and ran in for a touchdown. However, Trent's arm was moving forward when he was hit. I'm pretty sure that if I had challenged the call, it would have been ruled an incomplete pass, negating the touchdown. Following that, Trent threw an interception after he had stepped out of bounds. Again, I didn't challenge, but I think if I had, their interception would have been negated. Then the Giants would not have kicked their ensuing field goal—the difference in the 17–14 final score.

The replay system bit us a third time that afternoon. With just over a minute to go, we were attempting to drive for either a tying field goal or a game-winning touchdown. Our wide receiver Karl Williams made a twenty-eight-yard reception out across the fifty yard line. However, the replay official decided to review the call, and the completion was overturned, which ended our opportunity to score. Someone from the league office called us the next day to tell us that, in fact, it *had* been a reception. But by then the damage was done; we were 0–1.

Following the game, I made some ill-advised comments to the media, criticizing the officiating and the replay system, and Commissioner Tagliabue fined me ten thousand dollars. I know I deserved the penalty for having spoken out of my frustration. When I saw the deduction from my paycheck, I could picture my dad's smile and hear him saying, "Tony, I hope venting at least made you feel better at the time." My dad never mentioned the incident to me, but I knew better, and he knew I knew better.

Our defense had more great efforts in the two weeks ahead. We held Philadelphia to five points and Denver to ten points. But then we went to Minnesota and Green Bay and lost both games before returning home to face Chicago. I was debating whether or not to bench Trent Dilfer in favor of our backup quarterback, Eric Zeier. I found myself drawing on the lessons I'd learned from Denny Green when he faced the decision of benching Rich Gannon for Sean Salisbury. I decided to stick with Trent for at least one more week. We beat the Bears 6–3 but did not score a touchdown.

We were now 3–3, and I decided to make the switch at quarterback, putting Zeier in to start at Detroit. When he injured his ribs, we debated whether we should go back to Trent the following week against New Orleans or use our second backup, Shaun King. Since Shaun was only halfway through his first season in the NFL, we decided on Trent.

We beat New Orleans. Trent had begun to settle down, playing much better and with more confidence. In fact, Trent directed us on a three-game winning streak before breaking his right clavicle against the Seahawks. He was out for the season. So in came the rookie, Shaun King, in the fourth quarter. His plays helped us to put away the Seahawks, 16–3. In the following weeks, Shaun led us to wins against Minnesota and Detroit as well, giving us a six-game winning streak and a 9–4 record.

Despite our adversity through the first thirteen games, I continued to preach to the team to simply *do what we do*. Play solid defense. Don't turn the ball over. Force turnovers. Don't commit penalties. Don't worry about who is injured; just play with whom we've still got healthy. The players responded. They put us in first place in the NFC Central Division in December, a mark the Bucs hadn't held at that time of year since 1981.

Shaun was outstanding along the way. He didn't try to do anything spectacular; he just played solid football. He didn't turn the ball over, and he led us to win after win. Watching him, I thought back to how far we'd come as a league in assessing talent without respect to skin color. When we had evaluated Shaun for the draft, our entire focus was on how well he could play within our scheme. Nobody on our staff thought twice about skin color—which was quite a shift from years ago. Shaun was the sixth quarterback selected in the 1999 draft. Four of the six, including Shaun, were African American.

I think we've finally reached a point in the league where people have the creativity and imagination to see what a player can become and then determine whether it's the player or the team that should adjust. For instance, Vince Young had some obviously special talents when he was at the University of Texas. The Tennessee Titans appreciated those talents and drafted him. Then their head coach, Jeff Fisher, and their offensive coordinator, Norm Chow, clearly challenged themselves as they adjusted their offense to best utilize Young's talents, even in the middle of the season. This was a significant accomplishment that benefited both the Titans and Vince Young. Shifts like these represent tremendous strides in professional football—strides toward treating people right and doing what is best for the game.

Feeling pretty good about ourselves and our possible playoff position, we headed out to Oakland with a chance to clinch a playoff spot. Unfortunately, we fell just short of a victory—just forty-six points short, that is—as we lost, 45–0. It was one of those games in which nothing went right. While I hated for that to happen, I was calm in the locker room after the game. I explained to the team that this was only one game out of sixteen. The fact that we had lost so badly didn't make the game count for any more or any less. We just needed to correct the things that went wrong and move on.

And move on we did, winning our next game. That win against Green Bay was the second in our last three games against the Packers. We scored twenty unanswered points in the second half, for a final score of 29–10. With that win, we clinched a playoff berth.

Next we headed to Chicago for a chance to win the division, ensure a home playoff game, and get a first-round bye in the playoffs. We accomplished all those things by beating the Bears. On our sideline after the game, each of us got a shirt and hat proclaiming us the "1999 NFC Central Division Champions." If only it had been below forty degrees. Even so, being part of the first eleven-win regular season in Buccaneers history was spectacular.

Our first opponent in the playoffs would be the Washington Redskins, a team that had played a role in our early progress in Tampa. Two years before, in the preseason of 1997, we had practiced against the Redskins. We were getting good work done with them, but as the practices progressed, things got a little chippy. "Trash talk" flowed from both sides, and our guys weren't handling it very well. At a break, I gathered our team.

"Guys, they've got some talkers over there, but I don't want you to reciprocate. Just let them do their thing. Our thing is to simply play."

A few minutes later, we were in a drill with their offense against our defense. Brian Mitchell, a Redskins running back, said something to our linebacker Hardy Nickerson and pushed him. Hardy responded in anger, and a fight ensued. I told assistant coach Monte Kiffin to get Hardy off the field and into the locker room. Even the Washington coaches were saying I shouldn't take Hardy out, since he had only been responding to Mitchell. Again I told Monte to send him inside.

When I met with Hardy after practice, he was apologetic.

"Hardy, your response to a situation is always critical, but it's especially critical when you're on the field as a Buc, because you're one of our captains. I don't know exactly what happened out on the field, but I do know what I told all of you just minutes before about how to conduct yourselves. If I can't get the captains to respond appropriately and show the leadership I expect, how is anyone else going to respond?"

Hardy got the message. He apologized to the team and said he understood that in order to lead us in the right direction, he had to play with emotion but not lose his head. The next time he stepped onto the field, he went out as our leader and set the right tone for our team. I think it was important for the players to see this situation play out. Because I had been willing to send even Hardy from the field, they knew the rules applied equally to everyone. That day galvanized our growth as individuals and as a team.

The week of the Washington playoff game, I walked into the general manager's office and found that Rich McKay already had company. When the man turned around, I realized it was Rich's close friend Pat Haden, the former quarterback at Southern Cal. Rich and Pat had lived in the same house when Pat was in high school. I sat down in Rich's office and asked, "Have I ever told you guys the story of how I chose to attend Minnesota over Southern Cal? As I recall, the quarterback lived with the McKay family. . . ."

The Redskins had beaten the Lions in the first round of the playoffs the week before we hosted them in our new stadium.

We started miserably and trailed 3–0 at halftime. Our defense had been adequate, but our offense was misfiring. Before we headed out for the second half, I pointed out the obvious reasons for optimism.

"Guys, we're kicking off to them. Our defense needs to give us a stop. Then we'll get the ball back, score, and take the lead. Then we'll be in good shape. We'll keep playing our game, take control, and get the fans back into it. Take care of the ball. Don't panic. Just play our game. We've got thirty minutes to play."

Brian Mitchell ran back our kickoff one hundred yards for a touchdown. Trent then threw an interception, Washington kicked a field goal, and the score was 13–0. This was not the plan. Maybe I had given the wrong talk at halftime.

We gave the ball to the Redskins again, and as they were driving, our safety, John Lynch, stepped in front of their receiver and intercepted Brad Johnson's pass. We then drove the length of the field for a Mike Alstott touchdown. We trailed 13–7 at the end of the third quarter. Fifteen minutes to play.

During the next few minutes, two fumbles aided our cause. Our defensive end Steve White forced Brad Johnson to fumble, and Warren Sapp recovered on Washington's thirty-two yard line. As we were going in to score, Shaun King took the snap and fumbled on third down, but Warrick Dunn alertly grabbed the bouncing ball and ran for a first down. We went on to score a touchdown. Bucs 14, Redskins 13. Time was growing short.

I gathered the defense before they went back out on the field. "You've been waiting three years for this moment. The offense has handed you the lead—in the playoffs. *It's up to you.*"

The Redskins couldn't move far against our defense. With just over a minute to play, they had a chance to take the lead when they lined up for a fifty-two-yard field goal attempt. I found out later that our personnel director, Jerry Angelo, who had suffered through so many seasons of Bucs football and was watching from Rich McKay's box, crawled under a countertop because he couldn't bear to watch. "Tell me if he makes it," he said.

No one had to tell him. The stadium erupted in hysteria as the snap was low and the holder, Brad Johnson, couldn't handle it. The ball was never even kicked. We got the ball back on downs, and we ran out the clock using Herm Edwards's claim to fame, the Victory formation. Bucs 14, Redskins 13. 0:00.

We were moving on to the NFC Championship Game. One game from the Super Bowl.

It's difficult—no, impossible—to convey the excitement of that evening. It had been such a draining game and comeback, and then having to suffer through that field goal attempt—it was almost too much. To this day, that was the most excited I have ever been. After I did my postgame media interviews and headed back to the locker room, at least thirty minutes after the game had ended, my pulse was still racing.

Once again, Lauren honked all the way up Dale Mabry Highway. This time I rolled down my window on my own and joined in the celebration.

The news stories the next week focused on "The Greatest Show on Turf," as the St. Louis Rams offense had been nicknamed. The Rams had been terrific on offense that year, whereas our offense had really struggled to move the ball and score against Washington. We believed our defense was playing well, but nobody wanted to talk about defense. It was merely a tale of two offenses.

I learned the art of storytelling from my mom. Each week when I prepare my message for the team, I try to include something the guys can relate to, some image they can visualize. As I thought about what to say before the St. Louis game, hurricanes and tornadoes immediately came to mind. That year the Atlantic basin had been through a record-setting summer with the number and force of its hurricanes. Everyone in Florida was well aware of hurricanes.

Wednesday rolled around, and we'd already read three mornings' worth of newspaper articles about the mismatch. The Rams were heavy favorites, predicted to win by two touchdowns. At our team meeting I began my analogy.

"Guys, nature presents us with hurricanes and tornadoes. Hurricanes are powerful, massive storms. Meteorologists predict them, and we all track them coming in. This year they missed us in Tampa, but they didn't miss others. Hurricanes are dangerous and big, but they are also predictable.

"I grew up in the Midwest. We didn't have hurricanes there; we had tornadoes. Tornadoes arrive unexpectedly. They are unpredictable. They might come in the middle of the night or in the morning. And when they show up, it's already too late to prepare for them. You just have to live with whatever destruction they cause.

"This week we have a chance to be a tornado. Everybody knows about the Rams; they're a fantastic team, a hurricane. Everybody is predicting all the terrible things the Rams will do when they make landfall against the Bucs. But nobody sees the tornado coming. The Rams don't realize what they're getting into.

"You're going to hear me talk all week to the media about how great the Rams offense is and what a challenge it will be for us. But I promise you this: we can stop these guys. They're better on defense than anybody gives them credit for, and we'll need to come up with ways to move the ball and score. But we're not going up there just to play. We're going up there to win. The world's attention will be on the Rams, but the tornado is coming."

Sure enough, the only thing people talked about for the rest of the week was the Rams offense—how they had scored almost fifty points per game at home and even scored thirty points per game on the road.

Our guys were confident, but I wouldn't let them say anything to the media about us, only about the Rams.

In those days, the NFL required teams to arrive two days before a game. Once a team arrived, the head coach and selected players headed to a press conference. We headed to St. Louis on Friday, and Trent Dilfer, John Lynch, Warren Sapp, Hardy Nickerson, Paul Gruber, Mike Alstott, and I represented the team at the press conference.

I made the opening remarks, followed by the players. When it was John Lynch's turn at the podium, a reporter asked if he agreed with Rams receiver Isaac Bruce about the Bucs' use of so much zone coverage. Bruce had said we were either afraid or unable to play man-to-man coverage. John gave me a look—he wanted to say what he really thought.

My mind flashed back twenty-seven years as I gave John the same look Mr. Rocquemore had given me when he kept me from saying something rash to Coach Driscoll.

I mouthed one word. "Tornado."

Next to me, Warren hissed, "Come on, Coach. Come on. Come on."

"No, Warren," I whispered. "Remember what we talked about. We're the tornado. Unknown. Until it's too late."

Our guys held back the entire press conference, saying things such as, "We're just thrilled to be here," and "The

Rams will provide quite a challenge." I liked the way it was shaping up.

Game day finally arrived. Early in the game, our outside linebacker Derrick Brooks hit Rams receiver Torry Holt so hard that he was spitting blood and had to leave the game momentarily. All of a sudden, the Rams realized a tornado was upon them.

The Rams kicked a field goal in the first quarter, and we kicked one in the second. They added a safety before halftime when we snapped a ball over Shaun King's head and out of the end zone. We kicked another field goal in the fourth quarter, putting us ahead 6–5. With less than five minutes to play, the Rams' Ricky Proehl caught a thirty-yard touchdown pass from Kurt Warner. Now ahead by five, they tried a two-point conversion but failed. We tried to put together a final drive to win the game, but after a controversial replay ruling overturned a catch—the rule was changed the next year—we were unable to pick up a first down and lost the game, 11–6.

The NFC Championship Game brought out a wide range of emotions. We were proud of what we had accomplished, how far we had come since 1996. Still, it was bitterly disappointing to be so close to the Super Bowl and yet come up short. I couldn't wait to start the next year, but I also wished we were the team heading to Atlanta for Super Bowl XXXIV.

It hadn't been easy getting to the NFC Championship. I still believed we would get over that hurdle in the near future. As it turned out, I was wrong. It took me seven more years—and a move to a different city—to win a conference championship and get into the Super Bowl.

One of the most difficult challenges in football is for the

loser of a big game to come back the following year and reach the same height. It's difficult for winners as well. The pressure to repeat is intense. The losers of the last several Super Bowls have all struggled to get back to the big game the following year. Often they feel that they need to do something different. I have always preached to my coaches and players, "Do what we do." It's been our approach to the draft and free agency. The best solution for falling just short of the goal is to focus on the fundamentals but perform them better. Let's face it: if your system or approach hadn't been working, you wouldn't have come so close. So maintain your approach, and improve on it. There's a difference between making incremental improvements and making sweeping changes that take you away from your core values.

The master plan that Rich McKay and I operated under integrated both player selection and coaching styles. Using patience, we tried to build our core through the draft and teach our new players. Unless one of our players was a rare talent, we let them test free agency. I instilled the same philosophy into my coaching staff: be patient as you coach the players through their inevitable growing pains, and emphasize the fundamentals of sound tackling, protecting the football, and carrying out assignments. As long as a coach stuck to that philosophy, adding his own style, he was doing what I wanted.

That year, I attended some of the league events in Atlanta during Super Bowl week, just days after our loss in St. Louis. On Saturday, while an ice storm raged outside and paralyzed much of Atlanta, I had lunch with Rich McKay, Joel Glazer, and Bryan Glazer. This was the counterpoint to the lunch I had enjoyed with Joel and Bryan in 1996 when they offered me support to stick with my plan. I'd had a few days to reflect on things and watch the film of the game. Although I was still disappointed about not making the Super Bowl, I was feeling encouraged about the team and our prospects for the future.

The Glazers were not. They wanted to change a number of things offensively, starting with our offensive coordinator, Mike Shula. They wanted him fired. This was a problem for me. Mike was following our philosophy and doing a good job overall. After all, we had almost won the NFC Championship with a third-string rookie quarterback.

During the 1999 season, Mike had been forced to plan for three different quarterbacks, not one of whom was clearly the answer for the Bucs. Trent Dilfer had actually played better after being benched for a game, but then he had broken his clavicle and was out for the year. Eric Zeier had been injured before he could even get settled into the job. Shaun King had played well for us after Trent's injury, and Mike had coached Shaun effectively through the season and into the playoffs. He'd put Shaun in a position where he wouldn't make mistakes and where our defense could help us win. Shaun was young and held great promise, but it was only a guess how he might develop.

I believed that Mike was doing everything we needed him to do to give us our best chance to win. But the Glazers insisted that Mike had to go.

I was deeply concerned because I disagreed completely with their assessment. Two things weighed on my mind: First, I thought about the biblical teaching in 1 Peter 2:13 and 2:18—that we should obey the authority that is over us, even when we disagree. As the coach, I was under the authority of the owners. Second, I was concerned for the future of my other offensive coaches. All of their contracts had expired, including Mike's. As far as I knew, none of them had any job security beyond that lunch.

As our meeting progressed, I reiterated that I thought we

were on the right track and shouldn't make any changes. The Glazers repeated that they still wanted Mike fired—to them, it was in the best interest of the team. At the end of the lunch, I reluctantly agreed to fire Mike.

After the Super Bowl, the losing coaching staff from each conference championship game flies to Hawaii to coach the Pro Bowl. Our bittersweet experience of coaching the Senior Bowl after the 1998 season seemed like a luxury compared to this coaching assignment. I would much rather have coached the week before in the Super Bowl and watched the Pro Bowl on television. I flew back to Tampa after my lunch with the Glazers, packed for Hawaii, and changed my mind about firing Mike. I couldn't do it.

I asked Rich what he thought would happen when I informed the Glazers about my change of heart. He didn't know. I wasn't concerned for myself. I believed that even if I were fired, I could find another job quickly. My concern was for my staff, who were no longer under contract. My contract as head coach gave me control over the selection of my staff, but if I were gone, their protection would be gone too.

Our time in Hawaii should have been a time of celebration. However, while nobody knew exactly what was going on, my assistant coaches could feel that change was in the air. Additionally, I was struggling with what God wanted me to do in relation to the owners, regardless of what my contract said. Everyone was uncomfortable.

I called a meeting in the middle of the week to explain the situation. Mike said he saw an easy solution to keep everyone from losing their jobs: he would step down. Mike knew I was pleased with the job he was doing, but he had grown up in a football family, so he knew that sudden change was always a possibility. His father, Don Shula, was a highly respected coach in the NFL for many years, and I'm sure Mike had seen this type of situation before. I should have anticipated that he would willingly step down, but I hadn't. I was paralyzed by his resignation but accepted it. Mike and his wife headed back to Tampa that afternoon.

Clyde Christensen stepped in and called the plays in the Pro Bowl, and he did a great job. We scored 51 points to the AFC's 31, with the Vikings' Randy Moss and the Rams players doing most of the damage against the AFC team's defense. Despite the win, I still had a catch in my spirit. I felt I had mishandled the situation with Mike and had made the wrong decision, both personally and professionally, in allowing him to leave.

Later, I *knew* that I had made the wrong decision. Just because a decision is deliberate doesn't mean hindsight won't make it clearer. And walking closely with the Lord, trusting Jesus, and looking to the Bible for guidance doesn't guarantee that we'll always make the right decision.

Looking back, I think that decision was the first chink in the Bucs' armor, one that weakened our staff unity. Allowing Mike to resign was a superficial reaction rather than a measured response. It was a break from my philosophy. From that point on, we began a slow downward spiral, with more philosophical breaks. Although Mike and I are still very good friends today, allowing him to leave was the wrong decision, the one I most regret in my coaching career.

TAMPA 2 AND OPEN HEARTS

CHAPTER THIRTEEN

Football is not your life's work.
    CHUCK NOLL

OUR DEFENSE caused quite a stir after we held "The Greatest Show on Turf" to eleven points in the NFC Championship Game. During the 1999 season, people had talked a little about our defense. But after that championship game against the Rams, people began talking about our *defensive scheme*. For the first time, sportswriters and commentators started to use the label "Tampa 2," talking about the Bucs defense as if we had introduced something radically new. The funny thing was, our defensive strategy was merely the blending of a couple of concepts that had been around since my days with the 1977 Steelers.

Most teams, at times, play some form of what's called Cover 2 defense, even if it's not their base defense. The Cover 2 is a zone defense, in which players are responsible for covering receivers who enter their "zones." This is contrasted with a man-to-man defense, in which each player covers one particular person no matter where he goes on the field. Also, most defenses favor a "3 Deep" concept, in which the free safety and two cornerbacks protect the deep zones, the parts of the field farthest away from the line of scrimmage. Cover 2 has the two safeties playing deep and the cornerbacks and three linebackers covering the short zones. Many coaches think this makes Cover 2 more vulnerable to deep passes, but that's not necessarily the case.

We actually began to formulate this system back in 1992, when I joined Monte Kiffin in Minnesota. Monte was coaching the inside linebackers when I arrived, and the Vikings' defensive scheme was to rush the passer and have their secondary in man-to-man coverage. Ever since my days in Pittsburgh, I had always favored zone coverage, and I began to introduce those concepts. Monte, in turn, taught me about the "one-gap" style the Vikings used with their linemen and linebackers. Most teams ask their defensive linemen to protect two gaps, playing head-up on an offensive lineman, stalemating him, and then being able to tackle a ball carrier on either side of that lineman. The Vikings only asked their linemen to handle one side of the offensive lineman, using the linebackers and safeties to compensate. Because they never had to take on a man directly, Minnesota's linemen didn't have to be as big, and though they were generally smaller than the men on the other side of the ball, they were quicker, and they were exceptional pass rushers.

I inherited the perfect group of guys in Minnesota to blend Monte's run defense with my coverage ideas. We had a tremendous defensive line—John Randle, Chris Doleman, Henry Thomas, and Al Noga—along with a veteran group of linebackers and defensive backs. We played well enough to lead the league in defense in 1993, although not many people noticed because we didn't have a lot of success in the playoffs.

While most people saw the Cover 2 as a critical piece

of the defense we put together in Tampa, it really wasn't. We believed it was not our formations that made us good but rather how we played. We emphasized fundamental concepts, not making mistakes, and above all, eleven guys playing as fast and as hard as they could on every play.

The defensive line was critical to the success of our scheme. John Teerlinck was our line coach in Minnesota, and I saw how important he was in setting the tempo necessary for our undersized guys to excel. That was why hiring Rod Marinelli was such an important piece of the puzzle in Tampa. Rod could relate to, teach, and motivate each of our linemen, whether they were veterans or rookies, fast learners or not. He inspired all of those guys to play hard, fast, and smart. We used a number of high draft picks on defensive linemen, but Rod made every guy in his room feel valued and necessary, which they were.

During our first training camp in 1996, we were watching film as a staff, and Rod was particularly intrigued during the 7-on-7 drills. The 7-on-7 is a pure passing drill in which the linebackers and defensive backs work against the running backs and receivers. The linemen are usually at the other end of the field working on pass protection and rush. As a result, Rod never saw the 7-on-7 drills live. He kept stopping the film to ask the same basic questions after pass completions.

"How would you stop this one? Can you even cover that route? Won't they complete this pass all day?"

He loved my answer. "It all depends on the pass rush. We know there are holes in zone coverage if the quarterback has time to find them. But if he's under duress, he won't always see the open receiver, and he won't be able to hit him consistently."

From then on, Rod started each season by telling his players—our defensive linemen—that they were the key to our defense. It would not work unless they controlled their gaps against the run. Even more important, he emphasized that they had to put great pressure on the quarterback. Defensive backs can't cover every route in a zone unless they're guessing, and we didn't want them to guess. We didn't want to have to rely on feast-or-famine blitzes, so Rod made sure his defensive linemen understood how much every play depended on them. Rod—and his linemen—took the personal challenge to keep teams from completing passes against us. If a player didn't share his passion, Rod wasn't afraid to bench him until he consistently played with the energy Rod demanded.

We had gotten close to the Super Bowl in 1999, but rather than continue to do the things that had gotten us to that point, we began to tinker—at least in my eyes—with some of the basic tenets of our philosophy.

One of the biggest problems with becoming a head coach is that the higher up the ladder you go, the less actual hands-on coaching you get to do. Being responsible for more things means you can't coach every player the way he needs to be coached. You don't have enough time to be in every individual meeting to go over assignments and technique. You have to rely on your assistants to do that.

I knew from watching Coach Noll and Denny Green how I wanted to do things as a head coach. I hired top-notch people, trusted them to do their jobs, and then came to grips with the fact that I wouldn't be coaching as much. I missed that; coaching was what I had always done, and now I had to fight the urge to coach everyone. If I wasn't careful, I would end up coaching through or around some very good assistants, which would lessen their credibility with their players. I knew I had to make sure I didn't inadvertently devalue the coaches in the players' eyes by not letting them do their jobs.

As head coach, I also had more off-field responsibilities, and I could see how easy it would be to shortchange my family in an effort to do all that needed to be done. But I was determined not to neglect Lauren and our kids. I had resolved during those long days and nights in Kansas City that if I ever had the chance to be a head coach, I would not spend all night in the office. Rather, I would trust my staff and get us all home at a reasonable hour.

As a result, and in order to allow Monte, Lovie, Rod, and Herm the latitude to run the defense, I rarely attended meetings with the defensive players. I mostly sat in on meetings with the offense and special teams. Because I was a defensive coach, I thought it was important for the offensive players to see me in their meetings. When I played in San Francisco, Bill Walsh orchestrated the offense but rarely got involved with the defense. As a defensive player, I had felt unappreciated. We knew how smart Bill was, but it seemed that he put all of his concentration on the offense. We felt forgotten on the other side of the ball. Since I had been a defensive coach, I didn't want our offensive players to feel forgotten and unappreciated.

Even though I sat in on those meetings, I always made certain to allow Mike Shula (offense) and Joe Marciano (special teams) to coordinate their units, both in practice and in the meetings. I didn't ever want the players to question their authority. Because of that, I continued to feel badly about having allowed Mike to step down. I had been in those meetings, and I knew what a good job he had done. He had been thorough and well prepared, and he had taught exactly the way I wanted. I felt I had violated a basic principle we were trying so hard to instill in our team: trust.

Along with that, I felt we were moving away from our philosophy in the way we were building the team. Rich had never been afraid to trade draft picks for additional picks. Occasionally we would move up to get a particular player, but our philosophy had always been to build through the draft and improve our team for the long term.

Now, having gotten a glimpse of postseason success, we seemed to be shifting away from that philosophy to "get over the hump." Shortly after the Pro Bowl, we traded two first-round picks in the 2000 draft to the New York Jets for their volatile wide receiver, Keyshawn Johnson. My concern wasn't that we added him—Keyshawn was a great player who made us a better team the moment he stepped onto the field. My concern was that we gave up the two first-round draft picks to get him. The trade did pay dividends. Keyshawn played at a Pro Bowl level for us and eventually helped the Bucs win a Super Bowl. But I believed we were moving away from some core beliefs as an organization by looking for the quick fix.

Change isn't always bad; we should always be learning and improving. But the change I was seeing involved principles, not procedures. To my way of thinking, that was bad.

For the Buccaneers, 2000 was a good year—and very nearly a great year. We went to the playoffs again. We beat the Packers in Tampa again. And we lost a close game to them at Lambeau Field again.

I had hired Les Steckel, a good man and a fine coach, to replace Mike Shula. Our offense continued to develop under Les. In fact, we set a franchise record for points scored.

Yet we seemed to be a team of streaks. We won our first three games of the season, then dropped to 3–4 with a month

of Sunday losses. Included in that stretch was a loss to the Redskins in Washington. When Shaun King orchestrated ten points
in the final four minutes, the game went into overtime. But the
Redskins were able to get into position to kick the winning
field goal. Their kicker? Michael Husted. Even though it was
devastating for us, I was happy for Michael.

We won three games straight, lost to the Bears in Chicago,
and then won three more. At 9–5 we were on the verge of a
playoff berth and possible NFC Central championship again.
We only had two games remaining—the Rams at home and
the Packers away.

The Rams game was one of the most remarkable games I've
ever been a part of. It was hard to believe that our two teams
had ground out an 11–6 game only eleven months before. We
trailed 35–31 with less than two minutes to play. Shaun King
threw a screen pass to Warrick Dunn, who—seeing he had
nowhere to go—avoided being tackled by pivoting and flipping
the ball back to Shaun, who somehow ran for thirty yards. We
scored to take the lead, 38–35. Moments later, John Lynch
intercepted a pass to clinch the game. It was the Bucs' third
playoff berth in four years. The atmosphere in the stadium was
electric as we celebrated with our fans.

We headed to Green Bay for the season finale. Since I had
come to Tampa, we had never won at Lambeau Field. And
we still carried the never-winning-in-cold-weather jinx. That
day, the temperature was a numbing fifteen degrees with a
wind chill of fifteen below. Definitely sub-forty. With a win,
we would have our second division title and a first-round bye
in the playoffs.

The score was tied, 14–14, late in the game. Brett Favre
was driving the Packers toward the win. Then our linebacker
Jamie Duncan intercepted a Favre pass. Shaun King moved us
down to the 22 yard line to set up Martin Gramatica for the

game-winning field goal. Martin had not missed a big kick for us in two years; he missed this one just wide to the right. We lost the coin toss to start overtime and never got the ball. Green Bay kicked a field goal to win, 17–14. Our opening playoff game would be in Philadelphia.

We played poorly against the Eagles, losing 21–3 to end our season. But for the third time in four years, and the fourth in the Bucs' entire history, we had won ten or more games.

We had seen a number of positive results on offense and had set some team records, but I felt that Les's coaching philosophy did not quite mesh with mine. He is an excellent coach and a good friend, but thinking long-term, I decided we were better off making a change.

Had I known what lay ahead, I would not have fired Les and named Clyde Christensen as our third offensive coordinator in three years.

If you saw Clyde Christensen coming down a hallway, you'd never guess he had been a quarterback at the University of North Carolina. He's built more like a fullback. Clyde and I met at a coaching clinic and became friends through the Fellowship of Christian Athletes. When I was hired by the Bucs, Clyde left his role as offensive co-coordinator at Clemson to join me. It was Clyde's friendship with Mark Merrill that led to my involvement with Family First and All Pro Dad.

Clyde and I are both passionate about helping men become better fathers. Like me, Clyde is very close to his parents, a California minister and his wife. Like me, he has worked diligently to keep his children grounded and to spend meaningful time with them. Unlike me, Clyde's birth mother was a fourteen-year-old girl who put him up for adoption—insisting that he be adopted into a Christian home. Clyde's firsthand sensitivity to adoption has fueled his energetic support of Family First and All Pro Dad, as well as A Woman's Place, a Tampa crisis pregnancy counseling center.

✛   ✛   ✛

Just before the 2000 season, an unexpected part of God's plan unfolded on our team. Joe Marciano, our special teams coach, came to me and told me he wanted to adopt a child.

"I've thought it through, and I think I can make it work even though I'm going to be a single dad. I'll get help during the day, but if I can bring him here in the afternoons and then go home with him in the evenings, we'll be okay."

We talked it through for a bit. Joe knew I would make allowances for anyone's family issues, and I had always followed the lead of Denny Green and Chuck Noll when it came to scheduling. At the same time, football is a demanding profession, so even a family-friendly schedule requires a significant amount of time away from home.

On a typical Monday, we can be at the office from eight in the morning until ten at night, reviewing our film as well as film on our next opponent. Tuesday is our game-plan day, and it often goes just as late. Wednesday is our first practice day. We start around eight and stay until we finish reviewing the practice tape, which is usually about nine at night. On Thursdays we refine the plan and then try to be out by 8 p.m. Friday is a short dress rehearsal, and we're usually finished at 1 p.m. On Saturday morning, we have a "walk-through"—a slow-motion practice without full pads. Then we either fly out for an away game or go home and relax before checking into our team hotel that night for a home game. Sunday is a long day of pregame meetings and meals, the game itself, and return travel.

I knew we would have to be creative in thinking about ways to make this work for Joe and the Buccaneers. We decided that since Joe was the special teams coach, he didn't have to meet with the other coaches but could meet with me separately to review his plans for the kicking game on a schedule that worked with his childcare. He could probably even do a lot of his work at home. I hoped we could make it work.

Joe then began the process of adoption, and eighteen months later, he brought home his new son, Joseph.

One of the most interested parties in all this was my wife, Lauren. She wanted to help Joe all she could, but she also was interested for another reason—she wanted more kids around. Lauren was a twin and came from a close-knit, gregarious family. The Harrises were all very outgoing, and their household was always lively. By contrast, as Lauren had been known to say, "You never quite knew what the Dungys were thinking." We were a very quiet family.

When Joe adopted Joseph, Lauren and I had three children: Tiara, sixteen; Jamie, thirteen; and Eric, ten. But Lauren hoped for more. She wanted to adopt, as her parents had. They had taken in a number of foster kids over the years and had adopted two of them. Now in their eighties, my in-laws have a daughter in high school and a son in middle school.

Lauren and I had taken in foster children when we were first married, and I was at least somewhat interested. After all, God had blessed us with material resources that would allow us to take care of more children than our three. And Lauren really was cut out to be a mother.

At the same time, I'm not always quick to make a decision. I like to think things through and carefully weigh all the options whenever I can. Adding children to our family struck me as the kind of decision that was worth taking some time to contemplate. The fact that the process took eighteen months for Joe to complete gave me some comfort. Even if

Lauren and I decided to adopt, I knew nothing would happen immediately.

Having worked with the foster-care system in Pittsburgh, I knew the statistics. Well over half a million children were in foster care in the United States, and countless more awaited adoption both in this country and around the world. We had helped some of those kids for a short period of time—overnight, a week, a couple of months. But Lauren wanted to help kids in a more permanent way, and she also wanted the joy of having a new baby in our home. I knew we could make all the difference in the world to at least one child. But I needed to learn more, and I wanted time to think and pray through our decision.

We made an appointment to visit the same adoption agency Joe had used. Our purpose was to gather more information so we could better evaluate our decision. During the meeting, the woman asked us a number of questions, and then we went through ours. As more of a formality than anything else at the close of the meeting, we asked how long we could expect this process to take. The answer shocked me.

"If you're looking to adopt an African American or biracial child, you can have one immediately."

I was floored. My mind raced. My time to think things through had just been tossed out the window. "We . . . I . . . we thought it took like a year and a half."

"It does if you want to adopt a white baby or want to adopt internationally. However, the need is so great for domestic minority children that we are pretty much always in need of adoptive parents."

At that point, I knew my answer was clear. I had looked to God for clear signs when making career decisions, but this was probably the clearest sign I had ever received. I guess He had just been holding back His clearest sign for something critical like children who needed a home. That way, He could be sure I got it right.

Adopting a child—immediately—was quite a transition to contemplate. I was concerned with my ability to do my job and be a good father, not only to teenagers but now to an infant as well. Would I have the energy to do both now that I was in my forties? And what about our kids? Our three children were comfortably settled in their routines. Tiara was a good student and athlete, and she was enjoying high school. Jamie was growing tall and lean, and he was extremely sensitive, a lot like Lauren. Eric was most like me when I was growing up—always looking for a game. They were all good kids, and we wanted to make sure we didn't disrupt their lifestyles.

We all talked and prayed together about the impact adoption would have on our family. Everyone was in favor initially—except me. I needed time to think it through. Lauren finally moved me from my indecision when she said, "It's just like you always say to the team: 'If it's important enough to you, we'll get it done.'" There was no way I could dispute that.

A couple of months later, in August 2000, we adopted Jordan. He was in the hospital for a few days after birth before we got to bring him home. "Just running a few more tests," we were told by the doctors and nurses.

We assumed this was normal procedure when adopting a newborn, although we were a bit concerned that the birth mother might be changing her mind. The agency told us not to worry and that all the tests had turned out fine.

We thought it a was little odd, however, that Jordan didn't cry when he got his first set of shots. Then, one afternoon when he was about five months old, I was home alone with him—probably engrossed in a football game, I'm afraid—when he fell off the bed. And didn't cry.

We took him to a pediatric neurologist in Tampa and started asking more questions. We learned then that unlike most babies, Jordan hadn't cried in the hospital after birth when he was given eye drops. The neurologist suggested we take him to the University of Florida for more definitive tests. The doctors in Gainesville gave us an answer: Jordan was diagnosed with congenital insensitivity to pain. Jordan is missing a gene, it turns out, and therefore doesn't feel pain the way other people do. Some experts think he might not feel any pain at all.

Through Jordan, I realized that God allows us to feel pain for a reason: to protect us. God uses many things to show us what to avoid, and painful consequences often teach us lessons quickly. For example, like most kids, Jordan loves cookies. Warm cookies certainly aren't bad for you, at least in moderation. But they *are* harmful if they're *still in the oven*. Jordan would reach right in to pull out the piping hot cookie sheet with his bare hands. Then he would begin to eat the cookies without even realizing he was burning his hands and mouth in the process. Even a trip to the emergency room didn't help him understand that he was injuring himself.

I think at one time or another every one of our children has gone running through the house at full tilt. Looking backward at a sibling in hot pursuit or waiting for a pass, they inevitably slam into a wall with the side of their head. They've all done it—once—and then, because of the pain, they're careful not to let it happen again. Jordan, on the other hand, does this kind of thing repeatedly and gets up smiling. Without the painful consequences, how is he to learn?

Lauren and I have had to teach him the consequences of right and wrong and dangerous activities in order to protect him. Pain isn't available to him as a teaching tool. Before we had Jordan, I hadn't thought much about the way God uses pain to protect us from further negative consequences down the road. With Jordan, this has become obvious. Pain prompts us to change behavior that is destructive to ourselves or to others. Pain can be a highly effective instructor.

Lauren has done a great job with Jordan, as he has learned to thrive and survive even without that sense of pain. Jordan also has another special trait. He has an uncanny ability to process phone numbers. Now six, Jordan can see a string of digits come up on our caller ID and *immediately* identify any regular caller. I'm never surprised, either, when it works the other way and one of my friends tells me he received an unexpected phone call from Jordan. Those numbers are in Jordan's head.

In September 2001, we would bring home another child, Jade. Lauren felt that Jordan needed someone to play with—somehow I knew that was coming. When it came to adopting another child, we never gave Jordan's medical condition a second thought. Jordan's condition is difficult, but we realized it could just as easily have happened to one of our biological children. Plus, we believe God had a reason to send Jordan to us. We have a variety of resources that help us deal with his needs, especially Lauren's patience and nurturing spirit.

We view Jordan, our son, as a special blessing. We're grateful for our opportunity to impact and shape his young life. In the process, Jordan personally illustrates for us some of the wonders of God and His plan for us. Watching the impact of that single missing gene reminds me how intricately each of us has been designed and created. I am continually amazed at the wonder of God's most complex creation—people. The line between what we consider normal and what we consider special is so fine. So many varied, delicate pieces contribute to the balance and beauty of the whole picture.

Just another part of life's journey.

WALKING THE PLANK

CHAPTER FOURTEEN

It's always easier to do things the wrong way, but it's always best to do them the right way.
    CLEOMAE DUNGY

I HEARD RUMORS for the first time at the end of the 2000 season that the Glazers might be looking for a new head coach. Other people probably heard them earlier—Lauren says I'm usually the last one to pick up on things. I had two years left on my contract, but my assistant coaches were entering their last year. My agent, Ray Anderson, who knew more about the rumors than I did, felt we needed to approach the Glazers about an extension. I was against the idea. I believed I should coach out to the end of my contract if I expected to be paid fairly at the end of the day.

Ray, however, was worried about security, so we decided that he should talk with the Glazers. They refused to extend my contract but did agree to give one-year extensions to all of my assistants. That was fine with me; I didn't want to get into another situation like we faced at the 2000 Pro Bowl, when my coaches were out of contract and concerned about their immediate futures.

Lovie Smith and Herm Edwards left the Buccaneers in January of 2001. Lovie was hired to be the defensive coordinator for the St. Louis Rams, while Herm became the new head coach of the New York Jets. True to his word, Herm hadn't left for anything less than a head coaching position, though he had been offered a number of opportunities to become a coordinator over the years. I was sorry to see them both go—we hadn't made a change on the defensive side of the ball since we had arrived in Tampa in 1996, and now we had to make two.

As I began the interview process, Herm called from the Jets facility on Long Island.

"You should see my office up here, Tony! It's got a wall of glass that overlooks the practice field. But the best part is, they're concerned that it's not big enough! They want to know if I need it expanded! I said no, thanks, and didn't bother to tell them that it's twenty times larger than my closet in Tampa, and the door can be shut while I'm still sitting!"

Joel Glazer approached me in the visiting locker room in the Georgia Dome on the final day of August. We were about to play the Falcons in our last preseason game, and Joel and I found ourselves alone.

I figured he wanted to allay my concerns about my future and the rumors that were circulating. I was right.

"Tony, I know you're hearing rumors that if we don't win it all this year, we're going to make a change. I want you to know you don't have to win the Super Bowl this year. We don't want to extend your contract now, with two years left, but you're our coach, and we have confidence in you."

That was all I needed—to look him in the eye and hear him give me his word.

Lauren wasn't convinced, however. Something was different, and she could feel it. She always claims that I go through life with rose-colored glasses on, while she is more perceptive. She's right on both counts. Part of what she had always enjoyed about the Bucs organization was that the Glazers were so personally involved yet so deferential to her opinions. They regularly contacted her to get her thoughts on various issues and had allowed her to set the course for the Buccaneers Wives Organization.

But in 2001, the calls had stopped, and new leaders took over the wives organization. I believed there were other explanations for these things, but Lauren wasn't so sure. She believed the landscape was changing.

Tom Lamphere, my longtime friend and chaplain from Minneapolis, called me to ask about the rumors he had been hearing about my job security. I was hearing them as well but had chosen not to dwell on them.

"Worrying about my job is not my responsibility; it's God's," I told Tom. "My job is to coach."

I believed that. Not only did I have Joel's assurance that there was nothing to those rumors, I also felt that God was using this to test me. Just like when I had mono in 1978, the question was whether I would stay focused on the Lord or start worrying about things I couldn't control. I knew I needed to stay focused, continue to be the leader of our team, and let the Lord handle the future. Had I grown enough in my Christian faith to do this?

In 2001, Simeon Rice was a free agent. Rod and I took him to dinner when he was visiting Tampa. Simeon had been drafted third overall by the Cardinals in 1996 and had tied the NFL record for sacks by a rookie. He'd been a two-time All-American at the University of Illinois, and he continued with great sack totals in his first five years in the NFL. At an opportune point during dinner, Rod leaned across the table and, with a burning intensity in his eyes, spoke to Simeon.

"Simeon, you're a talented guy, but you're not a *great player*. You sack the quarterback and do some good things, but you don't play with the effort and intensity that it takes to be a winner. That's why you should come to Tampa. You need *me* to make you a great player."

Simeon looked at Rod like he was crazy, clearly thinking, *How can you think I'm not a great player?*

But Rod had him. Simeon signed with the Buccaneers, and Rod rode him hard through camp and into the season, trying to light a fire within him and get him to play up to his tremendous ability on every play. Rod was known to take Simeon out of games and talk about his intensity, then send him back in after a few plays. Out. Then in. Out again. Then back in. Over and over.

We played a home game against Green Bay in October. It was a typical Tampa day—muggy and hot, around eighty degrees. It was a tough, physical game, and we were fortunate to grind out a win, 14–10, after Brett Favre threw incomplete passes into the end zone on the last two plays of the game. Simeon fell to the turf on his back, exhausted. He, with his teammates, had played with the every-down passion that Rod demanded, so much so that he required IV fluids after the game.

Rod ran out onto the field, exhilarated by the win and the fact that he'd gotten through to Sim after all those weeks. He stood over Sim. "Now you're starting to understand! This—*this effort*—is what we've been talking about!"

Sim looked up and with typical Simeon Rice candor said,

"If this is what it takes to win every week, I'm not sure that I want it. It's not worth it." Rod's elation was immediately deflated. Eventually, though, Simeon became a player we knew we could count on.

For the fourth year in a row, we started the season 3–4. We lost to Green Bay on the road but defeated them at home. We swept Detroit but got swept by Chicago. We beat the Rams in St. Louis. It had been a roller-coaster year by the time we battled back to clinch a wildcard playoff spot during the next-to-last week of the season.

Along the way, we split with Minnesota, losing the game in Minneapolis but winning the game in Tampa. In that game we were faced with a situation in which league rules actually seemed to reward unsportsmanlike behavior.

Back then, if teams were tied for a playoff berth, one of the tiebreakers was point differential—which team had beaten its opponents by more points over the course of the season. The point differential wasn't the first tiebreaker, but it occasionally did come into play. When we played the Vikings in Tampa, we found ourselves inside Minnesota's five yard line with a 27-point lead and less than two minutes to play. We knelt on the ball four times, just running out the clock rather than trying to score. When we were winning with a big lead, I never liked to rub it in, especially when facing a good friend like Denny Green.

After the game, someone asked me whether I realized that my decision could cost our team a playoff spot if we ended up tied in the standings. "If the Buccaneers miss the playoffs because we refused to embarrass another team," I said, "then it's a lousy rule." Fortunately, that rule was later changed, so coaches no longer have to make that decision.

I hoped, of course, that my decision wouldn't end up hurting the team, just as I had hoped in 1997 with Michael Husted. But I believed that our principles were more important than worrying about the slight chance of missing the playoffs. I knew that if I was going to emphasize character, then I had to be willing to back it up with actions, even if those actions were difficult. Looking back, I still believe it was the right thing to do.

Although I've summarized our regular season in fairly short order, the season was anything but short for those of us who lived it. The NFL season lasts from July to January. It's a long grind in the best of years. But with the rumors of a coaching change circulating, the 2001 season seemed even longer for many of our coaches and staff and their families.

Lauren was especially sensitive to the changes in the air. Although she had previously been a sounding board for the Glazers, she now heard only silence. In the past, she often came by to spend time with me and our boys, who were in my office every afternoon after school; that year she decided to stay away.

Shortly before the end of the regular season, I had just finished a workout and was drying off in the cramped coaches' locker room after my shower. A member of our front-office staff was also in the locker room, getting ready for a run.

"Coach, I just wanted to say that I've appreciated seeing your witness in light of the circus that is occurring all around," he said.

I didn't really have a chance to reflect on my answer before I gave it, but I'm not sure that I could have improved on it much, even now.

"I think there are times when I believe God welcomes the circus into our lives to give us an opportunity to show that there's another way to live and respond to things."

Those words are no less true today than they were then.

Questions of faith—for all of us, I suspect—were pushed to the forefront of our lives and national consciousness by the events of September 11, 2001, just two days after we had beaten Dallas in our opening game.

The day before September 11, Jade had joined our family through adoption. When we got her, I had been so excited to think about all we could offer her as a family: love, stability, financial security. But on that Tuesday—the players' day off and a day we coaches are normally sequestered in a dark film room preparing for our next opponent—everything changed. We usually miss news events, but that day our thoughts of the Eagles stopped as we found ourselves glued to the television screens and wondering what was going to happen. Some of the staff left early. Others of us just stayed together to watch.

Suddenly, I realized how foolish I had been to think I could provide any kind of security for our new baby. As these events unfolded, it became clear to me that only God could do that.

As the day continued, it became obvious that we weren't going to play that week. In an unprecedented decision, Commissioner Tagliabue postponed all week 2 games, possibly to be rescheduled for a later date.

We were scheduled for a bye the following week, so we would not play again until the last week in September. By the time our bye week came along, the nation's resolve had become firm, unified, and pointed toward getting back into a normal routine. We did not want this act of terror to have changed our daily lives. I had never before attempted to convince someone that football was terribly important in the overall scheme of life, but as we prepared for the game against Minnesota that week, I told the team that the best thing we could do for our country and to honor those who had died was to continue to do our jobs with excellence in spite of our national adversity. Our country needed a return to some sense of normalcy. We needed to get back to work—for ourselves and our fans. This was like the five o'clock bus ride, an unforeseen obstacle we would have to overcome.

I don't remember much about that first game after September 11, but I know it wasn't the game itself I was looking forward to as much as just being out there again and getting back to work. It had been a while since I had given much thought to the significance of singing the national anthem before a game, since it happened so routinely every week. I was usually more interested in who was performing it. But this game, I was focused on the anthem itself—the words, the music, the meaning—as much as the game. I was focused on our team standing out there, ready to go back to work in honor of our country. It was a statement to the world and anyone who would seek to harm us: *You cannot stop us from pressing on.*

That was one of the few games in my life that I remember little about what happened or even whether we won or lost. What I do remember is that the Minnesota fans did a great job—as did fans around the country—of supporting us, our nation, and those who had died. We were all unified in our patriotism.

I have always felt that God remains in control, despite the situations we find ourselves in, and I believed He would use the tragic events of September 11 for His glory as well. I never lost faith that God loves us. He sent His Son, Jesus, to make it possible for us to have a full and joyful life here and to make it possible for us to spend eternity with Him in heaven. September 11 made me think about that a lot; compared to eternity, worrying about things like coaching jobs, playoffs, and even the Super Bowl didn't seem so important.

It was week 18 of the regular season. Usually the NFL season has seventeen weeks—sixteen games plus a bye week—but the commissioner had decided to reschedule those week 2 games for the week immediately following the normal end of the regular season, pushing the playoffs back by a week. Our matchup with Philadelphia, which had been highly anticipated by the fans and media in the preseason thanks to our playoff skirmish the year before, was now virtually meaningless. Both teams had already qualified for the playoffs, and the outcome wouldn't affect our seeding. Actually, it was beyond meaningless; we were scheduled to play the Eagles in Philadelphia the very next weekend in the first round of the playoffs. Both teams would be careful not to show anything in this game that we might use the next week, when the game actually mattered.

After our staff met, we decided to rest most of our starters and play a very vanilla offense and defense—a preseason game approach. The young guys would get playing time, and the starters would be protected from injury. We turned our attention to practice for the week.

On Thursday afternoon, January 3, I saw Rich walking out to the field. It wasn't unusual for him to come out and watch, but this time something seemed different. He walked straight toward me. In a very soft voice, Rich delivered the message from my dad: my mom had died.

My mom had been fighting diabetes for a long time, so I had known this was coming, but I had dreaded it. And yet, it was a relief. The disease had taken a physical toll. Her body had shrunk, and she had been confined to a wheelchair, in constant pain. As sad as her death was, I was overcome with a sense of joy because I knew she was in heaven. All that hit me at once: the sadness of losing my mom coupled with the joy of knowing she was now with God, pain-free. It wouldn't be the last time I'd experience those emotions simultaneously.

My dad was handling all the arrangements for the funeral, which was to take place the following Tuesday. I stayed in Tampa to coach our last regular season game, certain that my mom would have wanted me to. It was the first time I didn't care if we won or lost. It wasn't just because of my mom's death, although that certainly put things in perspective. Rather, it was because we were scheduled to play the Eagles again in the playoffs in six days.

I later learned that Rich had a slightly different perspective on that game in week 18. We had fallen behind early, and when we did, he said to another staff member, "Doesn't Tony realize how much harder it is to fire a 10–6 coach than one who is 9–7?" I can't say I did, because I still didn't think there was a chance I would be fired. So when our backup players couldn't hold a ten-point fourth-quarter lead, I didn't give it a second thought. I was only concerned with preparing for my mom's funeral and the next week's playoff game.

Throughout the course of my six-year tenure with the Buccaneers, the Glazers always flew with the team to away games. They sat in first class in our chartered 757 with the assistant coaches. Because there weren't enough seats for all the coaching staff in first class, Rich and I always sat in the last row of coach. I liked to sit in the back so I could see all the players.

That Friday morning, Rick Stroud of the *St. Petersburg Times* wrote an article, quoting unnamed sources, saying that I would be fired if we didn't win Saturday's playoff game against the Eagles. I really didn't worry about it, but I didn't want the players to get distracted. So I brought the paper with me on the flight so I could talk to the Glazers. I knew I could ask Joel, given our conversation in Atlanta and his assurance then that I was their coach.

None of the Glazers was on the flight with us that day. As Lauren says, I'm very naive, but that was the first time I felt that something was going on. How could the owners not fly with us to a playoff game?

On Friday afternoon we had a walk-through practice at Veterans Stadium in Philadelphia. It was cold and gray that day. Warren Sapp and a couple of other players took their shirts off in spite of the cold, trying to do their part to keep the others loose and relaxed.

It didn't help. For the third consecutive playoff game, we didn't score a touchdown. We lost 31–9. We couldn't make a single big play, and in the meantime, we threw four interceptions. Just like that, we were done for the season, and when we arrived back in Tampa, I wondered if those "unnamed sources" in the *Times* were correct.

Sunday came and went, and I didn't hear anything that would make me think I was about to be fired. We held our exit physicals and met as a team; then the players went their separate ways. Most of them wouldn't return until the off-season program began in March.

Rich told me that the Glazers were meeting as a family, but he thought we were going to be okay. The Glazers wanted to discuss some changes, but they were looking at continuing things for at least another year. I still had regrets about how I had handled the Mike Shula situation in 1999, so I was concerned about the kinds of changes they might ask for.

On Monday we met as a staff, reviewed Saturday's game film, and discussed our off-season schedule.

Rich called that afternoon and said the Glazers wanted to make a change. He asked me to come to his house to meet with them.

I knew then that my time with the Bucs had come to an end. Rick Stroud's article had been correct.

Rich lived in one of the oldest sections of Tampa, in an old, pretty home guarded by a huge oak tree in the front yard. The driveway wound around that tree, which made backing out to the street almost impossible. As I pulled up and saw the Glazers' cars, I made it a point to note how close I was to that tree so I could avoid hitting it when I left later.

As it turned out, I was backing out of Rich's driveway about one minute later. The conversation was short and pleasant and lasted about thirty seconds. As Rich had said, the Glazers wanted to make a change. Joel, Bryan, and Ed— the Glazers' three sons, who had been actively managing the team that year—were all present as they informed me I was no longer the head coach of the Tampa Bay Buccaneers.

I thanked them for the opportunity they had given me as head coach. My only question was about what would happen to my assistant coaches. The Glazers said they didn't know. After all, that would be up to the new coach. Since they had spent the last couple of days deciding whether or not to fire me, they said they had no idea yet who the new coach might be or what he would do with the staff.

Tuesday evening, after my nighttime excursion to One Buc to pack up, Lauren and I went back one more time to make sure I had gotten everything. Once inside, I suggested to Lauren that she go back outside and move the Explorer closer to the back door while I finished. The security officer who had let us in had given us some space, but I knew he was lingering somewhere nearby.

Lauren hesitated. She told me she was worried she wouldn't be able to get back in.

I tried to reassure her. "I think you're overly concerned."

"Really? Your keypad code doesn't work. The guard used his code and walked us in. And now he's around the corner somewhere, keeping tabs. Tony, we're not welcome here anymore."

She did decide to go move the Explorer closer to the back door, but I knew she was right. Everything had changed.

At the end of my tenure with the Bucs, I really had no one to be upset with. The Glazers owned the team, and they had to do what they thought was best for the Buccaneers. Yes, if it were up to me, I would have preferred that Joel and I not have had that conversation in Atlanta so I wouldn't have relied on it throughout the season. I would rather have been told that 2001 would be a make-or-break year, that we needed to advance deep into the playoffs and maybe win the Super Bowl if I wanted to keep my job.

At the same time, however, I have never lost sight of the fact that the Glazers saw me as an NFL head coach when no one else did. They gave me my first opportunity, and I'll always be grateful to them for that. So no, there was no one to be upset with. God just wanted me to move on to a different situation. His time for me in Tampa had been completed.

A SOFT LANDING

*"For I know the plans I have for you," says the L*ORD*. "They are plans for good and not for disaster, to give you a future and a hope."*
    JEREMIAH 29:11

I'M A FOOTBALL COACH. I always remember this fact to help me keep things in perspective. When the Glazers fired me, I was terribly disappointed that I wouldn't be able to stay the course with the organization we had built in Tampa. But I also recognized that I wasn't dealing with life-and-death issues. It wasn't as if I were helping women through high-risk pregnancies or helping people through physical problems, as my siblings were. They had what I considered to be critical jobs; I have never viewed my job as that important.

No, I am a football coach. And as a football coach in the National Football League, I know for sure that it's going to end someday. These days, about a quarter of the head coaching jobs change hands every year, and it's usually not pretty when it does come to a close.

At the time I was fired, I believed I would have other opportunities to coach in some capacity, but I also wondered if God might be transitioning me out of coaching altogether.

Maybe God had something entirely different planned for me. One of the best things to come from being head coach of the Buccaneers was the platform it provided me to speak on topics that matter to me. I enjoy speaking, especially to youth groups, and I've always believed that reaching young people is something I should do. We are all role models for someone, but as an NFL coach, my sphere of influence was broader than it is for most people. Now I had to consider whether I should start to be a role model in a different way.

I held a press conference the following day in Tampa. People might have expected me to be angry with the Glazers. I disagreed with their decision, but I truly believed that since they owned the Buccaneers, it was their decision to make. Plus, if I trust God that all things work together for good, then I have to believe it—even when it doesn't feel good to *me*.

Tom Lamphere and I had spoken the evening I was fired. He reminded me of two important points. First, if I had any bitterness in my heart, it would only hurt me. While bitterness is a natural emotion, I knew I needed to pray and let God remove it so I could press on. Second, I needed to remember that this was all ultimately designed for good.

Tom reminded me of Romans 8:28 and the Old Testament story of Joseph, which both have the same message: God is in control of our future, and He's working for our good—whether we can see it now or not. I knew what Tom was saying was true, and I remembered the story of Joseph clearly from my mom's Sunday school lessons. Still, it was great to have someone remind me at the very moment that I needed to put my faith into practice. After talking with Tom, I was able to go out and sincerely thank the Glazers publicly for giving me the opportunity to coach their team. That attitude didn't come from me but from the Lord, and I think it had an impact on a lot of people.

Over the next couple of days, Lauren and I spent some time with our feet up and a lot of time on our knees. I didn't know why we were leaving the Bucs, but I knew God was closing this door for a reason. First, we needed to determine if we even wanted to remain in coaching. I wasn't convinced that we should. I believed we had done things God's way, or tried to, and He was moving us in another direction. My time with the Buccaneers had given me a tremendous following in the community and an ability to rally interest and enthusiasm around things that were important to me.

One of those things was the All Pro Dad organization, which I had founded with Mark Merrill and Clyde Christensen. Our original goal was to try to reach dads everywhere, whether in the city or the suburbs, married or single. Our message was simple: dads—including us—need to spend more time with their kids. In four short years, All Pro Dad had grown into a national organization that sponsored clinics—called All Pro Dad Father & Kid Experiences—in NFL cities across the country and sent daily tips via e-mail to fathers around the nation.

As Mark studied family life in the United States, he had learned that two-thirds of African American teens have absent fathers. And I had learned from visiting prisons that the most common factor among male inmates was growing up without a dad in the home. When we put those two facts together, we knew we needed to focus our attention on fathers.

Somehow, through God's grace, it has grown in all those directions. When we started the organization, we weren't sure exactly how to go about it—we just prayed a lot. Today, 69 percent of all the All Pro Dad breakfasts we sponsor are in

Title I schools, many of which are located in inner-city locales. It has been wonderful to see those children with absent fathers bringing mentors, uncles, grandfathers, or even their absentee dads with them to the monthly breakfasts.

All Pro Dad chapters have grown from an idea in Tampa to a reality in schools everywhere around the country, from Los Angeles to the Bronx. They continue to grow today, and Truett Cathy, founder of Chick-fil-A, has even requested that every Chick-fil-A franchise in the country host an All Pro Dad monthly fathers' breakfast.

I had been visiting prisons with Abe Brown since 1997. Abe, a longtime coach at Blake High School in Tampa, had founded a prison ministry in 1976 after visiting one of his former players behind bars. I loved walking around Tampa with Abe. The man knows everyone in town and has probably coached half of them. He's the only person I could walk with in Tampa and have more people know him than me. Even when I was coaching the Bucs, I knew if we were together and someone yelled, "Hey, Coach!" they were usually talking to Abe.

Abe is an unassuming, low-key guy, and yet he has made a tremendous impact on the lives of many people in Tampa, including me. He started by visiting his former player, and when he learned the man had few—if any—other visitors, Abe kept going back, in part because he felt he had failed him as a coach. As Abe kept returning, he met other guys, talked with them, and tried to help them. Over time, these visits naturally developed into a prison ministry.

In 1997, I was looking for ways to use my platform in Tampa, and Abe invited me to visit a prison with him. I was intrigued by that because I had grown up in a prison town. I knew people who worked at the prison in Jackson, and today my sister works there. Although I really wanted to join Abe at the prison, I was a little afraid of going in.

When the day arrived for our visit to Polk Correctional Institution, I was very nervous. I still carried images from my childhood of the hardened men I had always imagined who lived within the walls of the prison in Jackson. Even though I was forty-two years old, no longer a child, I still pictured prisoners as old, belligerent, and calloused. I was coming with a message that there's always hope, based on the gospel of Jesus Christ, but I had no idea how that message—or I—would be received.

When Abe introduced me to some of the prisoners, I was shocked. Many of these "old men" looked like my sons Jamie and Eric—perhaps sixteen, seventeen, eighteen years old. And many of those who were in their thirties had actually come in as teenagers. This wasn't at all what I had expected.

Most of the men were into football, and I found I had a common bond with them—they read the sports page and the Bible. They loved talking about the Buccaneers, but they also wanted to talk about their dreams and what they might still accomplish when they were released. They were clinging to hope and seeking encouragement. A lot of those guys still stay in touch with me today, and for years I've been the beneficiary of all types of talent coming out of those prisons. I've received sketches, paintings, poetry—any means by which the inmates could express themselves. Many of them are very talented, and Abe is always looking for ways to create the right niche for them when they get out.

As coach of the Bucs, I had only been able to make summer trips to the prisons. But now that I was suddenly out of a job, I wondered whether God might be calling me to assist Abe in his ministry. After all, the inmate population had grown significantly since 1976, when Abe made his first visit. When he first started, he could visit every prison in the state in about three days; now that was impossible.

Abe had started out as a coach, but he had expanded his reach to working with these kids for the rest of their lives, and I found that fascinating. For Abe, the most important thing was not the football skills he taught. He derived his greatest joy from watching the young men he ministered to mature and lead productive lives. I just didn't have time during the season or through the draft to help Abe. But now . . . maybe this was what God was opening up in front of me.

Lauren and I were still seeking direction by the middle of that week. On one of those days, Lauren came home from running an errand, saw the light blinking on the answering machine, listened to the message, and saved it. When I walked in later, she directed me to listen to the message. It was from Jim Irsay, the owner of the Indianapolis Colts. He had just fired Jim Mora, and the message seemed to be expressing his interest in having me coach the Colts. It was difficult to know for sure, though, because this was not just a voice memo—it was a mission statement.

Mr. Irsay started by saying that he did want me to be head coach and then outlined where the Colts were at that time.

"Having only moved to Indianapolis in 1984, we don't have the long-established fan bases of Pittsburgh, Chicago, Cleveland, or other cities," he said. "But we're still trying to develop that base. I want an organization—and team—that emphasizes character, values, and family, and I want it to extend out into the community in a meaningful way."

He went on to say that when he was a kid, he had been a

ball boy for his dad and had watched the Steelers during the years I was playing. He said he aspired to be like the Rooneys and create that type of organization.

"You're the only person I want for this job," he said.

He concluded his fifteen-minute mission statement by saying, "Don't worry about your salary, and don't let your agent mess this up. I'll pay you whatever you want. We just need to talk man to man." Lauren looked at me, trying to read my face. Maybe God wasn't closing the football door after all.

Jim Irsay and I spoke by phone later that day for an hour, and none of it was about football. We talked about the Colts family, about values, about community. He said he wanted to win, but he wanted to win the right way. And if we ever did win the Super Bowl, he wanted Indiana to feel a personal connection, for it to be *their* team and *their* trophy.

I'm not sure I would have been interested in coaching at all if Jim hadn't left me that message with his ideas about my role as the new head coach of the Colts. It was exactly in line with the way I wanted to coach. In the next few days, the Carolina Panthers also contacted me. As I opened myself to that possibility, Carolina seemed like it could be a good fit as well.

While we weighed the options, Lauren and I spoke to people we respected about ministry, coaching, the Colts, and the Panthers. As usual, there was no clear voice from God—not even a muffled murmur. The people we talked to kept coming back to the same thing: follow your passion. "God has created you a certain way with certain interests and passions. Follow them."

Both Indiana and North Carolina were good options. My warm-weather wife was probably pulling for Charlotte, but in the end, we both felt the Indianapolis Colts were a better fit for us. Jim Irsay's phone message had touched both of us. We decided that God was continuing the football dream for the Dungys—and not just the game but also the ongoing platform and ministry opportunities. Hoping that we were still faithfully following God's leading, we joined the Colts.

Coming to the Colts in 2002 was significantly different from arriving in Tampa in 1996. For one thing, Jim Irsay flew Lauren and me to Indianapolis on his private jet, and then we were taken on a helicopter from the airport to the Colts facility. Even from the air, I could tell that this was no One Buc. For starters, the entire weight room was housed inside. There would be no lifting sessions on a patio.

Mr. Irsay introduced me to the press as the new head coach of the Indianapolis Colts. From the outset, he announced that we were looking to accomplish something special, on and off the field. The Glazers had always been terrific about supporting things in which I was involved, but in this case, it was as if I were supporting Jim.

I worked to instill the same basic principles we had used in Tampa: excellence in the giveaway/takeaway ratio, not committing penalties, excellence in special teams, and making—but not surrendering—big plays. Again, those aren't novel ideas, but they are critical building blocks for playing up to our potential.

From a football standpoint, the most notable difference from Tampa was having the offensive pieces in place already. The Colts were only a year removed from going to the playoffs and had been successful before that, so we didn't need to completely rebuild the organization as we had in Tampa. Indianapolis had plenty of veterans on offense, along with coaches I knew and respected. Tom Moore, my coach from the University of Minnesota, was the offensive coordinator. He had quarterback Peyton Manning running the same no-huddle offense he had run with me in the 1970s.

I also knew running backs coach Gene Huey and offensive line coach Howard Mudd, and I liked what they were doing on offense. I knew I wanted to change the Colts' defensive system, however, and sell my overall vision for the team and how I hoped to accomplish success.

Sometimes a new coach's biggest challenge is to sell a new vision, to overcome a losing mind-set. That's what we had faced in Tampa. My challenge in Indy was partially the same. The Colts felt that their offense was good enough to win but that their defense was not. We would have to rework the defense, but I also saw ways in which the offense could do better as well. More than anything, my challenge with the Colts was to sell them on the idea that *teams* win championships. We needed to come together as a complete team—offense, defense, and special teams.

My key sale in seeking to bring about this paradigm shift was Peyton Manning, the focused, talented quarterback out of the University of Tennessee. I had met Peyton once before, in 1997. He and I were in Philadelphia for the Maxwell Football Club awards—he was the Collegiate Player of the Year, and I was the Professional Coach of the Year. We had shared a limo to the banquet. When I arrived in Indianapolis to coach the Colts, after the introductory press conference with Jim Irsay, Peyton came back to the facility to talk with me. I was certain that he had forgotten all about our previous meeting, but as we walked into my office together, he commented that we had met before but that I probably didn't remember.

"I actually do," I said.

"Me too. We shared a limo ride together. I sat in the back

with you and your wife, Lauren, and you said you wished that someday you could coach me but that you figured I'd be the first or second pick, so that wouldn't happen." He then went on to recount the remainder of the evening, including details I had forgotten. I was amazed, and I had learned something important about Peyton—he remembers *everything.*

He went on. "Coach, I'm glad you're here. I want to be *coached.* I want to win. I want you to treat me like any other player and teach me what I need to do because I want us to *win.*"

At the same time, he was concerned because he perceived that I might want to be conservative and not score points. He'd seen many Buccaneers games in which my teams scored very few points.

"I like points," I told him. "I mainly like having more points than the other team when the game ends. What I want to teach our offense is how to avoid turning over the ball and putting our defense in a bad position. What I want to teach our defense is how to stop the other team so they get the ball back for you.

"If we're going to win," I continued, "you're going to have to trust me. You're going to have to trust that as we add defensive talent, it's part of a strategy to build a complete team so we can win. We're going to be one team, with all three units supporting and strengthening each other."

Peyton nodded, but I'm not certain he really believed it. He had played four years, and most of the time, the offense had needed to score a lot of points for the Colts to win.

I kept talking about my philosophy of building a total team. "We've got enough talent that if we have eighty snaps on offense"—an average game will have seventy snaps for each team—"we should score forty points. If we don't take plays away from ourselves with turnovers, not many defenses will be able to stop us. We can still play aggressively on offense; we just have to be smart. If our offense is executing well, we shouldn't have to take chances that lead to turnovers. We'll learn to score without turning the ball over, and we'll learn to close out games on offense without giving the ball back to the other team.

"I'm not saying, 'When the defense gets better, we'll win.' We'll win when we start to work together as a team and not as separate units. We have to complement each other. Your job is to get us ahead and then let the defense do its work."

I promoted this philosophy to the Colts for about a year and a half before I felt that everyone, including Peyton, really believed in it. That first year was a struggle in some ways. We went 10–6, a decent record, even though not everyone fully bought into what we were selling. But I was confident we would get there in time.

Peyton Manning is critical to our offense because Tom Moore's system emphasizes quarterback play. And not just quarterback play but quarterback smarts, too. We run a one-back, "check with me" system. It seems new, but it really isn't. Much like the "new" Tampa 2 defense, the concepts have been around for a while; we're just using them effectively in a slightly different way.

Most teams run their offense by calling a play in the huddle and then running it. To camouflage their intentions, they shift players and put men in motion, trying to create mismatches with the defense. The pressure is on the offensive coordinator to anticipate the defense and send in the right play to the huddle. The quarterback's job is to execute what the coordinator has sent in. If the quarterback sees a defensive formation that won't allow the called play to succeed, he can "audible"— call another play at the line of scrimmage.

Our offensive strategy is quite different. It dates back to 1973, when I was in college playing for Tom Moore. As offensive coordinator, Tom gives Peyton a "concept," telling him whether we would rather run or pass. He also sends in four or five possible plays for Peyton to choose from. Sometimes, to help Peyton sort out what's going on, Tom will specify in what order to think through those four or five plays. But beyond that, the pressure is on the quarterback after he gets to the line of scrimmage. Our offense lines up quickly to give the quarterback enough time to look at the defensive coverage, identify any weak spots, and select the right play. We don't go in motion; we don't change personnel groupings; we don't shift—we just line up. The defense will try to disguise what they're doing as long as possible, but eventually they have to get into a position to actually play. Once they do, Peyton dials up whichever play he feels gives us the greatest chance of success.

This system is easy to use at home because when we have the ball, our fans stay quiet enough for our offense to hear the quarterback. On the road, with the crowd making a lot of noise, it's not so easy, which is why we came up with hand signals. Fans often think Peyton is just being theatrical, but he's really communicating to the backs and receivers. It's a system that has worked well for the Colts, especially once we were able to get our ultracompetitive quarterback on board with the concept of not taking unnecessary chances.

One of the first things I did when I arrived in Indianapolis was to call the chaplain, Ken Johnson. I had met Ken at a Fellowship of Christian Athletes camp several years earlier. I asked him to come to my office so we could talk about our schedule and how I wanted to work with him. When he came to see me, Ken told me that although he had been the Colts' chaplain for eleven years, he had never once been inside the head coach's office. I explained that I believed it was important for our players and our coaches to be connected spiritually, so he'd better get used to coming by.

Three moments stand out from that 2002 season for me. The first occurred on a Monday early in the season. The offensive staff was meeting just down the hall from my office. Our running backs coach, Gene Huey, who had been with the Colts through the tenures of several head coaches before I arrived, froze.

"Did you guys hear that? What was that sound?" The group stopped talking and listened. There was no sound other than laughter. "That's it—the laughing! Who is that?"

Clyde Christensen, who had come with me from Tampa, spoke up. "Those are Tony's boys, Jamie and Eric." My boys didn't have school that day and were visiting me at work. They were doing the same thing they had often done in Tampa— hanging out in my office, playing video games, and watching television—and I loved it. I especially loved it when I realized that families had not exactly been welcome in the Colts building, at least during the last few years.

When Clyde told me this story later, I made it a point to let everyone on the team and staff know that their families were always welcome in our area of the building. "Be respectful of other people's spaces," I said, "but don't view this building as off-limits." The coaches who came with me from Tampa assured everyone that kids would now be a pretty common sight, both at practice and on the sidelines during games.

The second memorable moment was our win in the Vet over the Eagles in November. We had always struggled against

Philadelphia when I was with Tampa—not scoring touchdowns and getting knocked out of the playoffs. That day we scored five touchdowns against a great defense on our way to a 35–13 win. Peyton threw for three touchdowns, and James Mungro ran for more than one hundred yards. As it turned out, it *was* possible to score touchdowns against the Eagles. I knew how tough Philadelphia was at home, and that was my first indication that our offense was going to do some extraordinary things over the next few years.

The third special moment didn't involve the Colts at all.

Derrick Brooks called me from Tampa to relate a story he thought I'd appreciate. The Buccaneers were preparing to play their first game under their new coach, Jon Gruden. After pregame warm-ups, they were back in the locker room, and Jon addressed the team with his final points before kickoff. As the team got up to leave the locker room, a few guys hesitated. This would normally have been the time when the team prayed before heading out to the field. Jon obviously wouldn't have known that; besides, he was in charge of gameday procedures now. Suddenly, Warren Sapp ordered everyone to come back. "We're going to pray," he said. "We've been doing this for six years, so somebody's got to step up and pray."

Derrick thought that would mean a lot to me. He was right.

We made it to the playoffs that year as a wildcard and had to travel to New York to face Herm Edwards's team, the Jets. They had gone 9–7 during the regular season, and it was shaping up to be a relatively even game. As always, I believed that if we could take a close game into the fourth quarter, we could win, even away from home. I told the team I was not a betting man, but if I were, I would bet my house on us.

The Jets beat us 41–0. Another good reason I'm not a betting man.

For those of us who had come up from Tampa—Clyde Christensen, Jim Caldwell, Ricky Thomas, Alan Williams, and me—this was the fourth straight playoff loss without a single touchdown. The day after our loss, in our final team meeting of the season, I spoke to the players. Although some of the guys wouldn't be with us when the next season rolled around, many of them would. So I treated the meeting as I always do, as if it were the first meeting of the following season.

"Be patient," I told them. "Keep doing the ordinary things better than anyone else. Be uncommon. Do what we do."

Following our playoff loss, I headed back down to Tampa to rejoin Lauren. When I took the job as head coach of the Colts, Lauren and I had agreed that it would not be the best time to move Tiara, who was finishing her junior year of high school. So for two years we had two homes: Lauren and the kids in Tampa while the kids were in school, and me in Indy. The family would fly up for games and during breaks. Even though we reunited most weekends during the season, the separation and constant travel had become a grind. So as soon as my immediate postseason responsibilities were over, I went to Tampa to be with them.

Lauren had loved Tampa from the moment we first arrived in 1996. But now, the Bucs' popularity was becoming a little bit of a problem for her. In fact, the weeks leading up to the Bucs' Super Bowl victory in 2003 were really the only time that living in Tampa was anything short of perfect for Lauren.

We were both torn because we wanted our old team to do well. Bill Parcells had decided not to accept the Glazers' offer to coach the Bucs after I was fired, and a few weeks later the Bucs had hired Jon Gruden. I liked Jon, and many of my players were still on the team. What made it difficult for me, their former coach, was that Jon had them playing so well. They set a franchise record with twelve wins in the regular season and then won their playoff opener against San Francisco. And after the Colts had won 35–13 at Philly that year, I felt sure the Bucs could go and win there as well, especially since Jon had them playing with so much confidence. Once the Bucs beat the Eagles, I knew they would probably be able to handle the Oakland Raiders in the Super Bowl.

So the Bucs' success was great—kind of. One year after I had been fired by Tampa Bay, my family and I were in Tampa for the Bucs' magical three-week run through the playoffs. Super Bowl frenzy was everywhere—in the paper, on the radio, on television, in everyone's conversation. The comment we kept hearing was, "Thank goodness Jon Gruden came along to finish the job for Tony Dungy." That was painful to hear. Jon and the players were gracious in their comments toward me, and I appreciated that, but those three weeks were still difficult. I was excited for the team, and of course the players were ecstatic. But it still hurt, not being there with them.

Sometimes character lessons are hard to swallow, but I know that God used that period to stretch our faith and to help us grow and learn to trust Him more fully. Now I knew how Moses, the Old Testament prophet, must have felt. He had led the Israelites for forty years through the desert, but he wasn't allowed into the Promised Land. He got to see it, but only from a distance. That "growing experience" couldn't have been pleasant for him either.

A Super Bowl win with the Bucs would have been wonderful. I could have used that platform in a tremendous way. But I think my getting fired had an even greater impact. It's easy to be gracious when you're getting carried off the field in celebration. It's more difficult when you're asked to pack up your desk and your pass code doesn't work anymore. I think people look more closely at our actions in the rough times, when the emotions are raw and our guard is down. That's when our true character shows and we find out if our faith is real. If I'm going to call myself a Christian, I have to honor Jesus in the disappointments, too.

I believed then, and I believe now, that God is in control of everything. This was how He wanted it. I was certain there were things for me to learn and to accomplish for the Lord in Indianapolis. Otherwise we would have never left Tampa.

If we had stayed in Tampa, would the Bucs have gotten to the Super Bowl? Yes, I believe so, if we had stayed the course. But that's just speculation. Under Jon, the Bucs got the job done.

Those three weeks were the toughest part of the transition process for Lauren and me. But through it all, we never doubted that God was using this experience to mold and teach us.

A BIRTHDAY BLESSING

CHAPTER SIXTEEN

Talent is God-given; be thankful.
Praise is man-given; be humble.
Conceit is self-given; be careful.
  DAVE DRISCOLL

MIKE VANDERJAGT, our kicker, contributed to a rocky beginning for our 2003 season.

Shortly into the off-season, Mike gave a wide-ranging interview that . . . well, let's just say I wish he would have phrased some things differently. Coming off our 41–0 loss to the Jets, Mike appeared on a Canadian TV station. He mostly talked about how frustrated he was about our loss, but the comments that seemed to get the most notice were those aimed at Peyton Manning and me. Mike hinted that the leadership of the team was insufficient. He said the team needed "somebody who is going to get in people's face and yell and scream" and that I was too "mild mannered" and even-keeled for us to be successful.

My first reaction was that he was just going to have to get used to it. This is the way I coach, and I believed then and believe now that it is the best way to win football games and lead people. I had grown up with this philosophy. My mom used to say that a good leader gets people to follow him because they want to, not because he makes them—a principle reinforced by Coach Noll. He always told me that players want to be good and that the coach's job is to teach them and give them the tools they need to improve. I never have been the type to "get in people's face," and I never will be.

My second reaction to Mike's comments was to release or trade him. What he had said was completely unacceptable. We were a team, and neither he nor anyone else could put himself above the group. I called Mike at his home in Toronto and told him I needed to see him as quickly as possible.

I have never liked cut days during training camp. Those are the days when we have to reduce our roster from eighty players down to sixty-five, and then finally to fifty-three. Cut days are my least favorite days in coaching. No matter how long you've been a coach, I don't think you ever get used to it. Usually the guys you have to release have done nothing wrong—on the contrary, they have done everything you have asked and have gone to the limits of their ability. But in the end, they simply are not as talented or they don't fit our schemes as well as someone else.

I actually make it worse on myself because I bring each player in to talk with me personally, just as Coach Perkins did with me. Sometimes I have a great deal to say; other times I keep it short. But it's awkward and painful every time. I used to think that all head coaches did that, until I received a call from an agent who wanted to thank me for the way I had released his client. It was the player's third time being cut, he told me, but the first time that a coach had ever spoken to him personally. That surprised me, but it also reinforced my resolve to continue doing it that way no matter how tough it was.

A philosophical tension always seems to exist between personnel departments and coaches. As they bring in new players, the personnel people are usually looking for that diamond in the rough. The reality is, however, when you're releasing the eighty-fifth best guy on your roster in August and signing someone who isn't on a roster anywhere, that replacement is likely to be very rough—and usually not a diamond.

More important, however, is the fact that I believe strongly in the idea of the team as a family. I can't very well preach unity and tell the guys we're all in this together and everyone's important, then cut a guy because we *might* improve by one percent if we bring in someone else.

Again, it probably goes back to my playing days. I was never a star, and I know what it was like to be a bottom-of-the-roster guy. I will never cut a player just to keep the other guys on their toes, as some do.

I don't generally like to make individual cuts either, unless unusual circumstances force me to. But there are times when a player needs to be removed from the team, and that time was now. I was steamed. And after our loss to the Jets, no one else was in a good mood, either. At our final team meeting, I had told the players that we had to stick together, that people were going to try to pick us apart and get us splintered in different directions. I didn't think it would happen from within, but that's exactly where it was now coming from. I was burning.

Mike Vanderjagt was finished with the Colts, and the sooner he got to Indianapolis for me to cut him, the better.

Mike still had to travel from Toronto to Indianapolis. Before he arrived, my son Jamie intervened. Jamie and Eric were often around the facility in those days, hanging out in my office or around the guys. While Eric usually kept to himself, Jamie was always looking to make new friends. He generally believed that anyone he met was a potential friend. If anyone even so much as smiled at Jamie, it was confirmation enough that he had added another friend to the ranks. Jamie seemed especially drawn to people who were down on their luck—like talkative kickers. Jamie had been reading the sports pages, and he came into my office to ask me about the situation.

"Why is everybody mad at Mike, Dad?"

"Because of what he said."

"Dad, you can't get rid of Mike. He's my friend."

"I can promise you this, Jamie," I said, trying to reassure my concerned sixteen-year-old. "I won't do anything just because of what other people are saying or because of what's in the paper. I plan to bring him in here and talk to him. If I do decide to get rid of him, it will only be because the team needs it."

Jamie seemed pacified, at least for the moment, but I knew he was still giving it a great deal of thought.

Mike took two days to get to Indianapolis from Toronto. If he had arrived the night I first called him, I'm sure I would have cut him or asked Bill Polian, our president, to trade him. The following day I still felt the same way. But on the third day, I was reading our daily Bible passage—a number of us, both coaches and players, were still reading through the Bible each year. It was Matthew 21:28-32, a parable Jesus told about a father and two sons. The father told the two sons to go work in the vineyard. The first son said he would not go but later changed his mind and went anyway. The second son said he would go, but then he didn't. Jesus' point is that the first son was obedient in spite of his words. It's what is in our hearts that matters, even if our words say otherwise.

I immediately realized that my situation was very similar to this parable. I had heard Mike's words in the press and rushed to judgment without hearing his side of the story. Because he had done the very thing I had warned the team *not* to do during our last team meeting, I was still inclined to cut him. But I knew I needed to hear what was in his heart before I made my decision. I still didn't think there was anything he could say to change my mind, but I knew I had to hear Mike's side.

When Mike finally came in, he didn't deny making those statements, and he did apologize. He said he had been frustrated, and he explained that the media had not reported what he had been *trying* to say. Things had not come out the way he had wanted them to.

We talked through his comments at length. I told him he had done damage to our team that would be difficult to undo, and I would have to think that through.

Then I asked him the most important question: "Do you still want to kick for the Colts?"

He immediately said that he did, more than anything in the world. He had no desire to go anywhere else. He believed we could be successful, and he wanted to be a part of that journey.

It's amazing how many times my assigned daily Scripture reading has been something I needed to read, fitting exactly where I was and what I was going through at the time. That day, I decided that leading as Jesus would lead meant looking into Mike's heart.

After talking with Mike, I went against the advice I was getting from most of the football experts and decided to keep him on our team.

Later that summer, I found myself penning my annual letters to Warren Sapp and Derrick Brooks.

This tradition had begun in 1996, when I wrote a short

note to Warren about the things we were going to need from him if we wanted to win that year. Joe Greene, the cornerstone player of those great 1970s Steelers teams, had once told me about the way Coach Noll had challenged him to be a great player and a great leader. In 1996, I knew we needed Warren to play at an incredibly high level to set the bar for the rest of the team, so I wrote him a letter.

Warren Sapp is one of the most unique personalities I've ever had the privilege of meeting. Despite his reputation, he was always a joy to coach because he had a tremendous desire to win. He's tough to figure out sometimes and can be quite volatile, but he's genuine and—though he doesn't always want you to know it—he's pretty soft-hearted. He's also incredibly intelligent. He can—and will—give educated opinions on everything from global warming to Middle East politics.

That first year, Warren responded well to my preseason letter, so I kept it up. My letters moved from talking about individual goals for Warren to season goals, encouraging him as a leader of the defense.

Four years later, Derrick—Warren's roommate in training camp and on the road—found out about the letters. He insisted that I write to him as well.

When I left the Buccaneers, I faced a dilemma: should I stop writing to Warren and Derrick? They weren't *my* players anymore. But my relationship with those two guys was not just about their play on the field—I knew they would continue to be outstanding athletes.

What I really wanted was for them to step up and take leadership roles. They needed to make sure everyone stayed together, followed the new coach, and continued to improve. As long as they played, I would be watching them continue to make me proud. I decided to keep writing to them.

And if my words helped Warren and Derrick have more

productive seasons, I figured Jon Gruden and Monte Kiffin wouldn't mind.

+ + +

Despite the Vanderjagt incident, we started the regular 2003 season hot. At the end of September, we were 4–0 and looking for our fifth straight win. We were playing well on both sides of the ball, and Mike Vanderjagt was kicking well.

Our fifth game was a matchup straight out of a Hollywood script. On October 6, on Monday Night Football—and my forty-eighth birthday—we would play the defending Super Bowl champions and my old team, the Buccaneers. In Tampa, no less.

I tried to keep things as normal as possible that week. I remembered all too well a situation we had faced while I was at Tampa Bay, after we had traded with the Jets for Keyshawn Johnson. When we played the Jets the following year, Rich McKay and I let Key have a separate press conference before the normal media session. We figured that way he could address all the New York questions at once, then the distractions would die down and we could get back to normal. Unfortunately, it had the opposite effect. With all the attention focused on him, Key made some comments that really stirred things up in New York. I think it also gave our team the impression that there was something different about that game. Now, having learned that lesson, I was determined to keep the preparation for the Colts–Bucs game the same as it had been every other week. I didn't allow any extra interview time, even with those Tampa reporters I had known for six years.

I prayed all week that it would be a smooth return to Tampa and that I wouldn't get too emotional—high or low. The week went by fairly smoothly, but Monday night did turn out to be an incredibly emotional evening for me. Pregame was such a special experience as I visited with the Buccaneers coaches, players, and staff on the field. I was experiencing so many emotions and so many good memories, I'm afraid I wasn't of much use to the Colts during pregame, as I spent most of my time trying not to cry.

We headed off the field and returned to the visitors' locker room to await kickoff. Before that day, I had never been in that locker room, and I had never come onto the field through the visitors' tunnel. I was a little anxious about the pregame introductions. In the NFL, each team introduces either its starting offense or defense, followed by the head coach. I usually don't pay much attention to that introduction—that's my time to look at the corners of the stadium—but this time I wasn't sure how I would react. Jamie and Eric were with me on the field, and Lauren and Tiara were in the stands with friends. I wondered how the crowd would respond to me. I didn't know what they thought of me anymore.

As we got closer to kickoff, I realized that the crowd's reaction mattered a great deal to me. I knew I would get some boos—after all, I was now on the opposing sideline—but Tampa had been our home for six years, and the people of that community were an important part of our lives. I hoped that, in spite of my having left the Bucs, the people of our old community would be welcoming. I just didn't know what to expect.

I was caught completely by surprise when the crowd erupted with applause as soon as my name was called. I was overwhelmed. The tears I had fought back earlier could no longer be quelled. I didn't know it then, but this would not be the last time the fans of Tampa would rally around me.

The ovation was a very moving moment, but it was long

gone by the time we returned to the locker room at halftime, trailing 21–0. We hadn't played our game at all. The Buccaneers' top-ranked defense had given up only eighty-six yards to us in the first half, while our sixth-ranked defense had been torched for 239 yards. I was extremely disappointed. Here we had a chance to show the country what we were all about, and so far we had responded by self-destructing. We had nobody to blame but ourselves.

We couldn't have played any worse than we did in the first thirty minutes of the game, even though I had preached all week to our guys that we couldn't afford to fall behind against Tampa Bay. I had explained over and over that if the Bucs defense knew we had to pass, their pass rush would just tee off. Their defense was too strong if we were playing from behind. At halftime, I explained that we needed to "do what we do" with passion and execution and see what happened.

The guys responded—initially. We came out and scored on our opening drive to make it 21–7. But the Bucs then drove the length of the field for a touchdown, and the third quarter ended with us still down by twenty-one.

We scored another touchdown to start the fourth quarter, but then, with just over five minutes left in the game, Bucs cornerback Ronde Barber picked off a pass from Peyton and ran it back for a Tampa Bay touchdown and a 35–14 lead.

I had been in this position many times with the Buccaneers defense, and it was never pretty for the opposing offense. I turned to Tom Moore before the kickoff. Our offense was set to go back onto the field, but I felt there was no point in getting anyone hurt now; playing on Monday night meant we had a short week to prepare for our next game. I thought we ought to take the first group off the field, especially since the Bucs defensive line would be coming full bore with a big lead. "Let's get Peyton and the other starters out of there."

"Tony, let's just go one more drive and see what happens," Tom counseled.

Brad Pyatt ran the kickoff back eighty-seven yards to Tampa's twelve yard line, and we sent the first-team offense back out there. Four plays later, we scored. 35–21.

We tried an onside kick and recovered the ball. We scored again, stopped them, and scored a third time to tie the game and send it into overtime. We had scored three touchdowns in the last 3:43 of the game.

We won in overtime, 38–35, when Mike Vanderjagt kicked a field goal.

As I walked back to the locker room, it dawned on me. The Lord had allowed us to win, but only in a way in which *He* had to get the credit. No NFL team had ever come back from three touchdowns behind in the final four minutes, but we did it while playing poorly—on the road, on Monday Night Football—against the Super Bowl champions with the top defense in the NFL.

In Tampa, on my birthday.

It was nothing short of miraculous. Such a thing is almost impossible to imagine, but nothing is impossible for God to accomplish.

Back in the locker room, Lauren had a cake waiting, and the guys sang "Happy Birthday" to me.

John Lynch, Tampa Bay's All-Pro strong safety, waited for me to come out of the locker room so he could give me a hug, even though by that time it was approaching 2 a.m.

That game gave us all a new perspective on faith and the way God works in the circumstances of our lives. It also reinforced what we already knew—that if we do what we do without panicking, we can accomplish great things. We would draw on that lesson in the future.

A few weeks later, we again traveled to Florida for a division game against the Jaguars.

We were preparing for kickoff under the gray skies, with a light, cool breeze blowing off the St. Johns River across the stadium. Suddenly, I was tapped on the shoulder by a security officer.

"Coach, I'm sorry, but your son can't be on the sideline."

I was startled, and it took me a moment to realize he was talking about Eric, who was eleven at the time and had been at my side for various games—when it wasn't Jamie's turn—for the last four seasons.

"No," I said. "He's going to stay with me for the game."

The guard was firm. "Sorry, Coach, but he can't be on the sideline. League rules."

I was just as firm. As our debate continued, I heard through my headset that the guys were about to take the field.

"He's been doing this since he was seven. He'll be right here. With me."

"Sorry, he's going to have to go."

This had gone on long enough. "He's staying here with me—"

"Coach—"

I refused to allow the interruption. "—and if you remove him from this sideline, I'm taking my team to the locker room, where we'll change and then leave on our buses. You can explain to Wayne [Weaver, the Jaguars' owner] why he's refunding everyone's money."

The guard blinked, and I finished my thought.

"You might want to double-check with your head coach before you do that, however."

That was the last I heard of the issue. No one has brought it up since.

Of course, Eric is now as tall as I am, and I'm wondering when Jordan will be ready for a trip to Jacksonville.

✦ ✦ ✦

Two other games were noteworthy for me that season. At the end of November, we hosted the New England Patriots. Just like the Tampa Bay game, we played poorly at first and had to claw our way back, scoring a touchdown twelve seconds before halftime to cut their lead to 17–10.

One of the decisions I always have to make is our kickoff strategy. When the opponent has a dangerous return man or when there is very little time left, teams often "squib" kick the ball to prevent a long return.

With twelve seconds to go in the half, I inexplicably decided to kick it deep. Bethel Johnson ran it back for a touchdown and a 24–10 halftime lead for New England. One of my dumbest decisions ever.

In the second half, we fell behind by 21 again but came back to tie it—Tampa all over again. This time, however, New England scored, and the game ended with us on their one yard line, unable to score the winning touchdown.

The other memorable game was our final game of the regular season against Houston. We needed a win for the division title, but we fell behind by two touchdowns in the fourth quarter. Then Peyton handed off to Edgerrin James for a touchdown to start the comeback.

With 3:50 remaining, our wide receiver Brandon Stokely made an acrobatic catch to tie the Texans. We ended up winning the game on the final play—a 43-yard field goal by Mike Vanderjagt.

With that kick, Mike cinched a home playoff game for the

Colts and set an NFL record by making his 41st consecutive field goal.

As the guys carried Mike off the field, I looked at Jamie, who was running alongside me. "Good call," I told him. He flashed me his big, bright smile.

We opened the 2003 playoffs at home against Denver, who had beaten us just two weeks earlier. They had run against us at will in a game we had needed for a first-round bye. Instead, we lost 31–17. Now that we were in the playoffs, the media asked what we were going to do differently. "Nothing," I told them. "We're going to do what we always do, only do it better."

And we did. We drilled the Broncos 41–10 in a game in which everything went right.

We then traveled to play the number two seed, Kansas City. It was a terrific time for me, returning to Kansas City and the good memories of coaching with the Chiefs. They hadn't lost any home games during the regular season, and they had one of the loudest stadiums in the NFL. We stayed hot on offense, though, winning the game 38–31.

In two playoff games, we had scored ten touchdowns without a single punt. Now we were headed to New England for a rematch of the November game. The AFC Championship and a trip to the Super Bowl were on the line. Countless times that week, people pointed out that if we had only scored from the one yard line during the regular season game, we would be hosting the game in Indianapolis rather than playing in New England. I kept thinking about that kickoff to Bethel Johnson with twelve seconds to go in the first half.

The game started slowly for us. We had trouble moving

the ball and turned it over a couple of times. The Patriots controlled the tempo and kept the ball away from us with a good offensive game plan. They took the lead and held it throughout the game. As bad as it was, though, we got the ball back in the last few minutes, down 21–14. We needed one good drive to tie the game. All year we had converted in these situations, and I was confident we could do it this time. But once again, the New England defense stopped us when it counted. An insurance field goal by Adam Vinatieri made the final score 24–14.

The New England Patriots rarely made mistakes, and they knew how to capitalize on the mistakes of their opponents. They were the epitome of what Coach Noll had always talked about: they did the ordinary things better than everyone else. And because of that, I knew we would continue to have our problems with them, just as everyone else did.

Coaching the Pro Bowl that year was completely different from coaching it in 1999. Four years earlier, the Tampa Bay staff was excited about getting to the championship game but fearful because we didn't have the confidence of our owners. In 2003, we were down about losing the championship game, but we knew that everyone in the organization believed we were heading in the right direction. I was trusting that the Lord had our future in His hands, and I took comfort in these words of encouragement from Jeremiah 29:11: "'For I know the plans I have for you,' says the LORD. 'They are plans for good and not for disaster, to give you a future and a hope.'"

While I knew very well from my own experience that nothing is guaranteed, I also knew we were a good team. The guys were really beginning to buy into the mission and strategies we had been teaching. About halfway through the 2003 season, I could see the light go on for Peyton. He was seeing the progress our defense was making and didn't feel the need to take as many risks. Tom Moore and our quarterback coach Jim Caldwell had done such a good job preparing him that we were productive, with significantly fewer turnovers.

At some point during the 2003 season, Jim Irsay began having my dad fly with us to our away games. That was typical of the little things Jim does for all his employees, not just the head coach. So my dad was at the New England game, as he had been at just about every one of my games since I was twelve years old. For the sixth time, he saw my season end with a play-off loss. He was disappointed that we hadn't played well enough to win, but he never changed his expression or demeanor. He told me not to get discouraged and that he knew we'd get to the Super Bowl if we continued to persevere.

DEATH BY INCHES

CHAPTER SEVENTEEN

When you can do the common things of life in an uncommon way, you will command the attention of the world.
GEORGE WASHINGTON CARVER

I WAS EXCITED and believed that everything was moving in the right direction for the Colts. When the 2004 season rolled around, we felt as if we were on the cusp of taking that final step and making it to the Super Bowl. In the second round of the 2004 draft, we added another key piece to the puzzle with Bob Sanders, a safety from the University of Iowa. Right after the draft, however, that good feeling was temporarily interrupted when I received a phone call from my dad. He told me that although he felt great, a routine physical had revealed a problem with his blood work. Another test confirmed the doctor's suspicions: leukemia.

I was in shock because my dad was in such great shape for his age. Every day he woke up at five-thirty, rode his bike about five miles to Bob Evans for breakfast, and then rode back home. Two days a week, he went to the YMCA to swim. I could hardly believe this vigorous man had a serious health problem.

My sister Lauren, the doctor, brought my dad to Indianapolis for treatment at the world-class oncology center at the Indiana University School of Medicine. He went through an extensive chemotherapy regimen over the next couple of months. I loved that time with him. He didn't seem to be experiencing any of the side effects the doctors had warned us about. Just sitting together in his hospital room was wonderful.

We reminisced about fishing and hooks through the ear and Tigers games and Michigan and Michigan State games. I reminded him of the times when we had visited my aunt and uncle, staying up late to watch war movies and Westerns with them. Even though my dad had thought I should be in bed, my uncle Paul had always talked him into letting me stay up. My dad remembered playing catch and shooting baskets with me—all the quality moments that a father spends with his son. He especially wanted to know how our off-season workouts were going.

During my days with my dad, I thought a lot about the time I had spent with my own children. When I was growing up, my dad spent *quality* and *quantity* time with us. He always made sure he was around the house and at our games. I hadn't always done that with my children. I had tried to shorten my work days, to give the players Sundays off during the season whenever possible, and to make sure everyone got home at a reasonable hour. But the time I had spent with my children was nowhere near the amount of time my dad had made for us. I knew I was spending as much time as I could with my kids, but compared to my dad, it just didn't seem like I was doing enough. I was grateful for the times we had shared as a family but was disappointed in myself.

This was probably the first time I ever thought about purposely leaving coaching of my own accord. I had already made adjustments years ago—starting meetings later so I could take my children to school, never sleeping at the office, allowing families to be together in our offices—and short of leaving the profession, I didn't think there were any other changes I could make. I began to give the idea some serious thought. Football is a vocation and an opportunity for ministry. But it's not a life.

It helped a little knowing that Lauren and the kids would be moving to Indianapolis full-time that summer, even though we would still keep the house in Tampa. Tiara had finished high school, and after missing two years of driving my kids to school, I was eager to see them again on a daily basis.

In June we got some great news from my dad's doctors. The leukemia was in remission, and my dad was going to be able to go home to my sister's house. We were relieved and thrilled. My dad was excited because he wanted to be around when we made it to the Super Bowl. He had always claimed that a Super Bowl appearance was inevitable for us if we stayed the course and did what we did.

Less than a week later, the tide turned again when my sister called and said that we needed to come to the hospital immediately to visit my dad before he died. With his white-blood-cell count extremely low from the chemotherapy, his immune system had been vulnerable, and he had developed an infection. He died that night, June 8, only twenty-nine months after my mom had passed.

In the space of two months, we went from the fears of a leukemia diagnosis and the rigors of the treatment to the euphoria of his recovery to loss and grief.

A lot of family members came into town the next day, and I needed to attend to the last day of our off-season workouts. Actually I didn't really need to be there—the assistants could have handled it. It was only a couple of hours. But then I thought about my dad and the things he had always taught me. More than anything else, my dad loved watching us practice. I knew he would have wanted me to be with my team.

I arrived at the facility. Jeff Saturday, a great player and even better person, was one of the few players who knew my dad had died. After practice, Jeff let the team know about my dad's death before I explained why I was there with them that day.

"My dad always felt like practice was where you did your job. If a student learned during the week and studied hard, the test would be easy and take care of itself. It's the same way with practice. He liked you guys, and he especially liked the way you practice. That's why he always felt confident that we were going to do well."

Most of the veterans knew my dad because he had been around so much. But that day, our rookies learned a little bit about why I am the way I am.

Under a clear, blue sky, a man sprints to catch a speeding train. He has fired a machine gun at his pursuers—Nazis—and thrown grenades at them, setting various other charges and traps for them as well. Now, he has almost caught up with the German transport train that he and his fellow prisoners of war have commandeered and are riding into Switzerland. He closes in on the train, running with his hand out . . . and is shot and killed with his hand just inches from his fellow prisoners and only feet away from the Swiss border and safety.

Death by inches.

I showed that movie clip in the first meeting of training camp in 2004. When the clip ended, I explained the theory of *death by inches,* which Frank Sinatra suffered at the end of *Von Ryan's Express.* It was one of those movies I had watched as a boy late at night with my uncle Paul, my aunt Rosemarie, and my dad. I explained to the team that it wasn't the big things that had tripped us up in previous years but rather a combination of small details. By focusing on those details—inches—we could reach our goal rather than coming up just short.

"We're not going to reinvent the wheel. We're going to do what we do; we're just going to do it better. We're not going to focus on improving last year's 12–4 season, but we are going to look to improve and win our first game. And then we'll get better and win our second game. We're going to do it by doing the little things right."

Every year, the topic of my first talk at training camp is family. I want each guy to understand that his family is his first priority.

"Deal with them, focus on them, and take care of any issues or problems related to them," I said to the team in 2004. "If I ever learn that there was something with your family that needed to be addressed and you put team considerations before family without talking with me, there is going to be a problem. A big problem." *Especially now,* I thought. After reflecting on all those memories with my dad, I realized that we just don't have family forever. When you're thinking about death, you get more focused on time—the time you have today—and how it seems to be screaming past.

As a head coach, I'm interviewed by the media a great deal, and I pride myself in answering questions honestly without becoming a distraction. As a result, I tend not to find myself in the midst of controversy. But in 2004, I did—more than once. I don't usually think in terms of sound bites, but I've learned that I have to be more aware of the way they can be misused and the power they have to shape opinions.

The first incident occurred just after the Philadelphia Eagles played on Monday Night Football. At the time, ABC was opening those broadcasts with skits featuring star players. That week's skit showed a white actress from *Desperate Housewives* standing alone in the locker room with Philadelphia Eagles receiver Terrell Owens, who is African American. Wearing only a towel, she provocatively asked Terrell to skip the game for her and, after several rebuffs, finally convinced him, dropping her towel and jumping into his arms. TO grinned and said something along the lines of, "The guys will understand."

I didn't get home that night until after the game had started, so I didn't know anything about the skit until the next day. When I saw a tape of the opening, I couldn't believe it. I was disgusted. Later I asked Eric, who was then twelve, if he had seen the beginning of the game. He told me he had, so we talked about it for a while. Eric had been in the locker room before enough games to know that something like that could never happen, and he thought the skit was "dumb." I wondered, however, what other young kids might be thinking after watching that skit. I also wondered what Eric was *thinking* but not telling me.

During my next media session, I didn't wait for anyone to ask about the broadcast. I brought it up and said I thought it was totally inappropriate. I said I was displeased with the sexual nature of the skit and its being shown on prime time just before a nationally televised, family-friendly football game. I said I thought it was a slam on NFL football players, and I was upset with ABC for using an African American player.

Unfortunately, of the many things I objected to in the

skit, the only thing people focused on was that last statement. I began to hear comments that I was a "racist" and opposed to interracial dating, which isn't true and entirely missed the point I had tried to make. I did believe that ABC was either very insensitive or deliberately stereotypical in using an African American player for that skit, but my comments had nothing to do with the actress. I knew for a fact that the network had not approached Peyton Manning about being in the skit, and I was sure they would not have asked Bret Favre or Tom Brady either. I was disappointed in ABC for coming up with the idea, and I was disappointed in TO for going along with it. I was surprised that more players, especially those who were African American, didn't see anything wrong with it. Terrell had created the perception—even if it was in jest—that he would be willing to miss a kickoff to have sex with a stranger. The whole thing sent the wrong message about morality, responsibility, and NFL players to kids like Eric. But all of that got lost just because I mentioned race.

Some people did get what I was trying to say. Bill Belichick, head coach of the New England Patriots, was one of those people. He backed me, saying as I had that he'd be willing to take a pay cut if the NFL needed commercials like that to pay the bills.

The second media stir occurred when I tried to bring a little balance and levity to an incident involving Randy Moss of the Minnesota Vikings. Thankfully, this was a much smaller deal. After a touchdown during a playoff game at Lambeau Field, Moss pretended to moon the fans. His actions were clearly inappropriate, and I didn't want to excuse them, but at the same time, I was somewhat amused because I knew what was behind Randy's act. When asked about it, I said if there were ever a place we could count on for a mooning, it was at Lambeau. I had played there every season from 1992 to 2001, sometimes more than once, and I had learned that it was tradition there for a few Packers fans to drop their pants around their ankles and moon the visiting team's bus as it left, regardless of the temperature. When Moss scored the winning touchdown, I knew what he was doing; he was beating those Packers fans to the punch.

I got plenty of mail from people who thought I showed a double standard in defending Moss after being so outspoken about protecting the image of our players in the ABC incident, and they were right. In retrospect, I should have been much more clear in stating that I was explaining, not condoning, what Randy Moss had done.

Those two incidents made me even more aware of the need to think through the ramifications of everything I say as a head coach. I'm still learning.

That was off the field. On the field, we had another fun year. We went 12–4 and won the AFC South Division for the second straight year. Our defense continued to improve, but our offense, especially our passing game, reached a level never seen before. Marvin Harrison had been playing at a Hall of Fame level as our right wide receiver for several years. Reggie Wayne, our first-round draft choice in 2001, was now growing comfortable in his role on the left side, and the year before, we had acquired Brandon Stokley to play in the slot. In 2004, those three players became the first set of teammates in NFL history to each reach a thousand yards receiving and ten touchdown catches in the same year.

Peyton Manning set an NFL record with forty-nine touchdown passes. That was a great accomplishment, and I was especially pleased that he set this record while throwing only ten interceptions. Our prophetic conversation in 2002 was coming true, and the transformation of our offensive mind-set was clear. Peyton had thrown twenty-three interceptions the year before I arrived and nineteen our first year together. In 2003 and 2004 he had thrown only ten each year, and his touchdown passes were now coming in record numbers. We were finally playing explosive football without committing turnovers.

My biggest learning experience that year, however, was from a game we lost. We played Kansas City on Halloween. We had beaten them in the playoffs the year before in a shoot-out, but this year they lit us up, 45–35. We had just lost two games in a row, something that hadn't happened for a long time. I sensed that the guys were concerned, especially about the defense.

I was very direct at Monday's team meeting. "Men, we're not going to bring in any new players. We're not going to add any new defensive schemes. In fact, we're not going to change anything. We are the same group that went to the playoffs last year. We just have to do our jobs a little bit better, a little bit faster, a little bit sharper."

I really didn't think anything of it at the time—that's just what I thought we needed to do—but Gary Brackett, one of our linebackers, said later that because of that reassurance, the players were able to relax and concentrate on improving rather than worry about whether they still had a job. I would use that talk again during a critical time down the road.

Bill Belichick, New England's head coach, had supported me over the ABC flap, but of course he wasn't much support to me on the field—we still didn't break through and beat the Patriots. As sharp as we had played most of the year, we just couldn't seem to duplicate that sharpness against New England.

We lost the season opener to them in Foxboro, Massachusetts, 27–24. That was as disappointed as I've ever been after a game, and I let the players know I was upset. We fumbled twice (once at their one yard line) and threw an interception in the end zone. We gave up some big plays on defense but still had a chance to win at the end. We were driving in the last minute but gave up a sack with a missed blocking assignment. Then Mike missed his first field goal in over a year. We had lost to the Patriots again because they had done the ordinary things better than we had.

I knew we were going to have a good football team, but I had known New England would too. Over the rest of the season, we would have to win two more games than the Patriots to avoid coming back to Foxboro in the playoffs. It would be tough to do.

We played well the rest of the year, but we just couldn't make up that ground on the Patriots. So in January, we found ourselves back in Foxboro, and the game followed the same maddening script. We fell behind early, allowed them to control the football, and lost 20–3. New England had a great football team, and they would go on to win another Super Bowl that year. Through these painful defeats, we never had the feeling that we *couldn't* beat them; we simply had to play as well against them as we had played against other teams. Easier said than done.

Once again, I closed out the 2004 season in the visitors' locker room in Foxboro, telling our players that we would regroup, work hard, and do what we do in 2005.

I hoped they wouldn't lose faith, because I was certain that 2005 would be an unforgettable year.

AN UNFORGETTABLE SEASON

CHAPTER EIGHTEEN

And we know that God causes everything to work together for the good of those who love God and are called according to his purpose for them.
    ROMANS 8:28

I DON'T HAVE THE STRENGTH or wisdom to get through a single day without guidance and grace from God. That became apparent once again as the naysayers were out in full force after the 2004 season. Our offense had been so explosive and had set so many records. People figured if we couldn't win with that team, we might never win at all. They said the Colts' "window of opportunity" was closing. I didn't think so.

Some were saying the following year's regular season was irrelevant for our team, that we would be defined only by what happened in the playoffs. I didn't want that idea to sink into the team's thinking. I believed just the opposite: if we did what we were supposed to do—in the off-season, in training camp, and in the regular season—the playoffs would take care of themselves. Eventually. Getting to the playoffs is really difficult. As always, we would have to show up ready to do our conditioning work in March, trudge through the heat of training camp in August, and play one play at a time all fall until we won enough games to get in. Then we would have to trust that we were finally going to play well enough to advance. That was the formula—no shortcuts.

Just like the lessons *death by inches* had taught us in 2004, I wanted the team to remember that one detail at a time builds the whole. Like my dad always said, the test would be easy if you did what you were supposed to do in class every day. Practice was where we did our job.

The trick would be keeping everyone believing in that formula. I had said these same things for three years, and we hadn't yet reached the Super Bowl. I talked to several of the team leaders to make sure they were still on board and ready to continue selling our vision. We had become a good team by the way we had done things, and I wasn't going to make any drastic changes.

The 2005 training camp started as uneventfully as our prior camps. I spoke to the team about family, as always, and then I talked about a Michael Jordan interview I'd seen on ESPN Classic. The interview was conducted just after the Bulls had been knocked out of the playoffs for the second year in a row by the Detroit Pistons. "Do you ever think you'll make it to the NBA Finals?" the reporter asked. My players in the team meeting room chuckled. Of course, we all knew that Jordan would go on to win six NBA championships.

I wanted them to realize that there was a time when even Michael Jordan kept getting close but didn't make the finals. When Jordan was asked about his team's inability to beat the Pistons, he said they couldn't worry about the Pistons. They had to keep improving their team until they could beat *any-one*—and that's what they did. I wanted us to take this same approach. Even though we heard so much about coming up short against New England, I didn't want us to focus our attention on them. I wanted to concentrate on *us*. That classic Jordan interview during the Bulls' building years was laughable in 2005. I hoped there would be a time when the questions about the Colts would seem just as ridiculous.

After starting the season 5–0, Leslie Frazier, one of my assistant coaches, bought me a blank journal. He had been urging me to write a book, and he was convinced that 2005 was going to be a special season. In October, it sure looked that way. Bill Polian, our president, has a great eye for talent, and he had put together a tremendous team. Our high draft choices were all coming through for us. And some of our lower-round draft choices, such as linebacker Cato June and defensive end Robert Mathis, were starting to play like Pro Bowlers. Our only real question mark was in the middle of our defensive line. Just before the regular season began, Bill had signed Corey Simon, a former Pro Bowl tackle who had been locked in a contract dispute with the Philadelphia Eagles. Around the league, Corey's signing was viewed as a coup that just might vault us into the Super Bowl. The way we played that first month, it was hard to argue with that. I still didn't think I would ever write a book, but I figured it might be worth keeping a journal of the season anyway.

According to my journal, we were studying Acts 15 in our coaches' Bible study at the time, and we'd been reading about Paul, who on more than one occasion suffered in a cold and damp jail cell. "Patience in waiting out God's plan," I wrote. "Do what you're supposed to do while waiting." I wondered if I could do it. I knew I couldn't if I had to do it alone.

That week we beat the Rams on Monday Night Football, coming back from a 17-point deficit to win by 17. Quite a swing.

Three weeks later, we played the Patriots in Foxboro again. We were undefeated, and New England was not playing that well, but even so, the media made a big deal of the game. I kept preaching to our guys that we shouldn't think about it being New England. We just needed to focus on the Colts. We needed to think about what it took for us to play well and not worry about anything else. Going into the game, I really believed we would finally play well up there. It was a night game, so I had some extra time during the day. I took my customary late-morning walk through Providence and the campus of Brown University. It was such a pretty fall day, I wished we were playing at 1 p.m. As I walked, I had a calm feeling inside; I was sure we were going to execute well.

We did just that. Peyton Manning and our receivers had a big game, as did running back Edgerrin James. We won, 40–21. Walking back to the locker room, I started to get concerned about how the media would react to this win. After beating the defending champs in their stadium, I was sure they would be ready to anoint us the new kings. Since we were just at the halfway point of the season, I wanted to make sure we didn't fall into that trap.

I went in to talk to the guys, and as I had so many times before, I used a Bible verse to make my point. "Pride goes before destruction," I told them. "We won big today, but let's not forget how we did it. We worked hard. This was only one game, and now it's over. We need to continue to do what we do."

As we turned our eyes toward Houston next, I was concerned about our guys losing their focus. We were 8–0 and had finally beaten the Patriots, while the Texans were 1–7. Our guys were being told from every corner of the globe how amazing they were. As I was thinking about the illustration to best drive home my point to the team, my kids gave me the perfect idea—McDonald's.

"The beauty of McDonald's," I said, "is that they are consistent. The reason my kids like McDonald's is that they always know what they're going to get. It's not gourmet food, but the french fries they order in Indianapolis are just like the french fries they order in Tampa. Wherever they get McDonald's fries, they know it will be the same. That's what McDonald's does. They don't make french fries in New England more special than the ones they make in Houston. We have to do the same. We can't view any game as more important than another. Just like McDonald's, we need to keep making the same good fries."

After beating Houston, we played on the Sunday before Thanksgiving against Cincinnati. I was pleased to see that Marvin Lewis was turning the losing mind-set around in the city of Cincinnati much as we had turned it around in Tampa years earlier. During my pregame walk, I couldn't help but notice all the signs showing the city's support of the Bengals. Some local fans who recognized me assured me how much trouble the Colts would be in for later that day. It was quite a change from previous trips we'd made to Cincinnati. The atmosphere within the stadium was great, and we were pleased to escape with a 45–37 win.

I continued to journal, noting a memorable Thanksgiving holiday. Because our next game would be against Pittsburgh on Monday night, I was able to give our coaches and players all day Thursday off, which is rare. Normally we squeeze practices in on holidays—one of the downsides of our work. With an extra day to prepare, we were able to forget about football for once and just enjoy the holiday. Ricky Thomas, our tight ends coach, and Jim Caldwell, our assistant head coach and quarterbacks coach, brought their families to our house for the Thanksgiving celebration. Tiara flew home from Atlanta, where she was a student at Spelman College, and Jamie, who was attending Hillsborough Community College in Tampa, came for the gathering too.

During the season, holidays are always bittersweet for me. I'm always happy to spend time with family and friends, but I'm also reminded of how much I'm not around. Coach Noll always emphasized that keeping ridiculous work hours doesn't mean you'll be successful. After all, he kept reasonable hours and still won four Super Bowls. But when I think about the time investment my parents made, I know I'm still away from home more than I would like. Holidays remind me to reassess our schedule.

We had a lot of fun on Thanksgiving with family, coaches, and church friends. Lauren had begun a practice years ago that has since become a tradition for us, asking us all to select a meaningful Scripture verse and share something we are thankful for. Even though we were having a great year on the field—we were 10–0 at that point—not one person mentioned football. My verse was Philippians 1:3: "Every time I think of you, I give thanks to my God." I told everyone how thankful I was to have so many friends and family members to share the day with. God had really blessed us with so many special people.

At some point in life's journey, professionally and personally, we have to be able to trust our preparation. When we've done everything we can, we need to wrap things up and move on. Thanksgiving Day games require teams to prepare with less time than they usually have. But I don't ever remember watching a game on Thanksgiving and thinking, *These guys aren't prepared.* They simply have to figure out how to prepare in less time. It's a lesson we all could stand to learn.

Higher priorities, such as spending time with God and family, must not be afterthoughts jammed into your schedule. But doing so requires faith—faith in your preparation, faith in your outcome, and for me, faith that God is watching over me, even when I can't understand His plan.

I really enjoyed that Thanksgiving and our house filled with family and friends. In fact, we had so much fun that we lost track of time. Before we knew it, Tiara and Jamie were rushing out the door so that Jamie could catch his flight back to Tampa. They said a quick good-bye to everyone and hurried out to the car, without even time for a hug. I waved good-bye and got back to my guests, never giving it a second thought, other than hoping Tiara wouldn't get a speeding ticket on the way to the airport. I knew I'd see Jamie again at Christmas and get my hug then.

Back at work, the team continued making french fries on the field. We beat Pittsburgh that Monday night, and the RCA Dome was as electric as I had ever experienced. Marvin Harrison caught an 80-yard touchdown pass on our first play of the game, and from there the noise never stopped. It was so loud that some of the Pittsburgh writers accused us of piping in extra noise. We kept the enthusiasm going into December, beating the Jacksonville Jaguars to go to 13–0.

My journal entry of December 11 notes how excited we were on the flight home after winning in Jacksonville. We had kept our composure in a physical, hard-fought game. Toward the end, we pulled away to clinch a first-round bye and home-field advantage for the playoffs. The bye had been our primary goal, but we were also thrilled that we would be playing in front of our fans throughout the playoffs.

That was the last time I journaled in 2005.

✝   ✝   ✝

As a head coach, I occasionally receive middle-of-the-night phone calls, usually about some trouble one of our players has gotten into. At 1:45 in the morning, Thursday, December 22, the phone rang and Lauren handed it to me. *I hope one of our guys isn't hurt,* I thought as I reached for the receiver.

This time the call was not about a player. It was about our son. For reasons that will never be fully known, Jamie had taken his own life.

As the nurse was speaking to me, I frantically began to pray for Jamie. But as her words sank in, it became increasingly clear that we were beyond that point. Jamie was gone.

The next several days were all a fog. Lauren and I flew to Tampa on Jim Irsay's plane to make funeral arrangements and then flew back to Indianapolis for Christmas. Vikings chaplain Tom Lamphere called me while we were selecting Jamie's grave site.

"Tony, sit tight. I'm going to find a flight. I'll be in Indy tonight."

"Tom, just come down to Tampa for the funeral," I told him. "You can't be away from your family for Christmas." I tried to make him take no for an answer, but I knew he wouldn't. He's just one of those special people who would do anything for a friend. Over the next several days, our family would be surrounded by a lot of those people.

Tom sat quietly with us during Christmas. We attended the regular worship service at our church on Sunday, Christmas morning. Our congregation was unbelievable. People never quite know what to say at times like this; there really is nothing you can say. But we could *feel* everyone's love, and it was uplifting. Lauren and I weren't sure how we'd get through this, but we recognized that we were going to have to cling to God's strength and love if we were going to have a chance.

It wasn't until days later, when I was standing over Jamie's casket and preparing for the visitation, that it really started to sink in and become real. *I'm never going to see him again.*

At some point on Christmas Day, Tom had told us, "Life will never be the same again, but you won't always feel like you do right now." I clung to that statement as I looked down at my young son's face in that casket, just two weeks short of his nineteenth birthday. So sweet. So compassionate. So handsome. So gentle. So sensitive. So kind to kids who got picked on. So much like Lauren. So many people who loved him.

The next couple of days would bear out how loved Jamie was. Thousands of people attended his visitation in Tampa. It was a cold night, I'm told. I don't remember. People stood for hours outside in that cold. There were people we knew from the area and others who had traveled great distances—people from every team we'd ever worked for—mixing with people we had never met before then.

High school and college classmates of Jamie—or James, as he had begun to introduce himself—attended in great numbers. Folks from our church. Bucs fans. People who had watched us through the years. Those who just wanted to hug me or Lauren. People who couldn't stand football. People who understood when I said that it was *only* football.

The city of Tampa, our home, stood up for us once again—this time with a different kind of ovation.

We were determined to make Jamie's funeral a celebration of his life—a "homegoing," we called it. Jamie had accepted Christ as a small child and had stayed close to Him through the years. Because of that, we know his salvation was unchanged regardless of the demons he may have faced. We took comfort in knowing that his soul was in heaven even as we made our preparations to donate his organs and to bury his body.

The service was a blessing for us, and from the comments I heard afterward, I believe it was a blessing for others as well. I spoke for about twenty minutes at the conclusion of the service, not knowing if I would be able get through it. With the Lord's strength and wisdom, I talked about Jamie's life on earth and, more important, his *eternal* life through Jesus.

"It's great to be here today," I began. Then I paused, knowing that people felt I must have misspoken. "I know that's a strange-sounding message, but when you came in today, one of the first songs you heard was 'I Will Bless the Lord at All Times,' which says, 'I will bless the Lord, and praise for Him will always be in my mouth.'" I explained that those words were taken from Psalm 34, which David wrote.

"David didn't write that at a time of triumph. He wrote it when he was on the run from Saul, fleeing for his life in desperation. Even so, he was able to say that he would constantly praise God and bless Him.

"That's not easy to do. In fact, it's difficult at times. The only way we can praise God at all times is to remember that God can provide joy in the midst of a sad occasion. Our challenge today is to find that joy."

For our family, finding that joy had begun the night before, at the visitation. So many people came out and sparked so many memories that it actually began to bring back some joy for us. I told those who attended the visitation that we wanted to continue with the memories and the joy during the next day's service as well.

"I was thinking these last few days about a number of

things, primarily how I would like for you to remember Jamie," I said. Those thoughts brought joy as well. "As you've heard many people describe him already today, Jamie was compassionate and friendly."

I nodded toward the Colts organization, all of whom had flown down for Jamie's homegoing celebration. "So many of these guys sitting here were nice to Jamie. Players and coaches and others. You were great to him, and we thank you. We are grateful to you.

"I also want to offer a special thanks to Mr. Glazer." I looked over and saw Mr. Glazer, seated with his family in the middle of the large, packed sanctuary. "Jamie was nine years old when we came here to Tampa. While we were here, we took a lot of bus rides to the airport, and every time Jamie was with us, Mr. Glazer talked to him. Every single trip we took. He never talked about football but always about being a good son. Then he'd talk to me about taking care of my boys and being a good dad to my kids."

Everyone knew that if you were nice to Jamie you could be his friend, but I went on to share another way to be his friend—just *look* like you needed a friend.

"Jamie got a lot of spankings for having animals under the bed, and each time we'd find a turtle, dog, or other animal in the backyard, we'd ask what they were doing there. His answer was simple. 'Dad, nobody was there to take care of them.' Jamie was that way with our children, with kids at church, and with kids at the Y. He was a friend to everyone.

"The other thing he demonstrated was loyalty." I paused, and gathered myself. "If he was your friend, you had a friend forever, under any circumstances. I admired him for that. That's hard for teenagers. As you all know, there's an 'in-crowd' and an 'out-crowd,' and there's a great deal of pressure to remain in that 'in-crowd.' Jamie didn't care. If you were his friend, it didn't matter how anyone else looked at you. He introduced so many people to us over the years with the simple introduction, 'This is my friend.'"

I then recounted the story of Mike Vanderjagt and Jamie's concern over his continued presence with the Colts. I concluded the story by thanking Jamie for his example to me of being a loyal friend.

"The other thing I remember about Jamie—and nobody has said it up here today—is that he was a mama's boy. He loved me, but he *loved* his mom. I drive my kids to school in the mornings and Lauren picks them up, and you know how kids are as they hit high school. They don't always want their mom and dad around. Tiara used to say, 'Dad, you can just drop me here. The kids don't need to know that my dad's driving me to school.' It was the same with Jamie when I would drop him off. Lauren would come to pick them up, and Tiara would say, 'Just stay in the car, Mom. I'll come find you.' But not Jamie. He loved to have her come into the school to get him. And when she'd come . . ." I stopped again momentarily. "When she'd come, he'd say to everybody, all of his buddies, 'That's my mom!'"

This time I had to take a little longer to gather myself, laughing as I cried. The memories of Jamie and Lauren were so strong.

"He'd then tell Lauren, 'Some people think you're my girlfriend. And that's okay. I let them think that.' That's how I'll always remember him, as a sweet, young boy. But I'll also remember him as that young boy who was trying to change into a man and trying to find his manly identity. That's hard to do today."

Jamie and I had discussed that topic a great deal: what it means to be a man. One of the first times we ever talked about that was in 1995, when I was still with the Vikings. We had a player in Minnesota named Vencie Glenn, who gave Jamie a hat when he was about seven and attending his first train-ing camp. How he loved Vencie Glenn after that. But things change quickly in the NFL, and by 1995, Vencie was with another team. On our first day of camp in 1995, Jamie and I walked from the morning practice to lunch, and as we sat there and ate, Jamie had quite a long face.

"What's wrong, man?" I asked.

"I followed Vencie Glenn around all day and kept call-ing, 'Vencie, Vencie,' but he wouldn't even turn around. He wouldn't look at me, Dad." In light of his earnest, hurt little face, I tried not to laugh.

"Jamie, that's not Vencie Glenn. That's Alfred Jackson."

"No, Dad. It was number 25—Vencie Glenn. It's Vencie Glenn."

I explained to Jamie that 25 had been Vencie's uniform number but that now Alfred was wearing that jersey. Ven-cie wasn't there any longer, but he would always be Jamie's friend.

"No matter what jersey or uniform Vencie is wearing," I said, "the person inside that uniform will always love you."

Over the years we had continued to talk about changing uniforms and teams and cities and making sure that it didn't change the person inside, and I think he got it. As he got older, he was searching, as all teenagers do, for who he was and the kind of man he was becoming. And as he was making that journey, I knew he would never leave his compassionate, loyal, friendly, heartfelt roots. But like a lot of teenage boys, I think he was hit with messages from the world that maybe that's not the way boys are supposed to be. Like most of us, I think he went through a time as a teenager when he wasn't sure that his parents always had the best advice. He wasn't sure that we always had his best interests at heart. Tiara had said it best: "I just wish he could have made it until he was twenty, because when you're seventeen or eighteen, sometimes the things that you guys say to us just don't make sense. But when I got to twenty, those things started making sense again. I just wish he would have made it to twenty."

The memories continued to flood my mind as I looked out over the crowd of people gathered in the sanctuary.

"When Jamie needed to hear the right message, so many of you seated here today were there for him to reinforce that message and encourage him, and Lauren and I want to thank you for that," I said. "What's kept our family going these last couple of days is what we believe, and we believe God when He says that He works all things for His good for those who love the Lord. It's hard to accept because we can't always see it, but we have to believe it. I know that Jamie loved the Lord, and our hope is that God will be glorified today as we remember Jamie."

I urged those in attendance not to take their relationships for granted. Sitting there in front of me were parents and children, husbands and wives, friends and coworkers.

"Parents, hug your kids—every chance you get. Tell them that you love them every chance you get. You don't know when it's going to be the last time." I gathered myself and shared how I hadn't been able to give Jamie a hug at Thanksgiving. Although we had talked on the phone a good deal since then—including one call when he told me that he was sure we were going to the Super Bowl and that when we did, he wanted to be on the field with me—I was never going to get that hug.

"Hug them every chance you get. And for you kids—I know there are a number of you here today who are thirteen, fourteen, fifteen—maybe your parents are starting to seem a little old-fashioned, and maybe they won't let you do some of the things you want to do. Just know, when that happens, that they still love you and care about you very much. And those old-fashioned things will start making sense pretty soon."

I turned toward the Colts and addressed them again, as well as the other players who had attended.

"You are some great guys; you really are. Our guys don't always get great publicity for the tremendous things they do, while one negative thing will be replayed over and over and over. But I want to tell everybody here that these guys are the greatest role models we have in our country today. Continue being who you are, because our young people need to hear from you. If anything, be bolder in who you are, because our boys are getting a lot of wrong messages today about what it means to be a man in this world, about how they should act and talk and dress and treat people. They aren't always getting the right message, but you guys have the right message, and you live it, and we need you to continue to do that."

I finished my words with one final thought. "The last and most important thing I want to leave you with is this. Despite my having shed a few tears here, this is really a celebration in the midst of tragedy. When Jamie was five years old, he accepted Christ as his Savior. When Lauren and I would talk to him about his identity, about who he was and who he wanted to become, that was one thing that we could tell him for sure, for certain—that his identity was in Christ. The apostle Paul wrote that nothing can ever separate us from the love of God that's in Christ Jesus."

Just as Jamie and I had talked about that day in training camp in 1995 when he thought he saw Vencie Glenn, what's important is not the uniform or the number, and it's not what team you play for or whether anyone else sees your value; it's who you are inside. And when you're in Christ, that's never going to change.

"That's why we have joy today," I said. "We know that while we had him for eighteen short years, God has him now. And He will have Jamie forever."

It meant so much to us to have so many attend that day, role models such as Jeff Saturday and Reggie Wayne and Marvin Harrison from the Colts. And Tampa's Warrick Dunn, who buys homes for single mothers, and Derrick Brooks, who had asked Lauren and me to accompany him to Africa with a group of kids from the Boys & Girls Clubs. These guys all get it. They had all had a positive effect on my boys, and I thanked them for it.

Lovie Smith, Denny Green, and Herm Edwards were also there, leaving their teams' preparation to their assistants. I still don't know how Herm was able to get there on Tuesday morning after the Jets played on Monday night. But I knew that somehow my dear friend would be there for me, and he was.

The Buccaneers had chartered a bus for people who came from One Buc—people I'd worked with, as well as staff members and coaches I'd never met.

We rode on the Colts buses as we left the celebration and headed to the cemetery. All along the way, cars had pulled to the sides of the road. People stood beside their cars, waving and holding up signs about Jamie and us. I was stunned. It was as if someone had made an announcement letting the entire city know which route we would be taking.

My players marveled over it too. Edgerrin James turned to me and grinned. "Coach, you're big time to this city."

"No, Edge. Tampa is big time to *me*."

The next decision for me was when I should return to Indianapolis and go back to work. Jim Irsay and Bill Polian both told me to feel free to take the rest of the season off. They wanted me to make sure that Lauren and the kids would be okay. Lauren and I were grateful for this support from the Colts management. We talked it over, and we decided I should go back to work.

As painful as it was, we needed to move forward—getting back into our routine was important. Lauren knew me well. Work would help take my mind off my own pain. But I wanted to make sure that Lauren and the kids were as emotionally stable as possible under the circumstances.

We talked about the way this situation had forced us to practice what we preach. I had counseled so many players and others throughout the years, and now it was time to follow my own advice. These were certainly tough times, but our family couldn't quit living just because times were tough. Lauren and I knew our only option was to trust God and let Him lead us through the pain. Even though we didn't understand why Jamie had taken his life, our job was to persevere and continue to follow the Lord no matter what.

The Colts were surviving without me; Jim Caldwell had been running the team in my absence. They didn't need me, but I needed them. I thought back to the messages I had been giving for years. Times will get tough. God doesn't promise that once we accept Jesus as Lord and Savior we'll be protected from harm and pain and stress. But He does promise that He'll be there to lean on during those times. I thought it critical that, during this time of my own staggering loss, everyone watching our team see me live out those lessons rather than quit when times were tough.

I returned to work that Thursday. Jim Caldwell called a team meeting to announce that he was handing the reins back to me. Emotions ran high—the guys were extremely warm and welcoming, and I was overwhelmed by their love and support. As a group, we had always leaned on each other in difficult times; I needed them now more than ever.

Two days later, we played Arizona in the last game of the season. We were now 13–2, and like that Tampa-Philadelphia game at the end of the 2001 season, the game didn't mean anything in the standings. Our playoff position had already been decided three weeks earlier.

As we prepared for the pregame introductions, I was concerned. Unlike that night in Tampa in 2003, when I worried how the fans would respond, this time I was worried about how *I* would hold up. When I was introduced, the sound in the stadium was deafening. It was all I could do to keep from crying. I found the fans' outpouring of support and love to be extremely healing for me.

As we had in the previous game, we rested most of our starters, and our young players gave a tremendous effort. The game came down to the final play. We were leading by four points with the Cardinals at our one yard line on fourth down. They tried a quarterback sneak, and the official signaled a touchdown. Our players thought the quarterback had fumbled before he crossed the goal line—and that we had recovered the ball. Since there was no time left, it would be up to instant replay to decide the game.

The referee, Ron Winter, returned to the field after looking at the video monitor. He began to explain that the ball had come loose, and—

The crowd erupted as the referee overturned the touchdown. We had won the most meaningless—yet at that particular moment in my life, the most incredibly meaningful—game of the season. One of our defensive players, Mike Doss, handed me the game ball, and we exited the field to a very emotional locker room. Even though we hadn't needed to win the game, the players had wanted to win it for me and my family. It was great for me to be back with them.

We didn't play the next week because we had a first-round bye in the playoffs. I tried to stay busy, but it was tough. I gave the coaches some time off, but that left me with more time to think about Jamie.

How ironic, I thought. *Here I am, a spokesman for the All Pro Dad program, helping others be better parents, and my child took his own life.* I figured this would wipe out any credibility I might have had.

But then cards and letters started to roll in again. Many who wrote were parents who had been there, who had felt the same pain, loss, grief, and hopelessness I was feeling. Parents who, like us, were retracing their every step, trying to figure out what went wrong and what they could have done differently. I could tell their letters had been written from the deepest parts of very scarred hearts.

I used to think that teenage suicide was rare because it hadn't touched many people close to me. The fact is, teenage suicide is all too common. Sadly, those cards and letters we received were just the tip of an iceberg of grieving families who have lived through this. I realized that our young people are hurting—some so deeply that they're dying.

According to the American Foundation for Suicide Prevention, over the last four decades suicide rates have tripled for young men and doubled for young women. In 2005, 17 percent of high school kids seriously considered suicide. These kids don't necessarily have bad parents. Their thoughts of suicide can't all be explained. Bad things happen in life. Depression happens. All kids are susceptible. African Americans and whites.

Hispanics and Native Americans. Kids living with two parents, one parent, or no parents. Those who have turned their lives over to Christ and those who haven't. No one is immune.

Jamie's death will never make sense to me, and the pain of losing him will never go away. But in the midst of it all, I truly believe that hope is available to *all* of us—for joy in today and peace in the certainty that heaven's glory awaits us.

People often ask Lauren and me how we made it through something like the death of our son. Everyone is different, but for me, focusing on the things I knew to be true helped me find the path to recovery. First, I focused on my faith. Two years earlier, former Tampa Bay quarterback Trent Dilfer's five-year-old son, Trevin, had died. I clearly remember calling Trent and telling him that we were praying for him and that I appreciated his witness and the strength of his faith. Trent and I had been through a lot of ups and downs together, and when Trevin died, Trent was such an encouragement to me. I told him I was certain I wouldn't be able to handle the death of a child with the kind of grace and courage Trent had shown. His answer was immediate and direct.

"You could, Coach, if you had to. The Lord will give you the strength *at that time* to go through it, because you can't do it alone."

When Jamie died, I realized that Trent had been right. God's strength *is* sufficient. I would need to continue to rely on God's strength in the days, weeks, and months to follow. As Trent had done for me, I wanted to pass this encouragement on to someone else who might need it someday.

Moreover, I had always said that football was my job but that it was not the most important thing in my life. Jamie's death had reinforced that. Now I would learn if my faith and my ideals would hold up when put to the test. Over the years, many of my players had faced tragedies—their parents or siblings had died, or they were grieving over miscarriages or caring for sick children.

I had always said that trusting in the Lord was the answer. Now, facing my own tragedy, I knew I needed to accept the truth that God's love and power *were* sufficient. If I really believed it, I needed to use this personal and painful time to validate that belief. God would work for the good of those who love Him, even if we didn't understand how He was going to do it.

In those days following Jamie's death, I found great encouragement in the Old Testament story of Job.

Job was a godly man who was beset by a string of hardships that seemed to come for no reason. Some of Job's friends offered trite and unhelpful answers, but God let them know that they didn't—and couldn't—understand His ways. In essence, God is God, and we are not. God's ways are beyond our comprehension and our ideas of "fairness." He can see the entire picture even when we cannot. As Job grew into a deeper understanding of God, he trusted God enough to lean back into His everlasting arms.

Why do bad things happen? I don't know. Why did Jamie die? I don't know. But I do know that God has the answers, I know He loves me, and I know He has a plan—whether it makes sense to me or not. Rather than asking *why,* I'm asking *what.* What can I learn from this? What can I do for God's glory and to help others?

I'm definitely my father's son—his influence guided me through those days. I had two choices: I could either vent at

God or I could try to determine where to go from here. I knew I needed to figure out what good was supposed to come of this, even if it was still painful.

We had buried both of my parents not long before Jamie's death. Their deaths were traumatic for me but not totally unexpected. Sons and daughters, in their lifetimes, often bury their parents—but shouldn't have to bury their children. Again, those cards and letters from people dealing with the same issues I was facing poured in. People heard about our situation through the media coverage, but I was hearing from people who were going through the same thing we were but without the encouragement and support we were receiving. I've since written notes to grieving parents and visited those who are down.

In an effort to bring some good out of this, I have tried to assist others, to encourage people the way Trent Dilfer encouraged me. We began by donating Jamie's organs. Today two people can see, thanks to his corneas. A businessman wrote me after the funeral to tell me he's working less in order to spend more time with his son. A young girl wrote a letter to us, saying that although she's always attended church, she dedicated her life to Christ after watching our family at Jamie's homegoing service.

One worried father asked me to call his son, who he thought might be contemplating taking his life. We spoke several times over the next few weeks. "Why are you taking the time to call *me*?" the son finally asked.

"Because if someone had been able to help my son with a phone call, I hope they would have taken the time."

His dad called me later to thank me for helping his son get through that tough time. I was happy to know that our experience, as unbearable as it was, had actually helped another family.

That's the answer, I think. It's the best I can figure out at this time, anyway. God's grace is all I need; His power works best in my weakness, as 2 Corinthians 12:9 says. We live in a lost and hurting world, and God wants us to get beyond ourselves, whether it's to help hurting kids or grieving parents or artistic inmates or striving fathers. I'm not doing anything extraordinary. I'm just trying to do the ordinary things—as directed by God—well.

People sometimes ask if I went through a typical grief cycle and what I learned from having gone through it. I learned two primary things from our experience and from talking to countless other parents. First, there is no *typical* grief cycle, and second, it's not something I *went* through. I'm still grieving, as is Lauren. I don't know that I'll ever look at this in the past tense, as something I've emerged from. Getting back to work certainly helped me heal, and seeing the strength of Gary Bracket and Trent Dilfer and all those other parents who reminded me that we're not alone has certainly helped the process.

Pressing on to help others is all I can do. It's all any of us can do. I'm certain it's what God wants us to do, and He will use it all for good because He loves us. God's Son died too, but God willingly allowed Christ to die on the cross so that He could restore sight to the blind, heal broken hearts, and bring His children to Him for all eternity.

God so loved the world—and He still does.

We still weren't finished with the 2005 football season. We were the top seed, and after the bye week, we were preparing for Pittsburgh. The Steelers had beaten Cincinnati in the first round of the playoffs, and we were definitely not taking them lightly. We had beaten them during the regular season—soundly. But we had also had recent experiences in which we lost a regular-season game but beat the same team in the play-offs. We didn't want the Steelers to do that to us.

As the game began, we realized we had reason to be concerned. The Steelers jumped out to an early lead, and we started slowly—again. Even after a dramatic comeback, we trailed late in the game, 21–18. With less than two minutes to go, we were forced to go for it on fourth down. A sack by the Steelers seemed to end our chances. Pittsburgh had the ball on our two yard line with just over a minute remaining. As the defense took the field, I told middle linebacker Gary Brackett, "We've got to knock the ball loose." On the first play, Gary did just that, causing Steelers running back Jerome Bettis to fumble. Our cornerback Nick Harper caught the bouncing ball in the air and headed off toward a go-ahead touchdown, but their quarterback, Ben Roethlisberger, made a great tackle on Nick at midfield. We moved the ball but couldn't put it in the end zone. Even so, we were in field goal range and, with Mike Vanderjagt kicking, we were sure we would be heading into overtime. With seventeen seconds left, we sent Mike out to complete the miracle comeback. He missed.

It was an unbelievable end to an unbelievable year—the most accurate kicker in history missing a field goal to end our season when we were prohibitive favorites to go to the Super Bowl. The season was over. It had been a season of heartache, both on and off the field.

In the locker room, I faced a devastated group of players. I made it clear that we couldn't blame Mike. We had just dug ourselves too big a hole to climb out of. "And we almost *did* get out," I told them. "I wouldn't be surprised to see Pittsburgh win it all; they were confident and hot. We're just going to have to be better next year. Better in what we do, better in how we play. We're not going to change our approach. We'll stay the course, both on and off the field. "

Sometimes you get everything set up just right. We had worked so hard to earn a bye in the playoffs. To me that seemed even more important than the home field advantage, since winning only twice to get to the Super Bowl gave us more of an advantage than being at home. We'd had both. But having it all set up perfectly isn't enough. We had to go out and do our job when the time came, and we hadn't done it. So now we were going to push ahead to the next season. We were going to do what we do and see what happened.

Maybe 2006 would bring us another unforgettable season for different—*much* different—reasons.

STAYING THE COURSE

CHAPTER NINETEEN

Leaving the game plan is a sign of panic, and panic is not in our game plan.

CHUCK NOLL

SHOULD I COME BACK to coach the Colts in 2006? I spent a couple of days considering that question. After all that had happened, I wanted to make certain that I could focus and lead the team at the level the players deserved. I told Jim Irsay that although I planned to be back, I wanted to see how my mind and my spirit held up once the adrenaline of the 2005 season had worn off. And deep down inside, I wanted to show people that all the things I believed about hope and faith and dealing with heartache were more than just lip service.

Lauren and I prayed about it a lot before the playoff game against Pittsburgh. After that, I was sure I wanted to come back, and Lauren wanted me to as well. We felt it was the right thing to do for our family. I wasn't ready to give up coaching yet, and we needed to press on if we could. Within a week following the end of the season, I told Jim I was sure I'd be able to do it. I was coming back for 2006.

There had been remarkable similarities between my first

few years in Indianapolis and Tampa. Both teams had shown improvement, both had stretches of great play, both had reached the playoffs . . . and both teams had ended year after year with disappointing playoff losses. Just as the Bucs hadn't been able to get past Philly, the Colts had come up short against their nemesis, New England. The Glazers' response was understandable, and it's really the norm in the NFL. They decided to make a coaching change in hopes that something new and different would get the team over that hump. Jim Irsay's response was to stand by me. He never lost his belief that we could do it. Both strategies produced the same result the following season. I don't know what the lesson is in that, but I loved Jim's approach. With all the disappointment of the previous year, I really needed the support of my bosses, and it was great to know that he and Bill Polian were solidly behind me.

I remained convinced that we didn't need to change the way we did things. In the meantime, however, we were hearing talk from the experts that our "window of opportunity had closed," that we would never win the big one. This time, I fought the urge to do what we had done in Tampa—making short-term changes in an effort to get over an imaginary barrier. We had been putting ourselves in a position to succeed every year; we just needed to play up to our potential in the postseason. But even though I knew this, I also knew it would be a hard sell when so many people were telling our players differently.

During the off-season, we lost about 40 percent of our offense when running back Edgerrin James decided to sign with Arizona. The media saw this as the latest and clearest sign of the apocalypse—the Colts were finished. Inside the building, however, we were comfortable because we had Dominic Rhodes. We also believed that in time, Joseph Addai, our new first-round draft pick, could fill the position Edgerrin had handled for six years.

Mike Vanderjagt was a free agent as well, and he signed with Dallas. Ironically, we signed Adam Vinatieri from our archrival, the Patriots, to replace him. That miss against Pittsburgh had been Mike's last kick for the Colts, and unfortunately, even though he made so many big kicks for us, he'll probably be remembered for the one he missed.

Throughout the off-season, Lauren and I continued to work through our own feelings of loss and grief. Grieving parents and counseling pastors had told us that the death of a child can wreak havoc on even the best of marriages, but we were bound and determined that this wouldn't happen to us. Having said that, we quickly realized why losing a child is so hard on a marriage. No two people grieve in the same way or recover at the same rate. I don't think Lauren had very many good days at all during those first few months, and when she *would* finally have one, I would be having a bad day. And different things sent each of us into tailspins. Things that bothered her didn't always have the same effect on me, while some things that tore me up weren't a big deal to her. But gradually, we began to have some more normal days—together. Eventually, we began to return to the days when we could just talk and interact as husband and wife.

Eric and Tiara seemed to be healing a little more each day as well. Jordan and Jade talked about Jamie the most, often asking where he was and when they would see him again. This gave us plenty of opportunities to talk about heaven and God's gift of salvation. Although their young minds couldn't understand why Jamie wouldn't be coming back to see us, they could understand the concept of a beautiful place and a God who loves them.

In spite of our pain over losing Jamie, Lauren and I understood that we needed to keep living. In the summer of 2006, we went ahead with our prior plans and adopted Justin. When I see my in-laws, now in their eighties with a high schooler and middle schooler at home, I'm sure that I'm seeing my future.

Justin was born while Lauren, Tiara, Jordan, and Jade were in Pennsylvania visiting Lauren's family. Eric and I were in Indianapolis as the team finished its off-season workouts, and we were just about to join the family in Pittsburgh when we got the call that Justin had arrived in the world.

"Tony, just go by the hospital, pick him up, and bring him to us." Lauren tried to make it sound routine, like it was the kind of thing people do every day. She couldn't fool me.

"What? Does that seem like a good idea?" Lauren's plan seemed like a good idea to her, but I wasn't so sure.

"Of course it does. It makes perfect sense." Lauren's calm demeanor is tough to counter, especially when she couples facts with logic. I was valiant, but I could feel defeat right around the corner.

"But he's a brand-new baby. What if he cries or something? What do I do?"

"He'll need three things: to eat, to be changed, and to sleep. He'll probably sleep all the way, anyway. Just put him in the car seat and start driving. And if he doesn't sleep all the way here, I'm sure a fifty-year-old father of five and his fourteen-year-old son can figure it out."

Wily mothers and their logic. I'm glad Mark Merrill didn't post a transcript of that conversation on the Web site of All Pro Dad.

By the way, I'm embarrassed to say that it wasn't the last time we discussed the plan. I must have called Lauren back five times, trying to convince her to fly home and help me.

Justin slept the entire drive.

At the 2006 training camp, I explained our strategy to the players.

"We're going to be fine," I said, "as long as we *think* we're fine. If we don't, we're going to have problems. We're going to do what we do. Stay the course. Our biggest temptation will be to think we need to do something different."

That year, my word picture for the players was from a story Denny Green had shared with me about quarterback Joe Montana.

Joe had been with the San Francisco 49ers for a number of years, helping them win several Super Bowls. Year after year, the team ran head coach Bill Walsh's same offense. At the beginning of each season, Bill installed the offense the exact same way, with the plays installed in the same order. The first play he installed—every year—was "22 Z In." Joe Montana could run "22 Z In" in his sleep.

When Paul Hackett became offensive coordinator for the 49ers, he installed "22 Z In" just as Bill Walsh instructed him. Paul realized that Joe knew more about "22 Z In" than he did, but when the meeting was over, Paul saw that Joe had taken three pages of notes. He'd documented exactly how Paul wanted to run the play, as well as all of the basics of "22 Z In" and its details. That's what a professional does.

"That's what *we* need to do this season," I told the Colts. "You'll think you've heard it all before, but you can't get mentally lazy. We have to stay sharp and continue to work to improve—all through camp and all through the season. We are going to do the same things over and over—that's how we are going to win."

Then I ran through the same list of goals I use every training camp:

- Top 5 in the NFL in giveaway/takeaway ratio
- Top 5 in the NFL in fewest penalties
- Top 5 in overall special teams
- Make big plays
- Don't give up big plays

I talked about what we had done in 2005—things we had done well and areas where we could improve. Then I gave them a copy of an article I had read in the *Houston Chronicle*. They had often heard me paraphrase Matthew 16:26, my favorite Bible verse: "What good is it to gain the whole world but lose your soul?" To me, one of the implications of that verse is that Christ not only promises us eternal life but also a life that's more abundant here and now. But according to the *Houston Chronicle* article, many NFL players weren't finding that abundant life as evidenced by the following statistics:

- Sixty-five percent of NFL players leave the game with permanent injuries.
- Twenty-five percent of NFL players report financial difficulties within the first year of retirement.
- Fifty percent of failed NFL marriages occur in the first year after retirement.
- Seventy-eight percent of NFL players are unemployed, bankrupt, or divorced within two years of retirement.
- The suicide rate for retired NFL players is six times greater than the national average.

"Guys, please keep this in mind: football is a temporary job. We are going to do everything we can to win, but we're not going to ruin the rest of our lives over football."

Then I gave them a handout I've given every team that I've coached, entitled "Five Things That May Get You in *USA Today*." I had listed the five things in large print to grab their attention:

1. ALCOHOL OR ILLEGAL DRUGS
2. BEING OUT AFTER 1:00 A.M.
3. DRIVING MORE THAN 20 MPH OVER THE SPEED LIMIT
4. GUNS
5. WOMEN YOU DON'T KNOW WELL ENOUGH (OR THAT YOU KNOW *TOO* WELL)

I have always believed that if our players were careful in these five areas, they wouldn't have many off-field problems.

During training camp, I read another article suggesting that the regular season didn't matter to the Colts, that only the playoffs were important. The author said he didn't care if we went 16–0, because it was meaningless. The playoffs were all that mattered. I held the article up in front of the team.

"Don't buy into this trash. *Everything* we do matters. This kind of thinking will destroy us. We cannot have the impression that we will glide through the regular season and into the playoffs, that our wins along the way don't matter. That is the perfect prescription for *not* making the playoffs. This is the kind of thinking that destroys talented teams."

We wanted to start the season well. We knew the league would schedule the "Manning Bowl"—Peyton and the Colts against his brother Eli and the Giants—for opening weekend. Following that, we were set to play several division games. We didn't want to dig a hole for ourselves at the start. And we didn't.

We started 9–0, but it was different than the 13–0 of 2005. In 2005, we were playing well and winning by large margins. In 2006, we were struggling to win. We were coming from behind, sometimes on the final drive of the game. Often we were beaten statistically even though we were able to win the game. The media didn't think we were very impressive—and they were right—but I realized that this was a good sign. We were winning games the hard way, showing character and building resolve. We were playing together, even without playing our best.

I kept telling our coaches that here we were, undefeated, and we hadn't even played well yet. I thought we were in very good shape. Then we lost in week ten at Dallas and in week twelve at Tennessee, although both of those games were decided on the final drive. It wasn't as if we were being beaten badly.

In week thirteen, we headed to Jacksonville. The Jaguars always played us well, and we knew we would be in for a tough day. We didn't expect to lose 44–17, however, giving up the second-highest number of rushing yards in the NFL since 1970.

The players and coaches were stunned. We hadn't lost a game like that in a long time, and most of the concern was with our defense. But when I watched the tape, I didn't see anything that couldn't be fixed. I met with the coaches on Monday morning and told them we would be fine. We just needed to play a little faster, a little sharper, a little better. No personnel changes. No scheme changes. If anything, we'd simplify things a little to make sure the defense was playing fast and carrying out the correct assignments.

I told the team the same thing on Wednesday. My talk had the same effect as the talk I gave in 2004 when we gave up forty-five points to the Chiefs: everyone in the room exhaled. Sometimes change is needed, but usually people simply need reassurance and encouragement. This was one of those times.

We split our next two games and headed into our final regular-season game against Miami. We already knew we wouldn't get a first-round bye this year. No matter what we did against Miami, we'd have to play in the first round of the playoffs. But if we beat the Dolphins, we would at least ensure that we were number-three seed for the playoffs. Because only the top two seeds get that first-round bye, most people didn't think there was much difference between being seeded third or fourth, but I did.

I told our guys that 2006 might be the year the third seed mattered. San Diego and Baltimore were at the top of the AFC standings, but there wasn't a dominant team; upsets were still possible. With a couple of playoff upsets, there was a chance the third seed could end up hosting the AFC championship game. And if that happened, we wanted to be that third seed and host the game in Indy.

We came out and played well. Miami was a good test for us in many ways. They had a good defense, and their offense had really started to roll behind their running back, Ronnie Brown. We won, 27–22, and finished the year undefeated at home. Still, we had lost four of our last seven games.

None of the experts were picking us to do much in the playoffs, but I felt good about our chances. We would be getting a couple of defensive players back in time for the playoffs, including safety Bob Sanders, a physical and inspirational leader for us. He had missed eleven games with injuries that year and had not been able to play in any back-to-back games during the regular season. We weren't certain whether we'd have him after the first playoff game, but we hoped he would at least help us get off to a good start.

We opened the first round of the playoffs against the Kansas City Chiefs, Herm Edwards's new team, at home. Everybody outside of our building was certain that the Chiefs would be the end of us. We had had a lot of trouble stopping the run in the regular season, and the Chiefs had Larry Johnson, a big, strong back. All the commentators were having flashbacks to the Jacksonville game, especially since we were last in the NFL in rushing defense. One reporter asked me if I thought our run defense could even slow down Larry Johnson. I said that while I didn't think we would hold him to twelve carries for twenty-five yards, I thought we'd do fine.

When the Chiefs arrived in town for our Saturday game, Lauren and I went to dinner on Friday night with Herm and Lia Edwards. The Bears had earned a first-round bye in the NFC playoffs, so Lovie and MaryAnne Smith drove down from Chicago to join us at P.F. Chang's in Indianapolis.

Right off the bat, Herm brought up what we were all thinking: Lovie's Bears had the easiest road in the days ahead. With a bye and home-field advantage, they were the favorites in the NFC. After Saturday, either Herm or I would still have to win two more games to get to the Super Bowl. It wasn't out of the realm of possibility that either Herm or I would face Lovie and the Bears in the Super Bowl. If that did happen, we all knew the other one would be there to cheer.

After an early meal, I got up to go because it was time for both Herm and me to head back to our hotels for team chapel and meetings. They didn't think I saw it, but I caught the look that Herm and Lovie exchanged—a look that said, *Which one of us is getting stuck with the bill* this *time?*

Herm broke up laughing as I paid the bill. He claimed it was the first time in thirty years that I had paid. Who knows—he may be right.

A free meal was the highlight of that weekend for Herm, I'm afraid. While we didn't hold Larry Johnson to twelve carries for twenty-five yards, he ended up with only thirteen for thirty-two, and the Chiefs had only 126 yards of total offense. Our defense was stellar in our 23–8 victory—they had played better and with more energy.

In addition to our defense playing well, I was encouraged by the way we won that game *as a team.* Five years earlier I had stressed that every component was absolutely necessary to our success as a team. Now, on a big stage, Peyton hadn't played particularly well by his standards, but our defense had stepped up to help carry us to victory. In prior years, if Peyton didn't play well, we usually lost. This was a welcome change.

Next we headed to Baltimore to play the second-seeded Ravens. We had played them in Baltimore to start the 2005 season. Back then, the return of the Colts to Baltimore hadn't been much of a news item. Now it was *the* story line.

The Colts left Baltimore in 1984 when Jim Irsay's father moved the club to Indianapolis via a caravan of moving vans. We saw footage of those vans continuously during that weekend in Baltimore. As I watched the coverage, I noticed that while they may have been packing their belongings in the dark, it didn't appear that they were doing it in the rain.

With this matchup being portrayed as a "revenge" game for the Ravens—the team created when the Cleveland Browns moved to Baltimore in 1996—Clyde and I wondered if we should still take our customary walk. Baltimore's Inner Harbor is picturesque, but we weren't sure just how worked up the fans might have become about this game. We weren't looking for any excitement.

We decided to go anyway, and most of the people we saw greeted us and wished us good luck. And the Inner Harbor was beautiful, as always, on that unseasonably warm January morning.

The ride to the stadium was a different story. We've played before raucous crowds in Philly, New York, and elsewhere, but this crowd was vicious. As our bus approached the stadium parking lot, it was obvious that these fans, dressed in purple Ravens gear, were not the same people we had seen in the Inner Harbor.

Fortunately, I had warned our guys about this. I knew we would see the WWE wrestling-style introductions, with their defense coming out through smoke to whip the crowd into a frenzy. But eventually there would be a kickoff, and it wouldn't matter how much the crowd was pumped up. The crowd wouldn't be playing. After the opening kickoff, this was going to be a normal, sixty-minute game.

It was, and we controlled it. Baltimore had the league's top defense, so our offense wasn't able to get many big plays. We had a number of solid drives but had to settle for field goals. For the second week in a row, however, our defense played lights out, and we led 12–6 in the middle of the fourth quarter. We had the ball and were trying to run out the clock. We relied on our run game and held the ball for over seven minutes, throwing just one pass. We took the clock down to 0:26 as the Ravens called their last time-out.

We faced fourth down from Baltimore's seventeen yard line, and I had a decision to make. I had been thinking about this moment for the entire drive, knowing it might come to this. If we ran the ball again but didn't make the first down, they would have to go more than eighty yards to score. But we only had a six-point lead, and a fluke touchdown would beat us. If we kicked a field goal, the game would be over. They wouldn't be able to score twice in the last twenty-six seconds to overcome our nine-point lead. But disaster could still strike if they blocked our field goal attempt and ran it back for a game-winning touchdown. It was not unthinkable. Ed Reed, one of the Ravens' great players, had blocked many kicks in his career.

We had the best kicker in the game, Adam Vinatieri. Still the memory of my decision to kick deep to New England's Bethel Johnson in 2003 flashed through my mind. I've learned that our past often prepares us for the future if we allow it to. God provides us with opportunities to learn from those things that have happened to us. I remembered the New England game in 2003, and I remembered Herm's "Miracle in the Meadowlands." *Did I want to give the Ravens that remote chance to score quickly?* People sometimes ask me if I pray during the games. I certainly do, and this was one of those instances where I prayed for wisdom.

I decided to kick the field goal. Situations like this were exactly why we had signed Adam. He nailed the kick, tying a playoff record with his fifth field goal of the night. It was not until the next day, when I was watching the film, that I saw how close Reed had actually come to blocking it. Adam had gotten the ball up quickly, just over the tips of Ed's outstretched hands.

The flight home after a road win is always fun, but this trip was extra special. We were headed to the AFC Championship Game again, even if we didn't know who our opponent would be. We enjoyed celebrating on the plane.

The following afternoon, Lauren, Eric, and I were at home watching San Diego host New England. This was when that third seed might mean something. If the Chargers won, we would travel to San Diego for the AFC Championship Game. But if fourth-seeded New England won, we would host them here in the RCA Dome.

San Diego did some uncharacteristic things during that playoff game—going for it on fourth and long instead of kicking a field goal and passing when they usually would have run—things that were different from what they would likely have done during the regular season. Late in the game, the Chargers' Marlon McCree intercepted a pass that should have ended the game, but after being hit, he fumbled it back to New England. Watching the action, I kept thinking of the number of times I'd told our team not to do anything different in the playoffs. Marty Schottenheimer was San Diego's coach, and he prepares as hard as anyone I know. *Marty, just do what you do,* I thought.

It seemed like poetic justice, though. Somehow I knew that if we ever reached the Super Bowl, we'd have to do it by beating New England. Besides, I *really* wanted to play the AFC Championship Game in front of our fans in Indianapolis.

The buzz around town began as soon as New England upset San Diego, 24–21. Lauren and I took the kids to Chuck E. Cheese's after the game, and fans spotted us. "Coach, we're hosting the AFC Championship Game!" and "Can you believe we're playing New England again?" Indianapolis was alive all week.

RACE TO THE SUPER BOWL

CHAPTER TWENTY

And what do you benefit if you gain the whole world but lose your own soul?

MATTHEW 16:26

DAVID AND GOLIATH. I thought about that Bible story as I prepared for Wednesday's team meeting before our game against New England.

Even though we had beaten the Patriots during the season, I anticipated that we would hear all the reasons we couldn't do it in the playoffs: that was the regular season, but this was the postseason, where they play so well and we struggle; Bill Belichick and Tom Brady have never lost a conference championship game; they've got so many trophies and playoff wins; and on and on. Again, I reached back and drew on my mother's teachings with an apropos word picture for the team. Most of the Colts had heard the story of David and Goliath before. I wanted the players to remember three things that week.

First, the past had prepared us for what was to come. Although he was only a boy, David tended sheep and protected them from lions and bears. Unlike the Israelite soldiers, he didn't worry about Goliath's size or reputation. He saw the giant through God's eyes, as just another adversary. We had played three difficult games in the last three weeks—Miami, Kansas City, and Baltimore—and we had won each by playing as a team. We were playing well and had already beaten New England twice in a row, once this season and once last season. God had prepared us with situations both on and off the field, and we shouldn't be intimidated by their reputation. No fear.

Second, King Saul tried to outfit David with armor, a helmet, and a sword. But David wasn't comfortable. "I don't know how to use these; I know how to use my slingshot." Similarly, we weren't going to do anything differently to beat the Patriots. We were going to play our same defense and run our same offense. Do what we do.

Third, once he hit Goliath in the head with the stone, knocking him to the ground, David didn't take any chances. He took Goliath's sword and cut the giant's head off. Although the analogy isn't politically correct in this day and age, I wanted to make sure that when we got to that critical point in the game, our guys finished the job. I told them to get their swords ready.

My basic message was nothing different than it always had been, just a different way of getting them to remember it. I gave the team one final thought.

"People will tell you that in the playoffs we have to 'raise our game to another level,' whatever that means. The perception is that New England does this, and that they have such success in the playoffs because they do something special or better. But here's the reality: New England does so well because in the playoffs they play exactly like they play in the regular season. Smart. Energetic. Passionate. Disciplined. And then when the other team gets uptight and self-destructs, New

England keeps doing what they do. They play the same—day in and day out, play after play after play. Now we have the opportunity to match them, to avoid self-destructing and do what we do to the end of the game."

At our evening meeting on Saturday, I outlined the things we do well and what we needed to do the next afternoon. When I finished, Jeff Saturday, our center and a leader of the team, asked if he could say something. I was happy for him to address the guys.

"We have eighteen guys still with us from the 2003 AFC Championship Game," Jeff said. "Now we're getting a second chance. The other thirty-five players from that team are not with us, and they undoubtedly wish they could be here in the conference championship game. This is our team and our time. I know we're going to get it done."

The atmosphere in the RCA Dome was electric. After we took the field, the game immediately began like every other playoff game had begun against New England. I had already warned our guys that the Patriots might take some chances to score points early since we had scored a fair amount on them the last two times out. Sure enough, on a fourth down near midfield, when they might ordinarily have punted, they went for it instead, and Corey Dillon broke a long run. Three plays later they fumbled, but the ball went right through our hands and into the end zone, where it was recovered by one of their offensive linemen for a touchdown. We got ourselves in range and kicked a field goal, but then they drove right down the field for another touchdown. 14–3. In our first two playoff games we had not given up a single touchdown in the first half. Now New England already had two.

On the ensuing kickoff, we flirted with disaster when we fumbled, but we were able to recover the ball. We were not playing sound football.

Two plays later, disaster did strike. Patriots cornerback Asante Samuel intercepted Peyton Manning's pass and returned it thirty-nine yards for a touchdown. 21–3. The crowd was stunned. It was like every other playoff game against New England. So far.

Before the game, I had been in the locker room watching Lovie Smith's Chicago Bears play the New Orleans Saints in the early game, immediately before ours. When the Saints fell behind by eighteen points, I said to myself, *That's three scores; this game's over,* and headed out to our warm-up, feeling that the Bears were definitely going to the Super Bowl with that kind of "insurmountable" lead. For some reason, the fact that *we* were now trailing by eighteen points and needed three scores ourselves didn't seem a hopeless situation. The irony of that didn't hit me until much later.

Although the crowd was stunned, our players did not seem to be. I don't know exactly why, but I knew Jeff Saturday had been right. We were still in the second quarter, and while 21–3 was not where we wanted to be, we could score quickly—like many times in the past.

I went over to the offense before the kickoff and told them not to get their heads down. "Last night Jeff said it was our time. *It's still our time.*" They all nodded. "We're going to win this game."

We took the ball and marched down for a field goal. The score was 21–6 at the half.

In the locker room at halftime, I said, "Guys, we faced the same situation—against this same team—in 2003, right here in the same dome. The only difference is that we were down by twenty-one points then. Now we're down by only fifteen. We came all the way back in that game and had a chance to win from the one yard line on the last play of game. We're going to be in that situation again. So get your sword ready because this time we're going to win."

I really believed we were going to win, and my team knew I believed it.

We scored a touchdown to start the half. 21–13. We got the ball back after a New England punt, drove down the field again, and scored another touchdown. 21–19. Ordinarily, I would have just kicked the extra point, given all the time that remained. But we had practiced a two-point play, and we thought we could execute it against the Patriots. After a quick prayer, I decided I'd rather play from a tie. Our two-point conversion worked. 21–21.

This was a great comeback, but the tie didn't last long. New England ran back the kickoff eighty yards and scored five plays later. 28–21.

We drove right back down the field ourselves. On their two yard line, our running back Dominic Rhodes fumbled, and the ball went into the end zone. Jeff Saturday fell on the ball for the tying touchdown. This game was certainly different: two touchdowns on fumble recoveries by offensive linemen. 28–28. It was our time.

We traded field goals, and then New England kicked another to take a 34–31 lead with 3:49 left in the game. New England had the ball and needed only one first down to ice the game. Uncharacteristically, they made a mistake on that critical play. They had twelve men in the huddle—an automatic five-yard penalty. They were unable to get their first down and punted it back to us with 2:17 to go.

Every quarterback dreams of being in a situation like this, and Peyton met the challenge. He marched us down to New England's two yard line. Along the way, Reggie Wayne fumbled after catching a pass during the drive. I didn't see it; I was focusing on a flag thrown by the official in the back-field, away from Reggie. But I heard the collective gasp from the crowd. Moments later, I saw the replay on the scoreboard screen as the ball shot straight into the air in the middle of four Patriots, only to be plucked from the air by Reggie as he was being pulled down. We would have gotten the ball back anyway, since the penalty was on New England. Somehow this felt different than all the other games that had ended in disaster. It *was* our time.

Finally, we faced third down with 1:02 remaining. If we didn't score a touchdown on that play, we would still have fourth down to kick a field goal and tie the game.

I thought back to all the practices and all the times we'd come up short against New England. I thought about a year earlier, at 12–0, when Jamie asked if he could be with me on the field at the Super Bowl. The sharp pain of his death struck again, but I forced myself to return to the moment. I tell guys to hang on to memories but to live in the moment because we never know what will happen down the road.

I refocused. *Right now, at this moment,* I told myself, *we're* here. *Have faith. Faith in our guys. Faith in the journey. Faith in the practices, principles, and priorities that got us here.*

Faith in God, who had carried me through, both person-ally and professionally.

I was sure we would score.

Peyton took the snap. Jeff Saturday had a great block on their nose tackle, and a hole opened up like a path in the Red Sea. Joseph Addai carried the ball into the end zone. 38–34. The giant was down on the ground. But we knew the game wasn't over yet. The Patriots needed a touchdown, and they still had a minute left. Our Colts fans were caught up in the drama and intensity of the moment. The dome had never been louder. Even so, on the sidelines I heard our defensive players tell each other, "Get out your sword." It was time to finish off the giant.

Our defense took the field. The Patriots were moving the ball. Tom Brady dropped back to pass and fired the ball, and nickelback Marlin Jackson intercepted. With the clock at 0:16, the giant was down—and out.

People expect that winning the Super Bowl would be the bigger high, but for me this day was it. To *finally* win a conference championship. To know that we would *finally* have the experience of playing in a Super Bowl. And to have done it right there, at home in Indianapolis in front of our Colts fans. What a game. What a victory. What a feeling.

Confetti was everywhere—in the air, in our hair, on our clothes. Lauren and I stood on the podium with other Colts, watching the trophy presentation. All over the field I could see our coaches and their wives, our players and their kids, our staff and their families. *"We're going to the Super Bowl."* Unbelievable.

No one had left the stadium yet. I know. I checked the corners.

Standing on the podium, I had about two minutes to think. So full of emotion, I was having trouble grasping our achievement. I thought of how we had lost to the Patriots to end our season in 2004. And 2003. Losing 41–0 and not being in-your-face enough. Cleaning out my office in Tampa, wondering if I'd ever coach again. Not getting any interviews in 1993. Being traded from the Steelers to the worst team in football. Lauren. My children. My parents. Jamie.

A long journey.

The Lord had made this journey so awesome, even with

all of its disappointments. It was incredibly emotional, thinking about all we'd come through together.

For me, it wasn't even the Super Bowl itself that was uppermost in my mind. It was the thought of the journey and the way we had persevered through it all. Not giving up. Staying the course. The phone calls from Chuck Noll and Dick Vermeil saying, "Don't throw in the towel on what you believe in."

Coach Noll had always told me, "Being stubborn is a virtue when you're right; it's only a character flaw when you're wrong."

Through all those years, I had believed that the principles I was holding to were right, that the way I wanted to build a team and win was good. So many people had told me I couldn't get where I wanted to go while doing it the way I thought it should be done. Through it all, however, I had stuck to my principles—and getting to that point with my team was deeply rewarding.

On the podium, CBS broadcaster Jim Nantz asked me how we were able to come back and win the game.

"We have a great group of guys who are very unified," I said. "But I think God orchestrated this in such a way that we can't take credit for it. We just want to thank Him for giving us the strength to persevere."

Then he asked me what I thought about facing my close friend Lovie Smith in the Super Bowl.

"I'm so proud that Lovie is taking the Bears to the Super Bowl as well," I said. "And meeting him there will make that game extra special. But this moment is about us: the Colts and the fans in Indianapolis."

Indianapolis was wired, and so were we. Thirty of us went to dinner, and the restaurant stayed open for us until four in the morning. We sat there together, our extended family—

children and all—talking and laughing, enjoying the moment and all that it meant.

Some people say it's a letdown to finally reach a destination, but for us, reaching the Super Bowl was even more exhilarating than I had anticipated. That may be because it hadn't really been my focus. All along, my focus had been on doing things the way I thought was right—walking where I felt the Lord was guiding. Sure, I absolutely wanted to reach the Super Bowl, but I always tried to keep that goal in its proper place in my life. With the Lord beside me, I felt certain that whatever was supposed to happen was going to happen. He didn't call me to be successful in the world's eyes; He called me to be *faithful*.

I was bound and determined to stay with our schedule. On Monday, the day after the AFC Championship Game, the coaches met to watch our game film as we always did. On Tuesday, we put together our game plan. On Wednesday, Thursday, and Friday, we reviewed our game plan with the players. It was work as usual. Then I gave everybody the weekend off. I didn't want anyone to be at the Colts facility on Saturday or Sunday. Jordan and Jade had weekend basketball games at the YMCA, so we took those in as a family. It was the first weekend off for our team in more than three months.

Three Colts players—Adam Vinatieri, Anthony McFarland, and Ricky Proehl—had all been to the Super Bowl before, so I asked them to address the team before we left for Miami. They each did a great job setting the expectation level for our team—going to the Super Bowl was fun and an unforgettable experience, but the point of the game was to win.

We flew to Miami on Monday night. Some members of

the media were upset that we hadn't traveled there on Sunday. But I wanted our players to enjoy some family time—holding off the media hype as long as possible.

Tuesday is the big media day, when coaches and players handle interviews for television, radio, and other news outlets. On Wednesday, we started practicing with an eye on the Bears. I didn't want our guys to think anything superhuman would be required. Again, I tried to stick to our routine. Regardless of the stakes, I said that we didn't need more than three days to get ready for a game. Do what we do—as much as possible, anyway, in the Super Bowl environment.

Our players and coaches were able to bring family and friends to our last walk-through practice at the Dolphins facility on Saturday—to take pictures, see the field, and just enjoy that experience. We anticipated that each player would bring his dad or a brother; we ended up filling *seven* charter buses. I had the privilege of bringing a couple of my high school coaches, including Coach Driscoll, and my brother, Linden, and my brothers-in-law, Loren and Wesley. It was a surprisingly emotional time for a number of us and our guests. My dad would have enjoyed it. Actually, I'm sure he did.

On Saturday night, I addressed the team as I usually did. Calmly.

"Tomorrow night, there is going to be a storm in Dolphin Stadium," I told them. "We might get off to a slow start and have to claw our way back, but we can do it. We will do it. Do what we do. Don't panic. Stay the course.

"Remember New England? They overwhelmed us with a tsunami of points in that second quarter. We trailed for fifty-nine minutes in that game, but in the final minute, we showed everyone it was our time. Once again, it's our time. I believe God has prepared the leaders of our team for this time. Over the last four years, starting in 2003, we have had the most wins in football, yet each season has ended in disappointment. Until this one.

"Guys, it is *our* time."

I shared with them what had gone through my mind, standing on the podium in Indianapolis after that game. "We have not traveled an easy road, as a team or as individuals. But we have never wavered in our beliefs. Our perseverance put us on this doorstep.

"*It is our time.* Let's go win a championship."

On Sunday morning, Clyde and I went out for our usual hour-long walk. But two factors conspired to throw us off our routine. First, we were having a good time reminiscing about all the coaches and players in Tampa and Indianapolis we had known over the years. Some memories made us laugh; others made us more reflective. We were so caught up in the stories, we weren't paying much attention to where we were going. Added to that, we had switched hotels on Saturday night to a "getaway" hotel in order to escape the madness of the regular hotel. As best as we could figure later, we took a left when we needed to go right. Our one-hour walk lasted almost three.

During that extra time, I gave some thought to my post-game comments, win or lose.

The Super Bowl is great, but it's not the greatest thing. My focus over the two weeks leading up to the Super Bowl was Matthew 16:26, in which Jesus asks, "And what do you benefit if you gain the whole world but lose your own soul?" Our guys could gain all the accolades and success of this world yet lose touch with their priorities, their principles, and the

God who loves them. I knew that if my faith was that central to me, giving me such hope and joy and peace, it would be irresponsible for me *not* to share it on possibly the biggest platform I would have in my life. I had used every opportunity I could to do just that in the two weeks leading up to the Super Bowl. I believe that was one of the reasons the Lord had allowed me to be the head coach there that week.

I also thought about what it meant for me to be one of the first two African American head coaches in the Super Bowl. This was going to be a historic game, and I was so glad to share the honor with Lovie, who coaches the same way I do and shares the same values. We didn't want the focus to be on us individually, but we also knew how meaningful the game would be to black America. So many had coached in the league before me, yet so few had gotten the opportunity to be a head coach. Times had definitely improved across the league and in society, yet I still felt a burden to do more—to continue to do all I could do to level the playing field for everyone. I knew Lovie Smith echoed that.

Some of my daughter's professors at Spelman College told Tiara before the game, "This is why we marched on Selma. To see your dad standing up there." And all those who had gone before me in other walks of life—like my dad—paved the way for me and for those who will come after me.

I wanted to win so I could open people's eyes to the fact that skin color doesn't matter and to give other guys a chance when I could. I was proud of my accomplishments, but they weren't mine alone. I was pleased that children from every segment of society—some with hope, some without—might see that you can overcome society's racial limitations. Maybe now they would believe in themselves—and the God who created them—to reach for the dreams they held in their hearts.

I was also thrilled for older generations who thought they might never see the day that an African American would ever hold up the Lombardi Trophy. I hoped they would cherish the moment as if it were their dream, whether the winning coach ended up being Lovie or me.

It had also been a great week in terms of some of the other values that Lovie and I shared. Athletes in Action had approached us about taking out a full-page ad in *USA Today* on our faith. An individual was willing to donate the funds for the ad if we would do it. Lovie readily agreed with me, and AIA also set up a Web site that contained the ad content. That site received thousands of hits on the first day it went public.

In some ways, I thought, *it's just football.* At the same time, I knew it was a landmark, another step in our nation's history, and a memorable day for black Americans.

But as excited as I was about Lovie's presence at the Super Bowl and the joint appearances we had made all week, once the game began, I never had a second thought about Lovie being on the other sideline.

An actual storm hit early in the day on Sunday, and the rain began to fall. It poured all day, making ours the first Super Bowl ever played in the rain. All in all, it was definitely a unique moment in NFL history.

Even the pregame introductions were special as we waited in the tunnel. Being introduced as "the AFC Champions, the Indianapolis Colts," was a powerful moment for me.

People sometimes ask me who my bodyguard is with me at big games; it's my brother-in-law, Lauren's twin, Loren—not to be confused with my sister Lauren. The same Loren who had trembled with supressed excitement on the sidelines in 1997 in Detroit.

Even though wireless headsets have been used for years, Loren, my "bodyguard," stood by my side at the Super Bowl as the football storm hit us on the opening kickoff. Devin Hester of the Bears returned the kickoff for a touchdown. One play and we were down 7–0. Just like Bethel Johnson. Would I never learn? Actually, I would. We didn't kick the ball to Hester again that night.

Once again, we were off to a slow start, which continued for a while on offense. Then safety Bob Sanders changed the feeling on our sideline with a huge hit on Bears running back Cedric Benson, a hit that knocked the ball loose—win the giveaway/takeaway battle, remember?—and changed the momentum of the game.

We scored to tie the game, and then the Bears scored their final touchdown of the game, all in the second quarter. We led 16–14 by halftime, in spite of the fact that Adam Vinatieri shocked us all by missing his first field goal of the postseason. We felt good heading into the locker room with a lead, even though we hadn't played mistake-free football. And we would never trail again. We just kept plugging away, staying with our plan. Doing what we do.

Our defense was playing really well, but we couldn't put the game out of reach for a while. We were leading 22–17 early in the fourth quarter, when Kelvin Hayden intercepted a pass from Bears quarterback Rex Grossman and returned it for a touchdown and a 29–17 lead. When Bob Sanders intercepted a pass on the next series, it continued the ongoing theme of the postseason in which our defense, rather than our offense, was making the big plays for us. Time was growing short for Chicago, and we still held a two-score lead.

Later in the fourth quarter, we again chose to have Dominic Rhodes run the ball to run down the clock and ice the game. This time, however, unlike the divisional playoff game in Baltimore, I chose not to kick the field goal on fourth down. I was convinced that our defense would stop them and certain they wouldn't score twice, and I was determined not to give the Bears any other opportunities to score.

When the clock showed a minute remaining and I knew the Bears couldn't score twice, I began to think about how the whole journey had unfolded. I thought about how it wouldn't have been possible without my parents and how much fun it would have been to have them there. I thought about Mr. Rocquemore and the older guys in my neighborhood who looked out for me and kept me on the right track because they thought that I could "do something" with my athleticism. I thought about my Steelers teammates and Coach Noll and all the things I had learned from him. I thought about Tom Lamphere, talking about what it would take to lead a group of men well. And I thought about Jim Irsay and that fifteen-minute phone monologue five years earlier, just when I was thinking God was moving me out of football. Jim had been so sure we could win it all and that I was the person to coach his team.

I couldn't wait for him to get up on that podium and receive that trophy. I thought of all those things in those few seconds—and then came the Gatorade. Unlike in Tampa, when merely changing the mind-set in the organization warranted a Gatorade bath at 6–10, this was the first time the guys in Indianapolis had showered me with it. Although they never said it, the leaders in Indianapolis recognized that this was the kind of team we had: a team talented enough for their barometer of success to be the Super Bowl.

Stay the course.

Do what we do.

It had finally paid off in the final game. And Loren—along with Ricky Thomas—picked me up to carry me off the field, in true Harris fashion.

After the guys let me down from their shoulders, I thought about how disappointed Lovie must be. I knew he would be gracious, and when we hugged on the field, he was. I told him they had a great team and I was proud of how the week went. "You'll get one of these very soon," I whispered in his ear as he grabbed me in a hug. And I believe that.

The next thing I knew, I was doing a Disney World commercial, and then I made my way to the podium. I began to realize just how historic this moment really was. I thought of other African American coaches who might have done this had they gotten the chance. And I said a prayer thanking God for allowing me to have this experience of winning.

Getting to the podium was not easy; the place was a madhouse. Lauren had been sitting in the stands rather than in a suite, and although security told me they would be able to get her down to me, I wasn't so sure. When I looked around, however, she was suddenly there. We went up to the podium together, and then Tiara joined us. As we watched the celebrations all around us, we just kept looking at each other and repeating, "We did it. We did it. We did it."

I used to receive painful letters—not very often, thankfully—when I was the defensive coordinator of the Vikings and still opened my own mail. The letters may still come occasionally now, but if they do, they are intercepted before they ever hit my desk. They usually arrived with no return address and contained insensitive racist words of hate. As I held the Lombardi Trophy after winning the Super Bowl, I hoped the people who had written those letters were watching. I hoped their hearts had changed.

I didn't want to be an icon. I wanted to provide hope. I wanted my experience to open people's eyes to the opportunities available to all of us. Not necessarily just opportunities in football—although I'll certainly keep looking for those—but any opportunity to knock down the walls that divide us. That's how God wants it to be.

As we stood on the podium, I thought of my mom and my dad. Oh, how I wished they could have been there, celebrating in the rain with us. But I carried their memories in my heart. Memories of Bible stories and fishing and of their watching the only other Super Bowl I was in when I was a player for the Steelers in 1978. Miami, both times. Doesn't God have a sense of timing?

I thought of Jamie, too—the rain on my face mixing with tears. I always tell grieving parents to cherish the good memories they have. I know that Jamie is in heaven, and I wouldn't want to take him from there even if I could. What remains with me are the memories—warm and wonderful memories. At first they were too painful to think about, but I've come to realize that they're a gift—a healing gift.

And so we press on. We press on with our memories, our hearts buoyed by a God who loves us and wants us to know Him deeply. We press on with our sense that life's not always fair. And we press on with the knowledge—and assurance—that even though we can't see all of God's plan, He is there, at work and in charge, loving us. We press on with the conviction that even though we don't deserve the gifts and blessings we've been given, He gives them anyway. We press on into an abundant life on earth, followed by an eternity with God.

Someday in the not too distant future—no time here on earth is all that distant when measured against eternity—I'll be reminiscing with all my loved ones, talking of fishing or the Super Bowl or that stray dog that Jamie brought home or just how many children we ended up adopting, or getting fined for my outburst after the Giants game.

And my dad will probably ask me if I still think venting really helped.

EPILOGUE

Every time I think of you, I give thanks to my God.
      PHILIPPIANS 1:3

I WAS PRETTY SURE I didn't know anyone in Italy. Lauren and I were walking through Rome in the summer of 2005 when I spotted a guy who looked awfully familiar. As I walked past him, he immediately recognized me.

"Coach Dungy! It's me! Regan Upshaw."

Of course it was. Regan was vacationing with his wife and children in Rome, just as we were. We made introductions all around. And then, before I could say anything else, Regan brought up our time together with the Buccaneers.

"Coach, I just want to thank you," Regan said. "I remember how you were always talking about responsibility and doing things right and the importance of the off-the-field stuff. Every time you said those things, I always thought, *Dog, why are you on me about all this stuff that doesn't matter?*

"But those things you were telling us—those things are the reason I'm married today and why my kids are doing so well. Some of those things just made no sense to me at the time, but they make sense now.

"I can't thank you enough for staying on me."

The next time I would see Regan was at our hotel the night before the Super Bowl. Tarik Glenn, our Pro Bowl offensive tackle, had been Regan's teammate at the University of California, and Regan had come to see him play. Once again, Regan thanked Lauren and me for the example we had been to him and then joined Tarik at our chapel service. I could really see a difference in Regan—ten years after missing those appearances at that fourth-grade class.

Lauren has a friend whose brother watched the Super Bowl from his home in Michigan. He does construction work and had been wrestling for some time with a feeling that he should do something to help in the aftermath of Hurricane Katrina.

He listened to Jim Irsay speak during the trophy presentation about the Florida tornado victims of 2007 and the fact that the Colts shouldn't—and wouldn't—celebrate without reaching out to those who were hurting. Then he heard me talk about trying to do things the Lord's way. He felt moved to act. He placed his house on the market and sold it in one day. He is now living in Biloxi, Mississippi, working full-time to rebuild that area, helping one family at a time.

I had the priviledge of speaking at the Tampa Bay Festival with Luis Palau a month after the Super Bowl. Even though I had been gone from the Buccaneers for five years, I was presented with a key to the city. It was a thrill to accept that key—again in the rain—but even more of a thrill to watch so many young people dedicate their lives to Christ at the festival.

When it was over, I headed back to Tampa International Airport to wait for my flight back to Indianapolis. I found myself in the middle of a big group of Colts fans, and everyone wanted to talk about the Super Bowl, get autographs, and take pictures. However, there was one woman who waited until we were ready to board the plane before she approached. She told me that she felt she had something of a connection with me.

"My best friend had a baby in Indianapolis recently, and your sister, Lauren, was her doctor."

"My sister is really good," I said.

"No, no—your sister is *tremendous*," she said.

I nodded.

She continued, "When my friend's baby was born, his esophagus was not attached to his stomach. It didn't look like he was going to make it. Your sister not only treated him, she prayed with the family, gave them books on prayer, and spent a lot of extra time with them. The baby's doing well now, and they are so grateful—not just for the medical attention but also for what she meant to them emotionally and spiritually through it all."

At that moment, I was prouder of being Lauren's brother than coach of the Colts.

That's what this is all about. Touching lives. Building a legacy—not necessarily on the field but in those places that most people will never see. Trying to be faithful in the position God has given me. I love coaching football, and winning a Super Bowl was a goal I've had for a long time. But it has never been my purpose in life.

My purpose in life is simply to glorify God. We have to be careful that we don't let the pursuit of our life's goals, no matter how important they seem, cause us to lose sight of our *purpose*.

I coach football. But the good I can do to glorify God along the way is my real purpose. I want to help people see the path to eternal life through Christ, to enjoy an abundant life now, and to fulfill their God-given purposes here.

We are all role models to someone in this world, and we can all have an impact—for good.

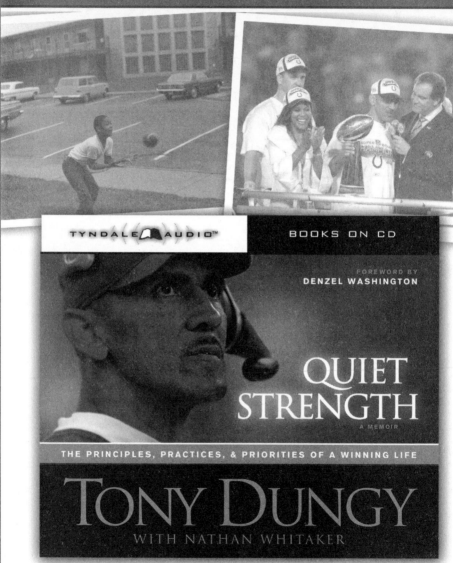